The Family Manager

The Family Manager

Kathy Peel

WORD PUBLISHING
Dallas • London • Vancouver • Melbourne

PUBLISHED BY WORD PUBLISHING, Dallas, Texas

Library of Congress Cataloging-in-Publication Data
Peel, Kathy.
    The family manager / Kathy Peel.
        p.   cm.
    ISBN 0-8499-3937-2
    1. Home economics.   2. Homermakers.   3. Family.   I. Title.
TX147.P34   1996
    640—dc20

                                                        96-9084
                                                        CIP

Printed in the United States of America
6 7 8 0 1 2 3 4 9 QBP 9 8 7 6 5 4 3 2 1

To Judie Byrd, Kathryn Waldrep, M.D., and Peggy Zadina
Three good friends and good Family Managers
who constantly inspire and encourage me.

Contents

Acknowledgments

No one can manage a family single-handedly—or write a book.

I give credit first to my husband Bill and our three boys, John, Joel, and James. You cheer me on, challenge me, and motivate me to strive for excellence as a woman, a Family Manager, and a professional. I love you.

To my "I believe in you" friends and colleagues who care enough about me to invest your time, money, ideas, and energy in this project: Dan Johnson, Kip Jordon, Nancy Norris, and Cynthia Romaker. I thank you.

Next, to Jan Johnson, my never-ceases-to-amaze-me book editor. Your insights and expertise make my books come to life.

And finally, to Nancy Guthrie, my gifted and never-tiring managing editor. If there's a Deliver-More-Than-You-Promise Award, you should get it. I appreciate you.

WARNING! If your home is spotless, your children never argue, your marriage couldn't get any better, you're never stressed out, you have plenty of extra time, money, and energy, and you feel completely fulfilled as a woman, then by all means, do not read this book. You don't need it.

But if your home and family aren't perfect this book is designed to get you thinking about how you'd like things to change. And remember, we're talking about your family, not the one across town, not the one described in anybody's latest study.

Twenty Questions

----

1. If a thirty-five-year-old man can learn to use a state-of-the-art computer program at work, can he learn to operate the microwave?

2. Can a woman whose mother founded the White Glove School of Housecleaning learn to live with dog hair?

3. Can a four-year-old set the table?

4. Can a teenager have fun planning and working on a garage sale? (Well maybe not fun, but tell her she gets to share equally in the profits and see what happens.)

5. Can a ten-year-old learn to fix a grilled cheese sandwich? (He can if he lives at my house and the alternative is a casserole recipe I made up.)

6. Can a forty-year-old woman tell her boss she can't work this weekend because she's going on a family-planning retreat? (If she can, can her husband do the same?)

7. If a man can learn to sort laundry and read clothing-care labels, can a woman learn to take the car in for regular check-ups? (And should she? Doesn't it all depend on who has the time, the inclination, and the skills, rather than what somebody else says we should be doing in our families?)

8. Can three growing boys, one right-brained mother, one rational-thinking father, and two dogs sit down every month or so for a family planning meeting? (That just about describes the Peel family in a nutshell. Our meetings are once every month or two. You may want to have yours more or less frequently. And they may look more like pizza parties than business meetings. The point is, you make them fit your own style.)

9. Can a woman who's used to doing things her own way allow her husband to plan and cook three meals a week? And live with a different standard of a "clean" kitchen for those days? (Or vice versa.)

10. Can a teenage boy learn to fill the gas tank after he drives his mother's car a hundred miles on a Saturday outing with his friends?

11. Can a middle-aged mother enroll in a geometry course at a community college for the sole purpose of tutoring her tenth grader who struggles in math?

12. Can a woman learn the joy of taking care of her family without feeling victimized and powerless?

13. Can a man learn that being available to meet the needs of his wife and children is a way that real men lead their families?

14. Can a husband and wife share a workroom, power tools, or a personal computer without killing each other? (We do, and we haven't, yet.)

15. Is it right to say that when a man does the dishes, he's helping? But when a woman does the dishes, it's her job?

16. Is it right to say when a woman mows the grass, she's helping? But when a man mows the grass, it's his job?

17. Is it possible for a family to enjoy a sixteen-hour car trip together?

18. Can a family weather a financial storm and come out on the other side of it stronger as individuals and closer as a family?

19. Can boys and men learn to put the toilet seat down and replace toilet-tissue rolls?

20. Can a husband, a wife, and sometimes children (depending on their ages and your family style) or any other combination thereof, determine who your family is and how it wants to live?

What's in a Name?

*"One should not be assigned one's identity in society by the
job slot one happens to fill. If we truly believe in the dignity of labor,
any task can be performed with equal pride because none
can demean the basic dignity of a human being."*
—Judith Martin

"Do you work?"

You're at a gathering, chatting with new acquaintances. Inevitably, someone asks the question, "Do you work?" Wives and mothers who do not work outside their home often flinch at this question. Why? They work all day, and it seems their work is never done. Yet, in recent years, the job of running a home and nurturing a family has not been considered a profession worthy of a title, stature, or esteem that reflects the true nature of the skill required to do it well. We pay lip service to something called family values, but that's about it. Most women I know who work at home don't want to call themselves "housewives," but they haven't had any other options. This question can be especially difficult for those women who have tabled other professional careers to raise a family. They find themselves not only defending their choice, but usually also suffering unwanted pity, "Oh, you poor dear, to think you gave up being a doctor, lawyer, marine biologist, whatever." Or anger, "How could you let your education go to waste?" People who ask questions like that have, in my humble opinion, never spent even one day with a curious three-year-old. Education is not wasted when you choose to care for your young children.

"Do you work?" The same question can cause women with jobs in the marketplace to roll their eyes. They may spend anywhere from twenty to eighty hours a week at work, be anything from a real-estate executive to a nurse. Ask a woman who works outside the home this question, and she probably will answer the question saying what she does for a living. Probe a bit and you begin to get the stories behind the statistic that women who work outside the home, no matter how much time they spend "on the job," spend twice as much time as their spouses working around the house. "I spend three hours every night doing laundry and cooking and cleaning just so we can have a few free hours on the weekend." Or, "It's all I can do to get dinner on the table. But that means the weekends are filled with chores left over from the week. Or, "I sure do work; I hold down two full-time jobs—one at my office and one at home."

Single moms, whether they work outside the home or not, carry an even greater burden since they don't have a husband to help them. They are often nagged by guilty feelings: Are they spending enough time with their children? Finding proper male role models for their sons? Stretching the budget to fit? The list goes on.

> **We all work hard,** and we are all looking for ways to do it better and smarter. The debate in the '80s between "working mothers" and "stay-at-home moms" a.k.a. "housewives," is really a moot question.

I believe it's time for a name change.

Now we all know that calling diet margarine "butter" isn't going to make it taste or feel like butter. I am not proposing we call a cabbage a rose. But what do we call a person who runs one (or several) departments in any kind of organization? Who's responsible for getting the right people and the right things, with the right tools, at the right time, to the right place, with the right attitude? We call that person a manager.

Women who run homes and raise families, who take responsibility for managing time, finances, food, special projects, home and property, needs of family members and friends, and their own personal growth deserve a new title that reflects their work: Family Manager.

The Family Manager's Creed

I oversee a small organization—

Where hundreds of decisions are made daily,

Where property and resources are managed,

Where health and nutritional needs are determined,

Where finances and futures are discussed and debated,

Where projects are planned and events are arranged,

Where transportation and scheduling are critical,

Where team-building is a priority,

Where careers begin and end.

I oversee a small organization—

I am a Family Manager.

Family Manager is a title that reflects the true nature of the work that millions of American women do every day, whether or not they have another full-time or part-time job outside the home. When we call ourselves Family Managers we see our jobs for what they are, and probably even expand our understanding of their meaning. The title acknowledges the importance of our work and reflects the legitimacy for our role in society. It also gives us a goal to aspire to—to become a Family Manager who is trained and efficient, effective and accomplished in our profession. It is my dream that every woman among us who dreads writing the term "housewife" on forms that call for "profession" will call herself a Family Manager, and that this title will gain household recognition in millions of homes across America—ushering in a new lifestyle of home leadership.

> "I looked on child rearing not only as a work of love and duty but as a profession that was fully as interesting and challenging as any honorable profession in the world and one that demanded the best that I could bring to it."
> —Rose Kennedy

The term Family Manager was actually born out of a meeting at which I delivered a speech to the editors of several major women's magazines in New York in 1992. I spoke about women in America and what their lives are like. It was as if a light went on in the room of career-driven editors as they, seemingly for the first time, began to realize how truly complex and demanding the job of raising a family and running a home is for so many millions of women. The editors also articulated the range of skills a woman in this role is called upon to use—many of the same skills needed to be a successful business manager. This confirmed my own thoughts about family management. I decided then and there to champion the title Family Manager, to figure out exactly what that term might mean for me and my family, and to share what I've learned with other women.

"We shape our houses, then our houses

I am, if you will, a woman with a mission—a woman driven by a cause: I want all of us, from the Madison Avenue ad executives, to the executives in boardrooms and manufacturing plants, to the men and—most of all—the women who have chosen Family Management as their only full-time profession to recognize the role women take in building strong families. I want every politician, preacher, and newspaper columnist who ever lamented the lack of family values to stand up and publicly pay attention to the role of women and how we help lead this country into the next century, with our values and ideals intact (or perhaps we should say restored). Mostly I want women to have pride in their work, to recognize its worth.

> "To nourish children and raise them against odds is in any time, any place, more valuable than to fix bolts in cars or design nuclear weapons."
> —Marilyn French

In writing this book, I reflected on books and magazine articles I've written, and I had lengthy conversations with dozens of successful Family Managers. But for the most part I've written about what I've learned—many times the hard way—from my own twenty-five years of family management.

Please don't think I'm a perfect Family Manager telling you exactly how it should be done. (You'll see in these pages that that's not true.) Don't for a minute imagine that our family is perfect, or even close. But our home is a good place to be. We maintain a good balance of organization and order, flexibility and fun. Our family is a team. We're each committed to working and enjoying the blessings of life together, and to helping each other develop to our individual potential.

This book is like a stew or a grab bag. Or, if you will, it's your management resource book, a manual you can read once and refer back to frequently when you're stuck or just looking for a new way to do something. After the first few chapters, which describe some foundational premises of Family Management—understanding your role, building

shape us." —Winston Churchill

your team, discovering your personal management style, you'll find a collection of ideas and observations about everything you oversee as a Family Manager. In a variety of ways, they cover a wide range of topics.

> "Any mother could perform the jobs of several air-traffic controllers with ease."
> —Lisa Alther

No matter what kind of family you live in, beginning to look at yourself as a Family Manager can mean a fundamental and dramatic shift in the way you view your work and its importance. When we start to take the business of managing families seriously, I believe that we, as a society, will start to take families seriously and pay more than lip service to the importance of caring for and raising children.

What Is in a Name?

Not much if we just substitute one word for another, I grant you that. But, if we begin to take ourselves and our work as seriously as, say, the manager of a manufacturing division of an automobile company, then, who knows what might happen?

I hope this book will help you understand this new concept and job title, and equip and encourage you in this valuable role. I also hope you find some fresh ways of looking at your life and your family and discover some strategies that will help you manage the time and energy demands of your family and outside involvements, adding fun and closeness to your home life and helping you feel good about yourself and what you do.

Kathy Peel

The Family Manager

chapter 1

Happy at Home:
The End Is the Beginning

"To be happy at home is the ultimate result of all ambition,
the end to which every enterprise and labour tends."
—Samuel Johnson, November 10, 1750

Sometimes I wonder what the world was like in 1750. Simpler surely, I think. In those days, nobody had to drive a carpool, be the computer-class aide for twenty-five fifth graders, present a marketing plan to the company vice president, and take the dog to the vet—all at 8:30 A.M. on Tuesday.

On the other hand, I haven't got a clue how I'd go about making soap—although I'm sure it's a smelly, time-consuming task. And, servants or no, I must admit it's a lot easier to throw a load of clothes into the washer and turn it on than to heat up water over a wood stove, fill a washtub, scrub seventeen petticoats by hand, not to mention wringing them out—I bet we didn't invent carpal tunnel syndrome—and then hanging them up to dry. I've toured enough of those working historical sites, where college history students sweat out the summer in layers of clothing, to know that I really wouldn't want to time travel back to the good old days, even if that were possible.

Some Things Never Change—But Need to

It's not a new idea that managing a family is an important job. In 1869 Catherine Beecher and Harriet Beecher Stowe wrote about their sympathy for the plight of women:

> "... the honor and duties of the family state are not duly appreciated, ... women are not trained for these duties as men are trained for their trades and professions, and that, as the consequence, family labor is poorly done, poorly paid, and regarded as menial and disgraceful ...

"Women's profession embraces the care and nursing of the body in the critical periods of infancy and sickness, the training of the human mind in the most impressionable period of childhood, the instruction and control of servants, and most of the government and economics of the family state. These duties of woman are as sacred and important as any ordained to man; and yet no such advantage for preparation have been accorded to her, nor is there any qualified body to certify the public that a woman is duly prepared to give proper instruction in her profession." (*American Woman's Home* by Catherine E. Beecher and Harriet Beecher Stowe, The Stowe-Day Foundation, 1869, 1975)

These words were written over a hundred years ago. When I read them, my first thought was: the more things change, the more they stay the same. Although the language is dated, and although I'm not saying women shouldn't be educated in law, medicine, divinity—or anything else they want to be educated in—Beecher and Stowe reflect both my frustration and my aspirations. I am frustrated because, despite our lip service to family values, women's unpaid work goes largely unnoticed and undervalued. Changing things begins with me. I believe that the first step is for women, ourselves, to recognize the importance of the work we do, and then communicate that to society at large. In that order.

When we recognize the importance of our role, others will. But, truth to tell, that recognition is almost secondary. It doesn't matter so much. What does matter is that when we take our role as Family Manager seriously (with a generous dollop of humor, which I, for one, believe makes us able to look at life in serious perspective) the quality of our lives and our family improves. We are on the road to the "ultimate end to all ambition."

"It's never too late—in fiction or in life— to revise."—Nancy Thayer

Small Pieces Make a Big Picture

When I first started thinking about myself as a Family Manager, it was a liberating experience. I didn't even have to do anything differently, I was just seeing the world through new eyes. But, as I thought more about who I really was saying I was, I realized that, like any manager, I needed a way to organize my head, my day, and my life. I went back to the journals I've kept over the years that helped me list my goals and aspirations for a year. I thought about what goes on in my family. I talked to other women, looked at their lives, and tried to learn from them. I wanted my family to think that home is a great place, and I wanted, for them and myself, to be the best Family Manager I could be.

Maybe you think I've been watching too many Donna Reed reruns. Maybe you think I don't understand the real world. Life is, after all, different in the nineties. Perhaps your home has become, at best, like a fast-food drive-thru, where family members rush in, grab a bite to eat and a clean shirt, ask for money, exchange a few words, then rush out again. Maybe that's all true, but is it how you want things to be?

My next question is how will things ever get better if we don't stop long enough to see what's wrong and start making it right?

Evaluation is important—I believe it's the first important step toward change. When my home and life were running out of control, I did something very painful, but very valuable. I wrote a description of what my family would look like if it were ideal—the atmosphere in our home, the relationships, our schedules, our activities, entertainment, everything. (I know that no family will ever be ideal, but I just  wanted to have a picture in my mind and a goal to move toward.) Then I wrote a description of myself and what I would look like if I were operating at peak performance as a woman and Family Manager. Again, no one is or ever will be perfect, or even close, but I believe that if we aim for nothing, there's a good chance we'll hit it. I decided there were some things I couldn't change about myself and my life, and I needed to accept those things and make the best of them. But there were a lot of things in my life I could take the responsibility to change.

My first attempt to describe our family the way I wanted it to be left me alternating between tears and laughter. I saw myself flitting around the house doing light housework (I hired the rest out) dressed in a leotard looking like Jane Fonda. I cooked and hosted parties like Martha Stewart, and carried on intelligent conversations about world affairs like Diane Sawyer. My husband instinctively knew how and when to meet my every need, so I never had to ask him to do anything. He lavished me with praise, adoration, and high-limit credit cards. My children never whined, never left wet towels on the floor, and never griped about food. As a family we'd spend Christmas in Connecticut, New Year's Eve in New York, summers in Colorado, and Thanksgiving in Jamestown.

Something (probably indigestion) brought me back to reality and I realized this line of thinking wasn't very helpful. So, I tried another approach.

4

I wrote a more serious description of my ideal family scenario, and it turned into kind of a "manifesto," which, to this day, we continue to strive for as a family. Here's what I wrote:

The Ideal Peel Family

I want my home to be a place where the members know they are valuable, where they feel loved for who they are as unique individuals, where they know they belong and can grow in their separate interests. I want our home to be a friendly place for everyone, those of us who can stand clutter and those of us who like everything in its place. There should be a balance in the "common" areas, the family room and kitchen, clean enough to be healthy, messy enough to be happy, so as not to offend either type. Every person's personal space should be his or her own personal space. Their personal belongings are theirs to enjoy, to share, and to take care of.

> "Every house has a voice."
> —Liz Seymour

I want our house to be filled with laughter. I want to have plenty of time to share our daily hurts and joys with each other, but we all have busy schedules. Therefore we designate certain times to spend together. Breakfast in the morning, starting the day off on a positive note is a must. At least three nights each week I want us to sit down as a family and eat together. We'll share the cooking on those nights, as well as the cleanup, and use the time to talk about each other's world. We'll have family meetings to iron things out, talk about schedules, or work on specific projects or problems. Each week we'll go someplace fun as a family, and we'll plan a fun weekend outing once a month. We'll take two family vacations each year. We'll look forward to growing up and growing old together.

I want to be my best so I can do my best. Therefore, I'll take time

"Much of the character of everyman--------

> "There is always hope for an individual who stops to do some serious thinking about life."
> —Katherine Logan

to take care of myself as well. I'll work time into my schedule to read books, take classes, learn new skills, exercise my body, and, even if everything else falls apart, I resolve to take time to think about my life.

"Running around the boat does not ensure progress through the water."—Anonymous

 THINK ABOUT IT

A Bolt of Lightning, Then Bit by Bit

I'd been making lists, calling family meetings, and trying to set goals for the coming year when it dawned on me one day that family managing was exactly that—managing. As I said in the introduction, the words "Family Manager" came to me all at once in a meeting with some magazine editors in New York in 1992. But calling myself something didn't make me skilled at it. Change didn't come overnight. It came bit by bit, as I looked at the problems and frustrations in my home and family, and my responsibilities from a different perspective.

Change came as I began to think about who a manager is and what she does and to see myself as a manager—much like being CEO of a corporation who oversees human resources, research and development, properties, purchasing, food services, health and safety, transportation, accounting, acquisitions—and more.

I want to be really clear here that I'm talking about efficient, streamlined, entrepreneurial, and innovative management. For the past few years, the business community has been talking about chaos and preparing managers to be able to deal with curve balls, and wanting to hire creative people who can be innovative in a crisis. I want to tell them, get a clue, people. Anybody who's ever spent three days with a sick three-year-old knows about chaos, knows about having to

----may be read in his house." —John Ruskin

6

implement plan b (and invent c and d) on the spot. Management guru Tom Peters should forget about interviewing sixteenth-floor management "experts." He could learn a lot more from mothers of preschoolers.

Finally one day, after I'd been thinking about myself as a manager for a while, I decided to get serious. I took myself, my favorite pen, and a yellow legal tablet out for a long business lunch.

I wrote down all of my chores and responsibilities—whether they had to do with our house, clothing, children, relatives, bank accounts, pantry, schools, vacations, furniture, holidays, etc., (the list was very long)—and studied them. Then I tried to place each item on the list into a general department, similar to those of a business. I wanted to see if any patterns emerged. They did. As a matter of fact, seven distinct departments emerged that made a lot of sense to me as a Family Manager.

> "Truth, which is important to a scholar, has got to be concrete. And there is nothing more concrete than dealing with babies, burps and bottles, frogs and mud."
> —Jeane J. Kirkpatrick, U. S. Ambassador to the United Nations

 Time—managing time and schedules—getting the right people to the right places at the right time—so that our household can run smoothly.

Food—efficiently, economically, and creatively meeting the daily food and nutritional needs of my family.

 Home and Property—overseeing the maintenance and care of all our tangible assets, including personal belongings, the house, and its surroundings.

Finances—managing budgets, bill-paying and a host of other money issues.

 Special Projects—coordinating large and small projects—birthdays, holidays, vacations, garage sales, family reunions—that fall outside our normal family routine.

Family Members and Friends—dealing with family life and relationships, and acting as teacher, nurse, counselor, mediator, and social chairman.

 Personal Management—growing and caring for myself physically, emotionally, intellectually, and spiritually (I figured that if I'm going to manage everything else, I've got to manage myself.)

You may move in and out of other careers, but you will, most likely, be a Family Manager for the rest of your life. THINK ABOUT

I was starting to feel good (and a little overwhelmed) about my role as Family Manager. It was definitely starting to make sense. Although I don't have a corner office with a view (the window near my desk has a perfect view of the basketball goal beside our driveway), I figured that I really am like a CEO of an organization.

Clothes Don't Make the Manager

Just because I now call myself a manager doesn't mean that I put on a business suit, pantyhose, and heels to drive carpool, unless, of course, I'm going to an appointment or meeting after dropping the kids off at school. And it doesn't mean that I set office hours and if a child needs me after hours, he'll have to talk to my answering service.

It does mean that I understand team-building, delegation, leadership, age- and skill-appropriate job placement, continuing education, and self-discipline—important terms to every manager, whether at home or at the office. And it means that every day I incorporate some basic management skills, simple strategies really, and that has made a huge difference in our home, our quality of life, and our relationships. To me, this was revolutionary.

Whether they're wearing sweat suits or business suits, managers are women who:

- Know how to get a household job accomplished by the right person using the right tools at the right time.

- Know how to stop the bleeding until they can get a child to the emergency room.

- Can drop everything to play a computer game with a child whose best friend just insulted her.

- Can figure out ways to meet deadlines, whether it's writing an expense report or getting a child registered to play soccer.

- Know how to stretch dollars—for a food budget or a building-project budget.

- Know they can spend quality time with a child while working together to cook the dinner. Dinner doesn't have to be at 9:00 P.M. because a nine-year-old needs attention now.

- Know how to create family fun without a fat bank account.

- Know where the fire extinguisher is, and that it's in working order, when things get out of hand in the kitchen.

- Know how to delegate responsibilities to people of all age and skill levels.

- Know how to make time for their dreams for themselves and their families.

First a Map, Then a Journey

After leaving careers in the marketplace, I've had a lot of women tell
me that they were afraid their new
"job" of staying home with small
children was going to drive them
crazy—until they started approach-
ing their new job as just that: a job.
Coming to an understanding of my
role as a manager was the easy part. The
next part was more difficult: deciding what I
wanted to accomplish as the manager of these
seven departments. I got out my trusty yellow pad
again and started a page for each department. On these pages I wrote
down these goals for each one, and my goals haven't changed since
that day.

Time Management:

*To see each day, each hour, each minute as a gift, not to be irre-
sponsibly "spent," but "used" in a purposeful way. Learn to use
small blocks of time to accomplish big tasks. To stop wasting time
with meaningless activities. To think and plan ahead so as to
eliminate as much chaos and stress as possible from our daily life.*

Food:

*To provide tasty, nutritious meals for my family. And even if the food
isn't gourmet, to make mealtimes especially enjoyable times when
we share laughter, tears, dreams, ideas—our worlds, as a family.*

Home and Property:

*To appreciate and take care of all of our belongings in such a way
that we can enjoy them as much as possible and they will last as*

long as possible. To create, through the decor and furnishings of our home, a warm and welcoming atmosphere for family and friends.

Finances:
To be alert for practical ways every day to live by the motto "Make as much as you can, save as much as you can, give as much as you can." To live within our budget and spend less than we make.

Special Projects:
To plan occasions and events to celebrate the special moments of life, and create and carry on family traditions. To put making memories high on our priority list. To make sure I (and others) aren't so overwhelmed with trying to do it right we don't have any fun.

Family Members and Friends:
To always remember that relationships are the most important thing in life, that people are more important than projects. To help those closest to me develop their full potential by providing opportunities for their growth and valuing them as individuals. To be, to the best of my ability, a good wife, mother, daughter, sister, relative, friend, and neighbor.

Personal Management:
To strive to develop my full potential as a woman. To be an avid reader and lifelong learner, to exercise regularly and eat wisely, to schedule times for personal recreation and refreshment, to grow in my knowledge of God. To take good care of myself and remind myself regularly of my value as a human being.

It All Takes Time

When I studied my goals, I saw that some departments that I manage need a lot more work than others. That's the way it will be for every Family Manager. None of us will be proficient in everything. And all of us have some things we are good at. It's important that we accept who we are as individuals—our weaknesses and our strengths. It's also important to realize that learning to be a good Family Manager is a lifelong process.

> "When I filled out my child's enrollment card for school, it felt so good to write 'Family Manager' in the blank for my occupation."
> —Mother of five children

After I studied my goals, I felt good about my ability to accomplish a lot because I am a proficient manager of time. I also do a pretty good job of managing our home and property, and I manage myself personally very well. When it comes to special projects and family members and friends, for the most part I'm pretty competent. But put me in the kitchen and get ready to take out extra insurance. And when it comes to finances—well, what can you say about a woman whose banker has her number on auto-dial? Just because I need a complete overhaul in the food and finance departments doesn't make me any less valuable as a Family Manager. It simply means I have to work harder and smarter in these departments. And, although I have a long way to go, I have made a lot of progress. I've had a number of hallmark experiences in my life—high school and college graduation, marriage, the birth of my children, having books make the bestseller list, speaking to audiences of thousands of people, being on national TV shows, but I must confess that the progress I've made toward becoming a better Family Manager ranks right up there at the top of my accomplishments that I feel really

"To tend, unfailingly, unflinchingly, towards a goal, is the

good about. It pleases me to no end that the household routines and strategies we've developed have reduced the amount of stress and chaos in our home. It gives me a great deal of satisfaction to see our family enjoy each other and our home and life together. And I feel pleasure knowing that each family member is flourishing as an individual, to a great extent because we are each committed to each other's best—we are on each other's team.

INSPIRATION + PERSPIRATION = PREPARATION

Be prepared" is the Boy Scout motto, but it could also be the Family Manager's motto. The Family Manager way of managing your home will do just that—help you be prepared. The Family Manager system doesn't prevent crises or chaos from happening. That's a basic part of family (and individual and corporate) life.

But if you have a drawer full of office and school supplies, you won't have to run to the store at ten o'clock at night in search of index cards and notebook paper for a report that's due tomorrow. If you've got a list of party menus, having to sponsor a last-minute get-together for an out-of-town friend becomes fifty times easier. If you're already operating by a budget you created, when you have a financial setback it will be easier to identify areas where you can cut back on expenses.

"Genius is 1 percent inspiration and 99 percent perspiration." —Thomas Alva Edison

THINK ABOUT IT

After the inspiration, there's the mundane part, the everyday perspiration, which as they say, is a big part of genius. Thinking about goals and working toward them, though, is useless unless you've decided what's important to you to be prepared for.

Right now, make a commitment to yourself. Set aside time to think about your own goals for each

ecret of success." —**Anna Pavlova, Russian ballerina**

of the seven categories of family management. What's most important to you and your family? What do you want to be prepared for? You might even want to get a notebook specifically for Family Management. Use it to list your goals and ideas and to personalize the principles in this book for your family. There are no right answers. The point here is to begin to think about what's important to you and your family.

Your Own Family Management Goals

Time Management: _____

_____

_____

Food: _____

_____

_____

Home and Property: _____

_____

_____

Finances: _____

_____

_____

Special Projects: _____

_____

_____

Family Members and Friends: _____

_____

_____

Personal Management: _____

_____

_____

A Personal Aside

Maybe you're starting to pick up on this, but I want to make it clear. There is something that I feel very strongly about. Oh sure, I believe it's smart to set goals and become a good manager of the seven departments. But there's something more important going on behind the scenes. I believe that a Family Manager has a great deal of influence over the development of human lives under her roof. It's important to me that my kids learn to be the best they can be, not what somebody else wants them to be, and not what society says is important. It's important to me that Bill and I have time for each other, and that our family continues to have fun and makes memories together. It's important to me personally that I continue to grow as a woman—bettering myself intellectually, physically, spiritually, emotionally, socially, professionally. What my goals and desires mean on a daily basis is this: The countless, mundane tasks I perform day after day are critically important to the development of lives I care so much about. This makes me feel very valuable, and it imbues everything I undertake as a Family Manager with a sense of significance. This means that making sure there's milk for breakfast is just as significant as making sure I get a magazine

> "He* is happiest, be he king or peasant, who finds his peace in his home." —Goethe
>
> ---
>
> * I would like to add "whether he be a man, woman, wife, husband, brother, sister, adult, or child."

article in on time. It means planning a party for high schoolers after a football game is just as important as a radio interview.

Do you know that when you take the time to play a game of Clue with your fourth grader, or fold what seems like at least the ninety-ninth towel, or get up twenty minutes earlier so you can make sure your family eats breakfast together, you are making a difference in our country? That may sound extreme, but hear me out. Every positive thing you and I do for our husbands and our kids, everything we do to

15

make our homes a greenhouse where human lives can flourish and grow toward their full potential, all of these actions and attitudes go a long way toward strengthening our families. And strong families build strong communities, strong communities build a strong culture, and a strong culture builds a strong country. Who can tell what might happen if we all began to find peace and happiness at home? This makes me know, beyond a shadow of a doubt, that my job as a Family Manager is very important!

Confessions of a Formerly Frazzled Family

The dictionary definition of frazzled is to be in or be put in a state of extreme physical or nervous fatigue or upset. And, believe you me, this is a word and condition with which I am familiar. I have a husband, three boys, and a dog. We create mounds of laundry and dirty dishes, and piles of clutter. Often we need a snowplow to clear a path through our family room. Time-release explosives may be the only hope for the mildew growing in our bathroom. Our pantry, gas tanks, and bank accounts often have something in common—they're empty. We have more practices, games, meetings, and errands than the day is long.

There are days when I'm not sure whether I need first aid—or brain surgery. At the very least, I probably need, as my mother says "my head examined." What could I have been thinking of when I committed to running a fund-raiser for James' baseball team, on the same day I'm supposed to be wallpapering John's room—transforming it from a mini-storage warehouse to a bedroom before he arrives home from college, going to the eye doctor with Joel, meeting Bill for lunch, and driving a carload of fifth graders to the museum.

> "I buried a lot of my ironing in the back yard."
> —Phyllis Diller

Okay, so maybe I'm exaggerating to make a point. Truthfully, there was a time when feeling overworked, overextended, and overwhelmed was standard operating procedure for me. For years I was frustrated in my own personal quest for balance, harmony, order, efficiency, and effectiveness. I attended countless time-management seminars and read volumes of organizational help books. All that left me feeling bewildered, incompetent, and guilty. I often wondered if I was the only domestically impaired woman in the world. My sanity and my health were at stake. I knew things had to change.

First Aid for Frazzled Families

After spending countless hours waiting with three children in various doctors' waiting rooms and after having struggled with numerous insurance forms that seem to require a Ph.D. in gobbledygook to understand, I have come to the conclusion, as no doubt millions of others have, that things need to be simplified.

Simplification, I thought. What is simple in health care? First aid. It doesn't substitute for overall reform, but it does fix problems as they arise. First aid requires some basic training, some simple supplies, some thinking about contingencies. And, in a way, that's exactly what Family Management is.

> "Healthy families are our greatest natural resource."
> —Dolores Curran

But preventive care comes into play as well. Do the things you need to do to stay healthy, have regular checkups, and things are not as likely to fall apart. Once you get on track with the Family Management System, you'll have the tools for preventive care. Of course, you'll still need first-aid tactics. This is, after all, family life we're talking about. Real people in daily situations. Crises do arise. But you'll also be more able to cope and innovate because you'll have a track record of managed preventive care.

Q: It sounds like you're saying it's the woman's job to run the whole household and take responsibility for everything. I'm not looking for more work.

A: The Family Management System isn't about working harder. It's about working smarter—delegating, team-building, simplifying—so you'll have more time to do the things you want to do, the things that are important to you. Neither is Family Management about inventing and encasing in stone a family bureaucracy that will give you headaches, make your children want to join a union, and have your husband filling out forms in triplicate just to get a Friday-night-movie date with you. That's not what modern management is about.

MODERN FAMILY MANAGEMENT

What's In	**What's Out**
Do it together	Do it yourself
Collaborate	Legislate
Brainstorming	Fretting
Cooperation	Do your own thing
Convictions	Convenience
Best effort	Perfection
Accept	Reject
Be good at a few things	Be mediocre at a lot of things
Mergers	Competition
Encouragement	Criticism
Flexibility	Rigidity
Faith	Distrust
Distributive authority	Dictators
Everyone contributes	Mother knows best
Serving	Servitude
Many ways to get it done	This is the way we've always done it

Working Smarter, Not Harder

Applying the principles of Family Management isn't about working harder. It's about working smarter so you'll have more time for the things you want to do.

I wish we could just sit down and have a cup of cappuccino together. Even if you don't want to drink cappuccino with a total stranger, don't you wish you had time to get together with your old college roommate, or play tennis with your best friend, or go shopping with your mother, or go back to school to finish that degree, or whatever? How many times have you had to say in the last month, "I don't have time for myself"? I know I find myself saying that all too often. There are some days when I feel like I'm sitting at my desk checking our calendar, holding a megaphone so I can cheer my kids along, while I organize our financial files, and make a grapevine wreath for the front door. And, then, if I could stand in two places at once I'd be at the stove cooking up some concoction for dinner, too.

> **Without a plan, your life will be tyrannized by the urgent.**

Of course, even if I could file with my toes, it's hard to hold a megaphone, a spatula, and unruly grapevines all at once. Last time I looked I only had two hands, two feet, one brain, and one life. And that's what becoming a proficient Family Manager is about. How best to use your one brain, two hands, and two feet to organize your family life so it's more efficient and more fun. In other words, to bring the tyranny of running a household under control by means of a well-managed plan of attack.

Getting a Grip on Time (Not Vice Versa)

"The average working mother spends forty-four hours at work and thirty-one hours on family responsibilities per week—in effect holding down almost two full-time jobs." ("Working Together: The New Rules and Realities for Managing Men and Women at Work" by Andrea Baridon, senior staff member, National Center for Higher Education.)

There's no doubt I spend at least this much time every week on Family Management—and maybe more. Every morning I get up and analyze the seven departments, and write down what needs to be done in each department. A typical day looks something like this.

Family Manager HIT LIST

| DATE | 5 | 10 | 96 |

HOME & PROPERTY	FOOD	FAMILY & FRIENDS	FINANCES
Take linen blazer to cleaners	Take muffins to school for teachers	Send Ann a birth-day card	Balance my checkbook
Paint spot on fam-ily room ceiling	Go to produce market	Pick up news-papers and get mail for Stevens	Mail check to camp for James
Plant flowers in front beds		Help Bill edit article	
Get oil changed in my car		Call mother	

SPECIAL PROJECTS	TIME & SCHEDULING	PERSONAL	NOTES
Start planning James' birthday party	Make dental appointment for Joel	Work out at YMCA	Ask Bill if he called the exter-minator
Call Destin Chamber of Commerce about vacation plans	Take James to baseball practice at 5:00	Read for 30 minutes	

Time Well Spent Equals Big Dividends

I keep saying I'm going to count up the exact hours I spend on Family Management. I know it would be a lot, but I know it would be less than it used to be—which is, to me, a big benefit of following the Family Management System. A second BIG benefit is that I'm spending more time with my family. And a third bonus benefit is that my kids are learning all sorts of wonderful behaviors because I've delegated many tasks and responsibilities to them—important life skills they need to know before leaving the nest.

A friend illustrated this principle for me in a story about her husband Sam. Sam was raised on a farm, and he had only brothers. (I thought, yes, farms are great models for Family Management Systems because they're family businesses.) She told me he was raised in the '50s, and probably, if there had been daughters, there would have been a more conventional division-of-labor scheme. But since there were none, and farm families all have to work together to have a successful farm,

> "In the end, what affects your life most deeply are things too simple to talk about."
> —Nell Blaine

Sam had a wide variety of responsibilities. In addition to driving a tractor, milking cows, and doing a lot of simple carpentry and machinery repairs, Sam learned to cook, plan meals, and clean up after himself. There is a great deal to be said for a young man who comes to a marriage already knowing how to make biscuits and sew on a button. May his tribe increase!

Changeless Truth in a Changing World

May, 1923: "Doing up cut fingers, kissing hurt places, and singing bedtime songs are small things by themselves; but they will inculcate a love for home and family that will last through life and help to keep America a land of homes.

"Putting up the school lunch for the children or cooking a good meal for the family may seem very insignificant tasks as compared with giving a lecture, writing a book, or doing other things that have a larger audience; but I doubt very much if, in the ultimate reckoning, they will count for as much . . . It belittles us to think of our daily tasks as small things, and if we continue to do so, it will in time make us small. It will narrow our horizon and make of our work just drudgery.

"There are so many little things that are really very great, and when we learn to look beyond the insignificant-appearing acts themselves to their far-reaching consequences, we will, 'despise not the day of small things.' We will feel an added dignity and poise from the fact that our everyday round of duties is as important as any other part of the work of the world.

"And just as a little thread of gold, running through a fabric, brightens the whole garment, so women's work at home, while only the doing of little things, is like the golden gleam of sunlight that runs through and brightens all the fabric of civilization." (Laura Ingalls Wilder, *Little House in the Ozarks*, pp. 206-207.)

"Eight out of ten Americans declared that they would sacrifice career advancement in order to spend more time with their families. . . . A majority of Americans report that they are willing to relinquish even current income to gain more family and personal time." (*The Overworked American*, Dr. Juliet B. Schor.)

". . . as we approach the 21st century, Americans will continue looking for ways to lay aside acquisitive consumerism for new priorities of family life and home." Dr. Jack Lessinger, author and professor emeritus at the University of Washington

"The whole term 'working mother' is kind of funny to me because every mother I know is hardworking. I have great respect for women who choose to stay home and strictly love their man and raise children. There is nothing wrong with making that choice."—Kathie Lee Gifford on *Larry King Live*

Taking Charge or Taking Responsibility

There's good news and there's bad news. In some ways, we're facing never-before-faced crises in family life, higher divorce rates, more children living at or below the poverty level, more children in emotional or legal trouble before they reach eighteen. The statistics are frightening. And it's not just "other" people these statistics affect. They affect us all. That's the bad news.

The good news is that women of all backgrounds, from all walks of life, from every socioeconomic and educational level, are talking about taking personal responsibility for their lives and the lives of their children. They are beginning to understand that they can make a positive difference in their own families, and ultimately in the world. That, in a nutshell, is what the Family Manager System is about.

"As the homes, so the state."—A. Bronson Alcott

Coming Home

"There's a shift from being achievement-oriented to getting your sense of identity and fulfillment in the family," says researcher Barbara Dafoe Whitehead at the Institute for American Values in New York.

I think this trend of getting our sense of identity and fulfillment in our family is not necessarily about NOT working at a career. It's about perspective. It's about seasons of life. It's about planning one's career, not taking promotions that disrupt your family, moving across country, uprooting everyone just for the sake of career moves. It's about simplifying lifestyles so that either or both parents can stay at home, work part-time or maybe do something he or she has always wanted to do. I think it's about more balanced living, and I think many of us are craving this.

I am not advocating that every woman who works in the marketplace should quit her job and come home. Of the five best Family Managers I know, one is a physician, one is an interior designer, one is a self-employed entrepreneur, and the other two have chosen Family Management as their only full-time career. These women live balanced lives, and their families take priority over their careers. (I might add that their husbands share that priority and their families work together as a team.)

I know some women who are full-time Family Managers and don't take their job seriously. They fritter away their time watching soap operas and shopping—adding stress to their family by running up big credit-card bills. Discontent and bored with their lives, they are not good mothers because they have low self-esteem and stay in a grumpy frame of mind much of the time.

Other full-time Family Managers consider their position to be one of great value. They understand the importance of running an efficient home and creating an environment where family members can grow and enjoy life together.

Each of our situations is very different, and every family is unique. But every woman who wants to lead a fulfilling life must be true to

24

her God-given gifts and talents, and pursue those abilities as she feels led—in the home and/or in the marketplace. She must at the same time balance her personal development with the responsibilities of family management.

Did You Know?

". . . the American household really is an economic institution. Food preparation, child rearing, laundry services, house cleaning, the transportation of people, care of the sick and elderly, the acquisition of goods and services (shopping), gardening and lawn care, home and car maintenance and repair, and financial accounting are all services typically produced in American homes. Perhaps the most convincing argument that these are economic activities—real and valuable work—is the fact that as the paid employment of women grows, and with it family income, more and more of these services are purchased in the market. Children are placed in day-care centers, meals are eaten in restaurants, shirts are sent to the laundry. Those who can afford it hire cleaning help, accountants, mechanics, gardeners, and people to paint their houses." (from *The Overworked American* by Dr. Juliet Shor, HarperCollins Publishers, 1991, p. 85)

S t r e t C H YOUR MIND:
"When you look at your life, the greatest happinesses are family happinesses."—Dr. Joyce Brothers

What It's All About

Some principles apply to every Family Manager—whether she's paid in sticky kisses or company stock, whether she's a happily married mom in an old-fashioned nuclear home or a single mom: Family management is serious business. It is not only a great privilege to have a family, but a big responsibility. And we need to take it as seriously as career success, because home is where success really matters. Every aspect of our work is very significant. Whether we're changing a diaper or closing a deal, our work has dignity, honor, and value. A woman's role in the family is powerful. To a great extent, we create the atmosphere and set the pace in our homes. We also play an important part in the development of the lives under our care. The family is a great invention. When it's working at its best, the family unit is a uniquely loving and supportive place. It's where unconditional love finds rich expression and produces lasting rewards. But whether we're office managers, Family Managers, or both, we are only human. We need help in balancing life's demands. We can't do everything by ourselves—that's what family is about.

Read the last sentence again, then go on to Chapter 2.

chater

Building Your Team

"We, rather than I."
—Charles Garfield

*"Managing requires setting aside one's ego to encourage
and develop the work of others. It requires a 'big picture' and
team perspective rather than an individual-achiever perspective."*
—Sara M. Brown

Remember the old adage: "If you want something done right, do it yourself"? Forget it. This is the future. To be an effective Family Manager, you have to figure out how to empower your team to work together to accomplish common goals. The key words in this new adage are: empower, team, together, goals.

Empower, Team, Together, Goals

It's important to consider what these four words mean to you and your family. In business, the term empowerment means giving people the time, resources, authority, and encouragement necessary to get done what needs to be done. It means the same thing to your family and mine. A team is defined by the members and their capabilities (your three-month-old is a member of your team, but obviously not capable of much). Together means just that: producing, working, cooperating, communicating, not alone, but with others—together. And your family goals cover everything from wanting to eat dinner together four nights a week, to planning a trip to Yosemite, to making your home a sane and sanitary place to be.

> **Women have finally learned that we can't do it all. We need HELP.**

Family Culture

Webster defines culture as the ideas, customs, skills, arts, etc. of a people or group that are communicated or passed along to succeeding generations.

Early in our family pilgrimage, Bill and I saw the need to spend some uninterrupted time together figuring out a "plan," for our family—what we wanted our family culture to be. We realized that if we didn't aggressively seek to create our own family culture—what standards we'd live by and teach our kids, what traditions we'd practice and pass on, what we'd place high value on in regard to education, morality, and spirituality—then someone or something else would do it for us. As they say, "Nature abhors a vacuum." And the problem with a vacuum is that it will suck up anything.

How could we become a unit, a people or group who passed along culture, if we didn't know what our culture was? Of course, as families, we all live in the larger society. And that society has changed dramatically in the last twenty-five years. Pick up the newspaper, turn on the television any day of any week, and you can see a definition of the American family, mostly concentrating on what's wrong with it. But who, exactly, is the American family?

It's me and my family, and you and yours, and you and yours, and you and yours. We all have the right and the responsibility of who we're going to be as a family and how we're going to work together to be that family. That's really what Bill and I were talking about when we decided we wanted to come up with a family plan.

Bill and I were products of the sixties: civil rights, women's liberation, and equal footing for all. So it made sense to us, from day one of our marriage, July 31, 1971, to begin on equal footing, doing something we called teamwork. Some people might have thought Bill didn't need to know how to sew, cook, or do laundry since he was the husband. And since he was the dad, and our children had a perfectly capable (most of the time) mother, there was no need for him to learn how to clean up baby vomit or build the Taj Mahal from Play Dough. I, the wife and mother, would have to assume most of the responsibilities for domestic chores and for these children who had come to live in our lives and hearts.

Bill and I didn't feel that way. We believed men were just as capable as women of mopping a floor and recognizing the aroma of a diaper that needed changing. We were in this together, we reasoned, and if that meant crossing some invisible, but deeply drawn, gender lines that say a woman does this and a man does that, well so be it.

We also believed (as we still do) that Dad is more than somebody who signs the checks and doles out praise or punishment at the end of the day. Bill wanted to be as involved with our home and children's lives as I did. We were naive at first, though, especially before we had our first child. Neither of us had a clue just how demanding a new baby can be, especially in the middle of the night. Since Bill had to get up to drive across town for an early-morning graduate class, it didn't seem fair that he should take equal turns at sleepless nights, so we reassessed equality.

Over the years we've reassessed our family and equality again and again. The first sixteen years of our marriage, except for a short stint of teaching school part-time before I had children, I chose to have only one full-time job—to stay at home with our kids and run our household. It made sense that I should bear most of the domestic responsibilities during the day since Bill had a full-time job outside the home. Then at night, we shared the responsibilities—kids, dishes, baths, spelling words. When needed, we helped each other out in our jobs. As our kids grew and were able, they began to help out as well. We wanted our kids to grow up understanding that being part of a family is a privilege, as well as a responsibility. But it was more than making sure the kids had regular chores to learn responsibility. We wanted them to feel the pride and responsibility of "ownership" and the independence of being able to, in part and according to their age, take care of their things and themselves.

> "Most people want to be part of a team."
> —Candice Kaspers

We also wanted our kids to grow up understanding that it's okay for men and women to cross traditional invisible territorial boundaries. Nowhere that I know of is it written that Dad is the only one who understands finances and Mom is everyone's live-in maid.

As our egalitarian arrangement has devolved and then evolved over the last twenty-five years, we've made some changes based on what we want for ourselves and our family.

When I began writing and speaking, which evolved quickly into a full-time job, we reassessed household responsibilities. We decided to divide and delegate even more chores between family members according to age, skills, and available time. Now we needed to work together even more. Our current arrangement involves Bill cooking two or three times each week; Joel shops at the wholesale club once a month and makes periodic grocery runs; everybody participates in a regular "cabin cleanup" —vacuuming, mopping, dusting. We all help with various aspects of the laundry. If James needs a patch sewn on his scout uniform, he asks Bill. Yes, Bill sews. He learned as a young child by sitting and watching his mother sew. His skill comes in handy since every time I pick up a needle I draw blood.

> "When men do the dishes, it's called helping. When women do the dishes, it is called life."
> —Anna Quindlen

Some families have a pretty traditional breakdown of chores around the house—she cleans and cooks; he takes the garbage out and takes care of the car. It may be, and usually is, the woman's responsibility to be the Family Manager. But husbands need to feel like they're an important part of the home team as well.

Where to Start

You may have a fairly egalitarian arrangement right now. Things may be running smoothly. Or it may be chaos. You may be, like I was, once upon a time, bound and determined to be Super Mom, Queen of Cuisine, and Ms. Better Homemaker all rolled into one. (Or maybe you catch on faster than I do and gave that all up long ago.) Despite our early we're-a-team mentality, I made myself and my family miserable, with self-imposed rules and regulations about how my house and my family should look and run. Notice those personal, singular, first person possessive pronouns: my, my, my, my. That was part of the problem. I wanted to do it my way.

Some women want to do it "my" way because that's what they've been trained to do. Their family isn't a team with shared goals. Some women want to do it my way because their self-esteem rests on whether or not THEY cooked the pot roast or ironed the shirts. I guess that's fine, if they aren't exhausted, if they don't take the lead in a family drama called "Martyrdom." It's like a Greek drama with the refrain, "I'm the only one who. . . ." Some women want to do it my way because nobody else ever said anything about doing it a different way.

For me, doing it my way meant I was succeeding at some level of perfection I'd set for myself to be the ultimate Mother, Wife, and Homemaker of the Universe.

"A good manager: Someone who has successfully trained others to discharge his or her responsibilities."—Unknown

 THINK ABOUT IT

Appealing to Your Husband for Help

Accept the fact that men and women tend to see different things. Often men focus on one thing and can easily miss things all around them—things that are very apparent to women. The reason your husband may not be helpful may not be because he doesn't care, but because he simply doesn't see what needs to be done. If you're going to be a team, also realize and say that you don't intend to call all the shots, decide what needs to be done, or become Inspector Magnifying Glass following him around as he cleans.

Guilt is a poor motivator. It accomplishes little, and many times worsens the situation. Instead of making your husband feel guilty for what he doesn't do, let him know how much you appreciate the help he already gives you. Then tell him you would like the whole family to work as a team. Appeal to his sense of fairness.

Talk to your husband in language he understands—use a sports analogy or an illustration from his work. In truth, men tend to understand the concept of teamwork more than women do.

Make your appeal rational, not emotional. Don't approach him when you are stressed out and feel overworked. Make a list of all the household tasks, then on a relaxed evening when no one is stressed, sit down and go over the list. Explain your dilemma, and ask his advice on getting the whole family in on the "fun."

 State your rationale for a team clearly. It's good for the kids to have responsibility to help, and bad for them not to. Things will run more smoothly, and you will have more energy for other activities.

Make sure he knows that you are on his team before you ask him to be on yours. I am NOT, NOT, NOT suggesting that you grab a rolling pin, corner your husband, and say, "The Family Management expert says you should do more around the house!" Men and women who demand their mate meet their needs first always end up empty. Go ahead—ask for help in lightening your load, but make sure you are doing your part to ease the stresses in his life. Your appeal will be immeasurably more effective.

> After a TV interview on family management and teambuilding, the producer of the show, who is also a husband and father of three, told me his wife's secret to success. "She gives me choices," he said. "Men don't like to be told what to do— especially if it involves things they don't like to do or things about which they feel inept. My wife will hand me a list on Saturday of maybe twenty chores than need to be done around the house, and she'll ask me to pick ten or twelve. This way I can pick and choose what I feel I can successfully accomplish."

Suggestion:

Choose a time when dinner's not burning, the kids aren't arguing, the roof's not leaking, and the electric bill isn't due—surely there is one such half hour in your life—to talk with your husband sincerely, and without blaming, about how you feel. Perhaps you'll find that he has no idea how hard you work. Perhaps you'll find that he wants to do more, but just doesn't know how to do it. Perhaps

he feels like he'd be intruding on your territory if he tried to do things. Perhaps he feels like he's tried in the past and your standards were so high or you had such strong ideas about the "right" way for him to do something that he felt frustrated and scolded, rather than appreciated for his effort.

Second; the two of you can look at each of the seven departments and delegate some of the chores and responsibilities in a way that makes sense for each member of your family. When we first did this at our house, our children couldn't do much to help, and what they did, they couldn't do well. But we decided it was more important for them to feel a part of the "team" and for us to praise them for helping as best they could, than for the job to be done perfectly. As they've grown older, their responsibilities have changed, and they do a much better job of their chores. It's no surprise that they do some things better than I do.

"If a job's worth doing, it's worth doing poorly—until you can do it well."—Bill Peel

Maybe you're not feeling overwhelmed, but things are changing in your family. This is an even better time to work on team-building strategies. Maybe you or your spouse are making changes at work—starting a new career, moving your office to your home, working a different shift—and that will require a change in the way you do things. You'll need to strategize about this. Maybe you've added a new family member—an aging parent, a new baby, a foster child. Maybe you've become a single mom and need to enlist the help of your children (and perhaps family and friends) to do things a new way. Maybe family members are getting

increasingly busy, starting to live in their own separate worlds, and you feel the need for cohesiveness. Whatever your reason or need, developing a team mentality is important. Your circumstances don't matter so much as your deciding to begin right now with how things are at your house and talk about how you want them to be different.

That's the plural you, the team you. Family management, like all other good management, is not about autocratic leaders imposing arbitrary standards from on high. It's about sharing responsibility, helping each person find their niche, and empowering them to succeed. Everyone gets a voice.

> "I don't believe you can effectively manage people without helping them understand where they fit into the goals of the organization. So individual goal-setting becomes an important means of communicating with a player and involving him in the team."
> —Tom Landry, former head coach
> of the Dallas Cowboys

Sure, Landry was talking about football, but it applies to the family too. If you're the only one who wants team effort and you want team effort because you want help doing things your way, you're probably going to have to rethink your wants and your ways. If you're having trouble getting the people in your family to sign up for the team concept, it may be because they don't have a clear sense or any sense at all of what belonging to the family means to them. Over time, practicing the team-building strategies in this chapter will very likely help the members of your family feel like a team.

But it may also help to look at Tom Landry's quote again. What are each of your family members' individual goals? If you're having trouble "selling" the team concept in your family, individual goals might be a place to start. What are your husband's goals? Yours? Your children's? How could working together as a team help each of you meet your individual goals?

If the concept of your family as a team and you as a manager is not new and is not meeting resistance, Landry's wisdom still applies. It's common sense. Even the smallest children will be more willing to cooperate if they understand that what's good for them is good for the family, that their contributions help get food ready, if their ideas for vacations and fun are honored, as well as their work appreciated.

You may want to set aside a regular time, maybe twice a year, maybe at the beginning of the school year or at New Year's (this is when we do it at our house) to set individual and team goals for your family. Then talk about how each individual's goals fit into the family's goals.

"Govern a family as you would cook a small fish—very gently."—Chinese Proverb

Happiness is . . . A Finely Tuned Team

When I got serious about turning my family into a team, it made a lot of sense to me to study how other people had been successful at turning a group of people into a team. I couldn't find anything written about family teams, but I figured a team was a team was a team, so

I looked elsewhere. Interestingly, all of the books, whether they were written by coaches, army generals, or management experts, stressed similar principles about team-building. Our family objective is not the ten-yard line (except in Sunday games of tag football) or the bottom line (except when it comes to balancing the monthly budget) or the first line of defense (except when we're trying to protect our children from detrimental influences). So, despite the fact that the principles I read were written for football teams, troops of soldiers, and corporations, I found, that with some term translation, they worked very well for families too. Here's my translation of twelve basic principles. I hope you'll find it useful as you go about your own team-building efforts.

1. Establish a clear-cut family goal or objective. In our family, our overriding goal is to help each individual strive for excellence and develop to his or her full potential—intellectually, physically, spiritually, socially, emotionally, and professionally. This objective influences every decision we make—how we spend our time, what we do for recreation, how we speak to each other, what we spend our money on.

We've found that having a clear-cut goal is critical to family team-building. When children know, beyond a shadow of a doubt, that Mom and Dad are committed to their very best and that their parents' main objective is to help them develop to their full potential, they'll want to be on that kind of a team.

2. Recognize the obstacles that can prevent your team from reaching your goal. Adapted to our family, this means we must constantly be on the lookout for attitudes, actions, and circumstances—not spending enough time together, becoming lazy about improving our minds, not encouraging each other, speaking unkind words, holding on to selfish motives—that run contrary to our goal.

3. Create and be committed to an action plan to overcome the obstacles. Here lies one of my greatest challenges as a Family Manager. Our family is no different from anyone else's. We meet with plenty of resistance to our goal. Often, identifying the resistance is the easy part. It's looking for ways to overcome the resistance that takes time, energy, and tenacity. It's easy to identify, say, that your family is watching more and more TV and communicating meaningfully less and less. Doing something about it—besides nagging everyone to turn off the TV—is the challenge. Taking the initiative to plan a fun activity or outing for your family usually means a sacrifice on your part. It's much easier to sit in the recliner comfortably and concede. But that kind of response doesn't encourage team-building. I've found that I must regularly look at the six areas in which we want to grow, identify obstacles, and orchestrate opportunities to overcome them.

4. Be persistent and willing to put in the time and effort required to help your team reach its goal. Persistence separates the teams that make it and those that don't. It's not enough to dream about having a peaceful atmosphere in your home, a family who is committed to each member's best, a family who works together at life. Though being a Family Manager already requires hard work, patience, sacrifice, tenacity, long hours at low pay, and resilience under fire, sometimes we have to be bulldog stubborn and take stands on what will and will not go on under the roof of our home—attitudes, actions, words, whatever. If it's not in line with who we are and where we're going as a family, we need to stand firm. We must persistently keep our family on course, understanding that the little decisions made every day in our home will make our family what it will be in ten years.

5. Be willing to take risks. Good coaches, commanders, and corporate presidents take risks—calculated gambles with people, money, and ideas. To them, the prospects of not trying are more onerous than not succeeding.

Family Management can be risky in a lot of ways. Maybe it's trying a new chore routine that may flop, giving children the freedom to fail, or choosing to spend more time with your family instead of trying to make more money. And, you must be willing to reassess your goals and objectives. If, for example, one of your goals was always to be in safe financial waters, but you're finding that you're spending more time making more money at the cost of your family life together, then you might make the choice to risk living with fewer material goods for a better quality of life.

In order to take risks, you must be flexible. For risktakers, routines are meant to be improved or amended. You can't do the same old things in the same old ways, which means there's a high likelihood that when you try to change some things, you'll make a few mistakes along the way. Risktakers are usually people who can admit their mistakes—and figure out what they learned from them. What if you risk going on a family rafting trip and it rains the whole time and everybody hates it? Well, now you know you won't repeat that—without checking out the weather first. But you might also discover, as we did, that recalling such a trip and how miserable we were, and how stupid we looked drenching wet, standing on the side of the road holding a raft over our heads hitchhiking back to the place in the river where we put in, makes us laugh and keeps us going under pressure. When it comes to taking risks, there is an old adage that's true: "Nothing ventured, nothing gained." A big risk can glean a big return.

6. Attract and energize your team members. Team leaders must ignite, inspire, and draw their team members around a common effort or goal.

What draws people to want to follow you to a common goal? Their sure knowledge that you are committed to each family member's best interest. You're not in their lives to make them miserable or to make them follow a bunch of rules that serve your interests and not theirs. We've all met mothers (and fathers) who look on their children as impositions—burdens they can't wait to get rid of. And what child wants to follow a leader who can't wait until he or she is gone?

This principle is really pretty simple. There are about a million aphorisms that demonstrate it. But consider two common household substances: honey and vinegar and what everybody's grandma said about flies. It applies to Family Management big time. If you offer the honey of encouragement, reward for work well done, affirmation, reassurance of love, and opportunities to grow and learn, you're going to attract family followers. Vinegar, well that's good for salad dressing.

7. Trust your followers. A good manager is able to establish relationships based on trust, respect, and care. She accepts family members as they are, doesn't dwell on past mistakes, and radiates confidence to her followers.

Anyone who is a Family Manager had best be ready to dish out forgiveness or else live in the garbage heap of her own hurt emotions. Kids need to be confronted with their irresponsible behavior, but they need heavy doses of forgiveness and unconditional love when they fail. (This is how they learn to give it back when we fail!) They also need to know that they can trust us—that we will keep our word, that we are committed to their best. They need to be able to say, "My mom is really for me. She is on my team. She is not trying to make me something I am not."

8. Know your own strengths and limitations. A good manager doesn't try to do everything. She knows what she does well and sticks to it.

Although I try not to dwell on it, I regret the many years I spent feeling like I was an inferior Family Manager because many domestic duties were a challenge to me. Now I'm committed to maximizing my strengths, delegating what I can that I'm not good at, and I'm always looking for shortcuts, easier methods, and fresh approaches to help me with my weak areas—even seemingly simple things.

For example, wrapping crisp-corner packages is a challenge for me. Lucky for me, Bill is great at wrapping packages, but he hates to make bows. I love to pick out beautiful paper and put the finishing touches on a pretty package. It's just getting the stupid paper around the box that I'm horrible at. The Christmas gifts I wrap are the most colorful ones under the tree, but if the paper isn't falling off, it's wrinkled and crooked. So, I could get mad at myself and think that I am a horrible person because I can't wrap packages like a good Family Manager should. Instead, I've learned to minimize my weaknesses and capitalize on my strengths. I ask Bill to wrap most of the packages. He's a detail person—he cuts and folds the paper precisely, and makes perfect corners. Then he hands the package to me, and I add the bow and trim. I still wrap a few gifts to put beneath the tree just to get a laugh on Christmas morning. I can always count on John saying, "Well, I wonder who wrapped this one?"

9. Be teachable. A good manager considers herself a student, not a professor. She is humble and can learn from anyone with something to teach. I, for one, do not know everything. My children already know this, so I figured I might as well give up trying to persuade them otherwise. I've found that it is important for family members that we set the model for teachability. Our kids may come up with a better way to clean up the kitchen. Our husband may have a more proficient way to do the laundry. (Mine did.) If we come across as Our Lady of Managerial Excellence, not only do we miss the opportunity to learn ourselves, but we set an example our kids will follow when we want to teach them something.

10. Love your work. If you have a zest, an enthusiasm about what you do, it will be contagious. I have many jobs. But, managing my family is the greatest job opportunity I've ever experienced. It is an incredible privilege and nothing, in my opinion, brings such lasting satisfaction. Of course, there are plenty of days I want to change my job description. And there are times I want to scream if I have to wash one more load of clothes, make one more peanut-butter sandwich, and sit through one more school program. But after twenty-plus years on the job, there's nothing I like to do better and nothing I consider more important. And my team members know this—my enthusiasm inspires theirs.

11. Have a positive attitude. Look at failures and difficulties as cleverly disguised opportunities to learn. Over the years I've failed at a lot of things. I couldn't begin to count the meals I burned, the whites I've turned pink, the times I've overdrawn our bank account, the decorating mistakes I've made, the "bargains" I shouldn't have purchased. But my father taught me to look at my mistakes and failures as opportunities to begin again more intelligently. Wallowing in mistakes has never helped anyone. When I make a mistake, which I do regularly, I try to think of Thomas Edison. He made over nine hundred attempts before he was able to perfect the electric light bulb. After failing so many times, his assistant asked, "Do you know that we've failed over nine hundred times?"

"No, no, no," Edison replied emphatically. "We've just found over nine hundred ways that won't work!"

12. Be self-disciplined. A good manager does not indulge her appetites or fears. She takes care of the inner part of her life. The result is integrity. What she says and does is who she really is. This speaks volumes to the people on her team.

Every Family Manager has to make some choices to limit herself in order to achieve a larger goal. I can be like a swamp or a river. A swamp has no boundaries, no limitations—and no impact. A river, on the other hand, is restricted to a channel—and flows with force. This means that I must know what my priorities are and strive to make decisions every day that point to those priorities. I can't afford to give into attitudes and actions that might give me momentary pleasure or immediate gratification if they conflict with the high ideals I have for my family and myself. No leader or Family Manager can make a positive impact without self-limitations.

> "Build for your team a feeling of oneness, of dependence on one another and of strength to be derived by unity."
> —Vince Lombardi

Team-Building Strategies

So maybe you've picked that time to talk about this team concept. Now what do you do? You sit down, perhaps the first time alone with your husband and talk about what it means to you to be a team. If this is not a new concept in your family, and you and your husband already pretty much agree on what it means to work as a team, and depending on how old your children are, you may want to begin by calling a formal family meeting.

"Nothing creates more self-respect among employees than being included in the process of making decisions."—Judith M. Bardwick

THINK ABOUT IT

One way or another, here are seven topics you might want to cover.

1 Look at the seven family-management departments one at a time and talk about what needs to be done in each department and how each family member can help. ("Talk about" means just that. It doesn't mean announce or declare.)

2 Make a list of the areas in your house and your family where teamwork could be improved. (**Hint:** Many managers, not to mention coaches, find that it helps to begin with a summary of what *is* working. "Remember that time we all worked together to get the house ready for Joel's birthday party? We all felt proud that the house looked so good—and we were able to find things for a change. Wouldn't it be great to have it looking like that on a regular basis?")

3 Start with a wish list. Again, let everybody participate. Maybe it looks something like this: I want the laundry room to be clean. I want the kitchen to be clean once a day. I'd like to be

able to invite friends over after school, but I know Mom (and/or Dad) works at home. So I'd like one room that can be kept for company and out of the way. I'd like to know that when I'm hungry the odds are pretty good that I can find something tasty and good for me to eat. I'd like to walk into the family room and not find crusty bowls that once held ice cream.

NOTE: When we delegate household responsibilities to children, it's important that we let go of any unreasonably high expectations we might have. There will be some things about the way our children perform that will annoy us. But before we get out the tool kit to fix this, we should stop and think, Is this my child's problem or mine? Is there a real problem in what my child is doing, or is she just not doing it my way? Is there really a perfect way to take out the garbage, clean a room, or mop a floor?

4 Take a lesson from business. Schedule some time for team-building. Block out an afternoon or evening on your calendar and turn off your phone. You might even want to go so far as to pick a weekend when you can get away to someplace with a retreat atmosphere. You might rent a cabin or camp out at a state park. While there, play some favorite or new games and then talk about the way you play together. Take some time for each family member to say what they like doing and why. Then ask questions about how those skills, hobbies, or enjoyable activities could be applied to making your family's house run better. (i.e., teenager who likes to drive the family car

could drive it more if he/she ran errands. A child who likes to arrange things in categories could volunteer to reorganize the games and sports equipment or the pantry. An artistic child could put a faux finish on an old coffee table.)

5 Clear the air. Give each person the freedom to talk openly and honestly about what makes him or her not feel like a valued team member. Talk about what would have to happen for those feelings to change.

Living as a family team means learning to put the feelings of others before our own. This means children, as well as Mom and Dad, exhibit self-control even though they feel like slamming a door, throwing something breakable, or hitting someone. It's important to learn to openly and honestly talk out angry feelings.

We're not a perfect family. But I have to tell you, that as I write this book, I am acutely aware that it is an indescribable blessing to be a part of a family of people who like each other, enjoy being together, and get along most of the time.

If your family, in your mind, doesn't bear any resemblance to a team, and you seem to be growing further apart by the day, it's never too late to start over. Maybe you blame yourself and say, "If only I had done this. If only I had done that. . . ." Focus your energies in a more positive way. Instead of saying "If only," try saying "What now?" Maybe you need to sit down with your husband or a child and ask forgiveness for your part in a relational problem—even if you think you're only 5 percent of the problem. Take responsibility and admit your own mistakes. Without blaming, confirm your love, and confess that you want to be a good Family Manager and on the same team. Ask family members to honestly tell you how you can be a better Family Manager. Your willingness to listen and learn will go a long way. Ask for honest answers to fill-in-the-blank questions to help, especially kids, get feelings out in the open. For example:

I would feel more like a team member if Mom or Dad would

_____.

Something I really like about my family is _____.

I feel less valuable as a team member when _____.

I feel like I add _____ *to our team.*

6 Commit to mutual problem solving. There are some private issues, of course, that should be discussed behind closed doors. But there are many problems—how to deal with a cantankerous neighbor, how to cut back on spending, how to de-stress mornings, how to adapt to a family member's illness—that you can brainstorm about together. When problem situations are approached with an attitude of "What can we do to solve it," not only will this allow the best possible solution to be implemented—because everyone the problem affects is involved in finding answers—but a spirit of unity will be promoted.

7 Write your own set of family team House Rules. Having a set of team rules that everyone agrees to abide by has been a big help to our family. We wrote them early in our family history, and they've evolved over the years to apply to the ages of our children. It's like having a standard operating procedure manual for your home. Think about it. A corporation wouldn't just let its employees start a new job without some guidelines and without knowing some basic company policies.

If you decide to write your own team house rules (which I highly recommend), feel free to use ours as a model. Our rules are not perfect, and they keep changing—which is an important point for all of us to remember: Stay flexible because kids grow, situations change, and schedules get altered.

Peel Team BIG Ten House Rules

1. **We're all in this together. The team rules apply to everyone—even Mom and Dad.**

Kids won't buy a double standard. When you give them permission to call you on the carpet for a violation they will feel ownership of the rules. Albert Schweitzer said, "Example isn't the most important thing, example is the only thing." (Note: If your children

> "It is not fair to ask of others what you are not willing to do yourself."
> —Eleanor Roosevelt

aren't on each other's team, ask yourself what kind of relational role modeling you and your mate are presenting. Is it evident to your children that you and your husband are teammates?)

2. **No yelling at anyone.**

Yelling and screaming are for emergencies only. Lay down a rule about yelling and enforce the consequences. Remember, authority doesn't increase with volume. The moment you are drawn into a yelling match, you surrender parental authority to the strength of the personalities involved. Margaret Thatcher said: "Being powerful is like being a lady. If you have to tell people you are, you aren't." If you have to raise your voice to prove you're in authority over your team, then you're not.

3. **Calling names or making unkind, cutting remarks to each other is strictly out of order.**

"To belittle is to be little." Help your children understand that you're being a small person if you find it necessary to cut someone else down. If feelings are hurt over a comment made in a joking manner, be sure to talk it out so it won't happen again. In our family we do a lot of kidding. The fact that we laugh a lot with and at each other is

47

one of the things I enjoy most about our family. But every family must have boundaries. Some comments—about someone's big nose, deformities, seemingly stupid mistakes —are definitely inappropriate and do not fall into the category of playful teasing. It's important that when family members poke fun at one another, it's fun for everyone. Don't tolerate disrespectful or devaluing words between team members. Enforce consequences for offenders.

4. Take responsibility for your own actions and words.

All family members are always responsible for their own actions—no matter what the other person does. This principle goes a long way toward promoting healthy adult relationships, as well as relationships with children. Children need help learning how to work through conflicts. When they're fighting, sit them down and hear both sides of the story. Ask questions that make each one think about both sides of the problem. Guide them to discover what the root problem really is and focus on their behavior—not what was done to them. Remind them that they're on the same team.

5. Keep confidential what you share with each other.

If your family is going to be a team, you must be able to trust each other. Not only Mom and Dad, but kids too. Your children need to know they can trust you. Don't talk about one child's problems to another child. And don't talk to your friends about confidential family issues or matters your child shares with you. One mother I know virtually ruined her own daughter's reputation and their relationship by openly talking to other mothers about how she couldn't trust her daughter. Although the daughter had abused her mother's trust only once by sneaking out with an older boy, when the news traveled—as it unfortunately does—the occurrence was blown totally out of proportion in the minds of those who heard it.

6. Ask forgiveness when you have hurt or offended someone, even if it was an accident.

Sometimes it's hard—really hard for kids—to see the importance of restoring a relationship—especially if they can't see that they did anything wrong. Make sure you set the example by apologizing when you hurt or disappoint them—even if it was unintentional.

Saying "I'm sorry" or "I was wrong" won't undermine your authority—living a double standard will.

7. Respect each other's space.

Team or not, everyone needs a degree of ownership and privacy. We make a habit of knocking before opening someone's closed door. Talk openly about giving each other space and respecting each other's feelings. For years our teenagers shared a room. They learned to give each other privacy when needed. And since one of the boys is a creative slob (to put it mildly) and the other one likes order and neatness, they had to learn to think of each other's feelings and cut each other some slack.

8. Respect each other's stuff.

It's important for all family members to respect the property of others. And kids need to learn to share their belongings with others. To do this, they must have a sense of control over their things and respect the control someone else has over their things. This means if James has a friend over and they want to play with something that belongs to a big brother who isn't home to give his permission, then they find something else to play with. It means if Joel wants to wear a sweater of John's, he asks John first. It also means that Bill and I respect their property.

9. Agree to abide by a family chore system.

Work out potential problems ahead of time. Identify the consistent conflicts in your home—whose turn it is to feed the dog or do the dishes, how many minutes someone gets to play a video game, how much time is spent on the telephone, etc. Meet together as a family and map out simple guidelines of fairness.

At one point in our family life, It's-your-turn and I-did-it-last-time arguments were causing me to give my kids a piece of my mind—which I could ill afford to lose. We were all wasting precious emotional energy on small issues. We agreed on a fair way to rotate privileges and responsibilities. We decided to rotate monthly who got to ride "shotgun" in the car and chose which cassette to play first. (To some this may sound trivial, but those of you with elementary- to junior-high-age children understand me perfectly.) As for responsibilities, we set up a chore system so each person knows exactly whose responsibility it is to do what. This has worked well for a number of years. Now they know who has kitchen duty and when. And there's no need to bicker over whose job it is to feed the dogs and take out the garbage.

10. Agree to get together regularly for family team meetings.

It's important to keep the communication lines open—to talk about ongoing problems and share successes. Make sure everyone has an opportunity to add to the agenda. (One Family Manager told me her secret to getting her kids to attend team meetings without griping: that's where she distributes their allowances.)

STRETCH YOUR MIND:
Take a piece of paper and draw a picture of your family
and write a one-line caption. Have each member
of your family do the same.

12 Easy Ways to Build Team Spirit

"Celebrate what you want to see more of."
—Tom Peters

1 Show support and active interest in your husband's work and your kids' world.

2 Don't expect your kids to act beyond their understanding and skill level, but sometimes give them assignments that will be challenging. Be sure to cheer them on.

3 Try not to ask your kids to do things where their weaknesses will prevail over their strengths.

4 Thank your children for the small things they do, even if it's for chores they're supposed to do.

5 Remind your husband and your children regularly that you're glad you're all on the same team.

6   Look for ways to make jobs fun.

7   Aggressively look for activities and outings you can participate in together.

8   Bring back family dinnertime. Eating together is an unparalleled opportunity for family discussion of issues both large and small. Encourage conversation by not allowing television or phone calls during dinner.

9   Turn off the TV and play a game together.

10   Turn off the car radio and talk about what's going on in each other's world.

11   Do something special for a family member that they don't expect—like a chore they don't want to do.

12   Be flexible.

> "The key to developing people is to catch them doing something right."
> —Ken Blanchard and Spencer Johnson,
>   *The One Minute Manager*

---

12 Easy Ways to Demolish a Team

1   Let your kids know that your adult world is more important than their world.

2   Make sure each family member has his or her own TV in their bedroom so they can spend a lot of time alone.

3   Be too busy to attend your kids' school and athletic functions.

4 Call it "baby-sitting" when your husband takes care of the kids instead of "parenting."

5 Talk about doing a job like it is punishment instead of making it seem like the job is part of being in a family.

6 Be a martyr. Nag or complain regularly about how much work needs to be done and how you never get any help. Sigh a lot.

7 Don't go to the trouble to plan family outings.

8 Don't take family vacations together.

9 Regularly criticize family members for not meeting your expectations.

10 Whine about how one family member's circumstances are affecting everyone else's life.

11 Be rigid.

12 Disapprove of family members' performance and belittle their efforts. Always make them redo the job.

Who "Makes" the Team

I've talked to single mothers over the years who are, in many ways, even more proficient Family Managers and team builders than married women with cooperative husbands. In a very real way, necessity is the mother of invention. If you are a single mother and the concept of building a team is new to you and your children, particularly if your children are small, you may want to talk with a trusted friend or extended family member about the changes you want to begin making. Use that person as a business manager might use a consultant: as a sounding board, as a person to help you brainstorm ideas and ways to implement them. Then, involve your children as soon as you can. You

"I am only one; but still I am one. I cannot do everything,

can explain basic team concepts to very young children in a simple way. They can begin to have a "we're all in this together" spirit from an early age.

Given the realities of being a single mom, it's important to reassure your kids that even though you are all in this together, you're the mom and you will be there for them and take care of them. Too much sense of responsibility (in a single- or two-parent family) can be as detrimental to a child as too little.

Single-parent families especially might want to get creative about who's "on the team." Consider banding together with other families you might know from school or church or day care to share special occasions. Plan shared work days for larger projects like cleaning the basement or painting the house. Talk with your close friends about becoming a support system for each other. Although you may not live day to day with these "team members," they can be like special consultants.

If you are the only person in your family committed to being a team, don't give up. You don't know what good your efforts may accomplish. Resistance from older children or teens to the new idea of being a team is probably normal and to be expected, whatever your family constellation. Rome wasn't built overnight. Worker accountability wasn't implemented in one eight-hour shift. And you might need to suffer through some dramatic consequences when your son discovers that he has no clean jeans for his date because he didn't do the agreed-on job which was to put his laundry in the hamper. Or when there's no dinner one evening because your daughter decided to hang out at a girlfriend's house after school and didn't come home to cook on her designated night.

A Dozen Team Benefits
----

1. Two (or more) people can accomplish more than one. It's simple arithmetic—two people times two hours cleaning

but still I can do something; I will not refuse to do--------------

equals a clean house, an attic or basement where you can actually find things, a formerly trashed minivan that's neat as a pin on the inside and waxed to a high gloss on the outside.

2. An overwhelming task often becomes manageable when it's shared. That's true for tangibles that one person can't do alone, like moving furniture around, and intangibles like brainstorming ways to trim the budget.

3. When you work together, you get through faster and have more time for the whole family to spend on more meaningful activities.

4. Teamwork develops team-member skills—cooperation, communication, sensitivity—in children and their parents preparing them to be better team members at school and at work.

5. No one person has all the skills and abilities needed to manage a family. A team allows family members to focus on individual strengths.

6. The family team provides a safe and loving environment in which to learn new skills and work on weaker areas.

7. The team approach stimulates commitment to the family. Someone who is not required to help usually doesn't value the family.

> "Leaders do not give up easily. Whether attributable to patience, perseverance, or even tenacity, effective leaders are not easily discouraged. They find successful courses of action by refusing to acknowledge failure and by continuing to work to resolve the problem."
> —Mary McClure

--------the something I can do."—Helen Keller

8. Working together is usually more fun and always more encouraging—we're in this together!

9. Teamwork provides daily opportunities for family members to demonstrate trust and confidence in each other, building up that invaluable asset—self-esteem.

10. More than one head working to solve problems from different perspectives makes for creative solutions.

11. Since no one person is trying to do everything, all of you have more energy to overcome obstacles.

12. The family that works together is there for each other. One of the great blessings of a family team is having people to go through the good times and the bad times with you.

STRETCH YOUR MIND:
Set a goal as a family to look for ways that "two are better than one . . . ." Not only will you share the load, but you'll multiply the pleasures along the way.

One for All and All for One

California's giant Sequoia trees have stood for almost two thousand years and grow to over two hundred feet high with a seventy-foot circumference. You'd think trees that big would need gigantic deep roots to help them remain upright in the face of wind, rain, and years. Not so. They have shallow root systems, barely below the ground. But they also have a competitive edge in the tree world. They grow in groves, and their roots intertwine with each other so when the strong winds come they hold each other up. This is what a team is all about—holding up each other, helping each other, being there for each other.

One for all and all for one, the Three Musketeers and your family, having adventures, building a team. Before you go on, I want to invite you to come back to this chapter when the going gets tough, or any time at all. In fact, I encourage you to pick a couple of times during the year to sit down with your team. Celebrate and affirm what's working for you. Assess and make plans to change what's not.

I've saved perhaps the most important thing to remember for last: Team-building is a process. It's not something you do once and then it's done. In that aspect it's like cleaning the bathroom, although a whole lot more fun!

c h ap t e r

Discovering Your
Family Management Style

"I don't know the key to success,
but the key to failure is trying to please everybody."
—Bill Cosby

"Each mind has its own method."
—Ralph Waldo Emerson

I grew up in a home that was a bit unusual for its time—the time of June Cleaver anyway. Both of my parents were professionals. Mother owned her own business, and she had a full-time housekeeper/cook to help at home. Consequently and unfortunately, I never learned to clean house or cook.

Since Mother's business was women's clothing, she had a tailor on duty at all times. If I needed a zipper replaced or a hem raised, the tailor took care of it. I never learned to do even the basics.

Although I was aware of my domestic shortcomings when I married Bill, I didn't let this get me down. I love a challenge, and I simply ignored my first setbacks. (And I'll admit they were legion.) I was blazing new territory, and I figured that anyone with a new college degree should be able to figure out how to serve a romantic candlelight dinner for two seven days a week, clean the bathroom twice daily, color coordinate her husband's outfits with tags for days of the week, be there for her husband when he needed to talk about his problems in graduate school, read three new books a week, teach school, jog five miles a day, and still have time to plan fun outings for the weekends. I mean we're not talking brain surgery here. (Little did I realize that, in some ways, brain surgery is probably less complicated.)

It took me awhile, but finally I realized that in my quest for domesticity, I was mostly asking the wrong questions. They went something like this: What does a homemaker look like? Does she wear an apron all day? Does she have cooking substitutions memorized? Can she make a bed with hospital corners? (The right question here, of course, is does anyone care, unless she's a nurse or in the army?) Does she grow her own vegetables ? Can she operate a pressure cooker without summoning the fire department or ending up with third degree burns on her arms? Does she make all her clothes? Can she work full-time and host a dinner party for eight on Friday night? Can she see her reflection in her dinner plates? Does she rotate her husband's underwear in the drawer? Should her apartment look like she's expecting a photographer from the Style section any minute, all the time? Should her husband's favorite (ugly) reading lamp be donated to charity?

I didn't give up my domestic ideals all at once. I remember the Saturday I decided to go to the park rather than clean our apartment.

The photographer didn't show up, and we lived through the week with dust bunnies under the bed. What a relief! I gave up growing vegetables when I figured out that I'd spent $159 on fertilizer, nursery plants,

> **"Effective management always means asking the right questions."**
> —**Robert Heller**, Editor, *Management Today*

gardening tools, and a cute little outfit. At the end of the summer, I harvested about $25 worth of vegetables—except for the zucchini; I had so much I baked zucchini, stuffed zucchini, stir-fried zucchini; and made zucchini cake. On the seventh day, Bill rebelled.

Learning Curve on a Long Downward Slope

Over the years, as our family has grown, my questions have changed. For a long time that didn't stop me from my one-woman crusade to become, if not the perfect homemaker and mother, then at least a candidate. I attended seminars that were supposed to help me organize my home and manage my time better. I usually came away with a glow of inspiration. I would buy each "expert's" philosophy hook, line, and sinker, sometimes along with a week's grocery budget worth of materials that would make it so easy to organize our belongings and manage time that a toddler could do it. I think the longest the glow ever lasted was about eighteen hours. Then feelings of guilt and inadequacy set in. What was wrong with me? How could hundreds of thousands of young mothers have time to make their homes perfect havens from the world, and I couldn't get dinner on the table if the baby was crying?

I have never been one to give up easily. Bound and determined to get this homemaking thing down, I watched different friends in their homes, figuring I could pick up skills and techniques by imitation and osmosis. I tried to be like them, which made me feel even worse about myself. I pretty much stopped that method when I realized that my friend Susan, who could whip up a seven-layer chocolate cake from scratch—without a recipe, had an MA in home economics. I told myself I didn't have her training.

But did that stop me from comparing myself regularly to friends like Lindsey? Not a chance. Lindsey didn't live in a home. She lived on a different planet. Her pantry was alphabetized—artichokes in the upper left corner, to zoo-animal crackers in the lower right corner. She had menus planned through Thanksgiving 2001. She ironed her children's shoelaces and stored them in graduated lengths. Once, after Lindsey attended a home organization class (which is tantamount to Julia Childs attending a cooking class), she took inventory and made a list of everything they owned, where it belonged, and how often it needed maintenance. She knew exactly how many dry-cleaner bags were in her closets at any given moment (they were perfectly stacked in eight-inch squares), where to find the warranty card on her twelve-year-old fondue pot, and how long it had been since she oiled the nutcracker. She regularly purged her home of useless knickknacks so that it had the warmth of an operating room. I didn't like it. So why did I feel guilty every time I left her house and went back to mine?

"The lure of the distant and the difficult is deceptive. The great opportunity is where you are."—John Burroughs

THINK ABOUT

Finally I almost gave up. I decided that some women are born to be homemakers. Their touch brings order to the messiest drawer. They can alphabetize and categorize the mail with the speed of a Pentium 120. Their families can eat off the kitchen floor. Unfortunately I wasn't one of them.

Some women regard housekeeping as an annoying news bulletin during a Tom Cruise love scene. They find almost anything more interesting than housecleaning and cooking. They would rather walk barefoot on hot coals than clean a closet.

For years I struggled with trying to understand which kind of woman I am. I longed to be able to open up my lingerie drawer and not have to spend twenty minutes untangling my pantyhose, only to find I didn't have a single pair without a run. I was getting tired of my kitchen getting a four-star rating in *Exterminator's Quarterly*. And it bothered me that solid air fresheners melted in our bathroom in five minutes. (Okay, it wasn't quite that bad, but it was close.)

Finally things started to come together for me. I realized that I'd been trying to be all things to all people, live up to someone else's ideal, and do ALL things equally well.

A New Light Was Dawning

At the same time I was going through this tunnel of domestic despair, and totally unrelated to my struggle, I happened to be reading a couple of business and management books. I realized that maybe some of the same principles that helped corporations run efficiently and effectively could be applied at home. From the vantage point of business man-

agement, homemaking started to make sense to me. I started over, reading the same books with my home in mind and took notes. Lots of notes. I wrote down principles and ideas, the first of which was a description of a good manager. This was the beginning of the end of my domestic despair.

Seven Strategies of Smart Managers

1. **Maximize your strengths.** For example, I have a good eye for style and color, and I love to entertain people in our home. But I hate to cook. So my parties tend to either have simple, but nicely presented, food, or I plan parties when I know Bill can give me a lot of support in the kitchen. Or, if I have the money, which happens about once a decade, I hire a caterer. No matter how the food gets on the table, I always have fresh cut flowers arranged in various containers, the table always looks great, and house is decorated according to the season or occasion.

   "Too many people overvalue what they're not and undervalue what they are." — Malcolm Forbes   THINK ABOUT IT

2. **Minimize your weaknesses.** Asking for help when you need it, many times, is a good way to kill two birds with one stone, as it were. When I get an idea for a valance over our bedroom window, I have two choices. I can put myself down because I don't know how to make it myself, and I can't afford to pay someone to do it for me. Or I can pick out the fabric, set up the sewing machine and supplies, and ask Bill to do the measuring and stitching. This way, we enhance our bedroom and spend time working on a project together.

3. **Use the resources at hand.** I am a fortunate Family Manager. I have the resources of three strong sons and a willing, helpful husband. Some of our best times together have been working on home remodeling projects together. The home itself, of course, affects resources in more ways than one. For instance, when we remodel our family room in a teenager-friendly motif, it becomes a resource for them when choosing where to go on the weekend. When the boys learn home-improvement skills, such as painting or laying wood floors, these skills become

resources they can use to get jobs elsewhere to make extra money. And also on the money-resource front, we've made quite a bit of money remodeling rundown houses and then selling them. We've financed several wonderful family vacations, bought appliances, and helped pay for college tuition with the money we earned together.

4. **Delegate as much as you can.** When I read that the average family of four produces two tons of dirty laundry each year, I thought, "Small wonder I feel like I spend half my life folding clothes." Surely, I decided, if the men I live with can learn how to program a VCR so they won't miss game four of the World Series, then they can learn some basic laundry skills. Actually, when I approached the men in my house about sharing the laundry load, they were quite receptive, especially the older boys. They were tired of my shrinking their knit shirts.

5. **Set your priorities.** Remember Lindsey? Her house was always perfectly clean, her closets and drawers were perfectly organized, every month her checkbook balanced perfectly, her hair was always perfectly in place—and her husband and children were perfectly miserable. Somewhere along the way she had forgotten how to have fun. She took life and herself too seriously. Household responsibilities had become more important than relationships. I may be slow on the uptake about some things, but I was a fast study this time. I clearly saw that although I wanted to run my home more efficiently, I didn't want to run it into the

- What are you really good at?
- What are your limitations?
- What strengths do your family members have?
- What can you delegate?
- What are the most important things to you? your priorities?
- What is the fun quotient in your family?

ground. And I wasn't going to beat myself into the ground for being the kind of woman who has to rake the kitchen floor before I can mop. In my mind I'd rather my home be a fun place than a fastidious place.

STRETCH YOUR MIND:
Learning to be a fun person means being willing to laugh
when you discover mildewed gym shorts under your
teenager's bed, and to leave dishes in the sink
and go on a spontaneous family bike ride.

6. **Work smarter, not harder.** It occurred to me one day—maybe it was when I was standing at the sink scrubbing a pan and I figured out that if I sprayed every pan I cooked in with nonstick vegetable spray, whether the recipe called for it or not, I could cut down on cleanup time. Or maybe it was when I'd been standing in the grocery store checkout line for twenty minutes I decided that if I went to the grocery store when other people didn't, like early in the morning, I could get out faster. Or perhaps it was when Joel woke up in the middle of the night with a sore throat, I realized that if I'd keep my medicine cabinet well-stocked, we wouldn't have to make midnight runs to the drugstore when someone got sick. Now, I'm in the habit of looking for ways to take a little time now to do something that will make more time for me later.

THINK ABOUT

"The best way to clean a frying pan that has burned food cemented to the bottom is to let it soak in soapy water for several days and then, when nobody is looking, throw it in the garbage."—Dave Barry

"A home in which there is no laughter

7. **Outlay should not exceed income.** It doesn't take a master's degree in finance to understand that whether it's a multibillion-dollar corporation or a family with two kids, a dog, and a cat, you can't spend more than you make—or at least you shouldn't. In this day of easy credit and long payouts, it takes a savvy Family Manager to operate her household within her family's means and without running up big debts.

Family Management Is . . .

A woman told me recently that she didn't see how I could call myself a Family Manager. When I questioned why she would say that, I realized that her image of a Family Manager was a 1960s housewife. She thought I should be the consummate cook, a wonderful seamstress, and that I should enjoy housework—traditional descriptives we think of when we use the term housewife. And she knew I wasn't big on or good at lots of those things.

I explained to her that even though none of the above described me, I was a pretty darn good Family Manager. Every morning I get up and think through the seven departments I manage. Then I make lists and jot myself notes about responsibilities and tasks that need to be done in each department. Some of these things I delegate—which is part of being a good manager—especially those things where I lack skill. I might delegate to Bill the job of barbecuing chicken on the grill for dinner, or I might delegate helping James with a science project to one of the older boys. Or if I have to take a pound cake to a mothers' meeting at school, I might delegate that to Sara Lee. (The way I see it, if she does it better, why not let her do it?)

Vive La Difference

It's important for each Family Manager to discover her unique, I repeat *unique*, family-management style. To do this you need to know where

is only a house." — G.H. Knight.

your current picture of a good Family Manager came from, and you need to know yourself, your own style, so you can work on your strengths, compensate for your weaker areas, and choose your priorities.

That last sentence was very important. Please read it again.

I meet countless women across the country who feel frustrated. They are weary of disorganization and clutter. But interestingly it's not just those who live in chaos who feel that way. Some of the tidiest women I know are frustrated as well. They feel inadequate because they'd like to be more flexible and creative. The common thread in this is that both types of women seem familiar to me because they're essentially trying to do the same thing I was. They're trying to be perfect. Or at least exceptional in all categories—and, believe me, it'll never happen. They're trying to be the one type of manager that never works: SuperMom. She might make a good cartoon character, but she sure doesn't make a good Family Manager, mostly because she doesn't exist in the real world. Her corporate counterpart is the boss who tries to do it all, who doesn't value creativity or self-direction in team members, and therefore doesn't get any. Sooner or later the super-manager, in the home or in the workplace, feels frustrated because things aren't going well despite best efforts, and she usually becomes bitter because of lack of cooperation.

How We Learned to Do What We Do

There are three ways we've learned our style of family management.

> "Believe in your limitations and sure enough they are yours."
> —Richard Bach

Assimilation:

This is the way Mother, Grandmother, or Great Aunt Susie did it—the way you were raised—and you simply accepted it, no questions asked, as the way it should be done. But now that you're grown up, you feel pressured to conform—whether the style fits you or not. It's the accepted way to do it, and you want to please.

A friend of mine told me a story that gets right to the point. She said that for many years a woman she knew would buy a ham for holiday dinners, bring it home, and lop the end off. When asked why she was throwing away a perfectly good end of the ham, she said, "My mother always did it. That's what you're supposed to do." She thought the end of the ham was somehow tainted. So, finally, one day she asked her mother why she cut off the end. Her mother replied, "Because my roaster pan wasn't big enough."

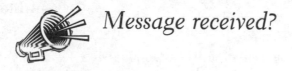 *Message received?*

Adoption:

You idealize and idolize someone else and try to be like her. You do certain things because your college roommate, a famous expert, or a major TV personality does it this way or that way. In fact, people often move from assimilation, once they discover there is not a "right" way to do something, to adoption. Adoption can work just fine, and is a good way, to bring new ideas into your life, unless you aren't aware of your own strengths and weaknesses when you're deciding what to adopt.

I had a major crisis in my life a number of years ago over Thanksgiving dinner. First, I tried to cook my turkey in a pastry crust. It looked so easy on TV, but at my house Tom Turkey didn't work as a doughboy. Then I tried a new cranberry salad. The photograph on the magazine cover was beautiful and the cover-line said it was a salad anyone could make. Wrong. My fresh-from-the-bog cranberries were sort of still stuck in the bog. Let's just say that nobody ate them because nobody could pull the silver serving-spoon out of them.

Personalization:

You value your uniqueness as an individual and figure out how you are wired. You're energized because you maximize your strengths and downplay your weaknesses. You pick and choose how to do something because it fits or doesn't fit you. You can remember your mother's homemade angel-food cakes, thirteen egg whites, from scratch fondly. And then go buy a chocolate cake at the bakery for your dinner party because cooking isn't your gift. You can read a magazine article about how to start a home-based decorating business, and then decide, yes, I would like to do something to make some extra money. But make it a bookkeeping business because you're good with numbers and details.

> "You cannot make a crab walk straight."
> —Aristophanes

I believe that each of us has a unique style—a certain energizing way of doing things. And when we cooperate with who we are and our unique style, it brings an incredible amount of joy. And joy always brings energy with it. To me, this means that I don't have to feel substandard because my clothes don't all hang the same way in my closet, and sometimes they don't even hang. I am, more often than not, in a hurry and have about ten things on my mind. Therefore, I dress quickly and sometimes don't stop right then to pick up the clothing and accessories I leave in my wake. I clean up my closet twice a week—which means the other five days it may be messy—and that's okay with me. It also means that if you come to my house, you may see dust on the coffee table, but you'll also see fresh flowers in a vase—because I'd rather spend ten minutes adding beauty to a room than taking away the dust.

Work with What Works

Now I don't claim to be a psychologist or social scientist by any stretch of the imagination, but I've learned that an important key to managing your family well and feeling good about yourself as a Family Manager is not only discovering your personal management style, but also how to motivate yourself to get done what needs to be done.

Some of you like to make lists and handle details. You enjoy systems and routines, and you usually put things back where you found them. Others of you can tolerate some degree of disorderly mess, and you like to keep everything you're working on in sight. Over the past thirty years researchers have learned that to a great extent, our behavior, our learning and work styles, and our personalities have less to do with Freudian potty-training theories than which side of the brain dominates our thinking process. Individuals dominated by the left side of their brains tend to express themselves through order and organization. People dominated by the right side of their brains tend to express themselves through creative means. Whichever you are, it's important—for your family's good and your own mental health—that you accept and work with your natural style when it comes to managing your family and anything else for that matter.

For the most part, management theories have been dominated by left-brain thinkers. So, most of us have learned left-brained kinds of rules for organization and management, such as "Handle each piece of paper only once," "Finish one thing before you start another," and "Schedule certain task at certain times for certain success." This fits left brainers, who carefully plan out each day, set their priorities and schedule everything precisely. But it overlooks a part of the

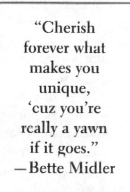

"Cherish forever what makes you unique, 'cuz you're really a yawn if it goes."
—Bette Midler

mental process some creative people use. They like to juggle a number of different projects at a time, tend to file in piles and live in a somewhat cluttered environment. This looks irresponsible and sloppy to left-brainers. But to a right-brain dominant person, this "mess" works as visual organization and order. My life changed incredibly for the better when I discovered and accepted my natural brain dominance and developed a family-management style that is in sync with it.

The term "brain dominance" refers to a person's tendency to think and act according to the characteristics of one side, or hemisphere, of the brain cortex, rather than the other side. It's important to understand that there is a constant give and take between the right and left sides of a normal brain. The two sides of a brain are constantly "in touch" with each other. Many accomplishments such as decorating a room, performing in a musical, writing this book require continual cooperation of both sides of the brain, because all these activities need an emotional and aesthetic response, as well as logic, analysis, and language skills. This same cooperation is needed in managing a family.

There's no right or wrong style of managing a family.

 THINK ABOUT IT

Recognizing which side of your brain dominates your thinking helps you develop your own unique style and methods of managing your family. I tend to be right-brained, which means, for one thing, I like to be flexible. If you tell me I have to clean house a certain day each week, I'll get bored. I enjoy change. I like to rearrange the furniture just to rearrange it. I like to vary schedules. I don't care what time we eat dinner, just so we all sit down at the same time and enjoy each other's company around a beautifully set table. I like to work spontaneously. A spur-of-the-moment-attic cleanout is much more attractive to me than putting it on the calendar and dreading the time I've set to do it. I like experimenting with something new, like trying to paint a wall to give it a marbleized look. I have no problem leaving dishes in the sink while I'm painting. And I enjoy working on several projects at the same time. Even while I write this paragraph, I've got a load of clothes in the washer, I'm cooking chicken breasts to make two casseroles (I'm not contradicting what I said about my deficient culinary skills. The recipes are easy. After all, my family does have to eat.), I'm watching our new, not-yet-housebroken puppy out of the corner of my eye, and I'm glancing at the clock so I won't be late to a mothers' meeting at school. I work well under deadlines (maybe that's one reason why I like to write) and get energized by challenging or unconventional situations. I like to have lots of sensory stimulation in my work areas—bright colors, artwork, photo-graphs of family and friends, and music. And my desk usually looks messy because I like to have my work within view. Stacks and piles don't bother me.

My left-brained friend Peggy is completely different. She has created housework methods and routines that run like clockwork. She gets pleasure from developing a system or procedure to tackle a task, then following that procedure every time until the task is complete. She would rather focus on one job, do it well and do it thoroughly, than have a lot of projects going at the same time. She, too, likes to learn new things, but she wants detailed, step-by-step instructions when learning something new. Her closets and drawers are impeccably organized and efficient, and her desk is rarely in disarray. I don't think I've ever seen dirty dishes in her sink for more than five minutes. Peggy and I, although we're very different, are both good Family Managers. We just manage in different ways.

> "Respect . . . is appreciation of the separateness of the other person, of the ways in which he or she is unique."
> —Annie Gottlieb

S T R e t C H YOUR MIND:
Don't try to recreate yourself. It won't work.
Figure out how to best use your talents
and make your unique personality work for you.

Understanding your right- and left-brain tendencies can help you understand why you manage your family the way you do and why you get frustrated with some of the things you do. It can also help you discover more efficient and effective ways to manage your family that are compatible with who you are. Both right- and left-brain forces are equally valuable and necessary in this world. What matters is that you learn to work and manage your family in sync with your natural design—which is the most productive and energy-efficient way for each individual to work. Learning how to be whole-brained—integrating both sides of your brain into a harmonious working relationship—you become more well-rounded and able to meet a wider range of challenges in life. (For further reading, see *You Don't Have to Go Home from Work Exhausted* by Dr. Ann McGee-Cooper, Bowen & Rogers, 1990.)

Whatever side of the brain you think dominantly with, it's time to look at how you operate and how you might like to change. Take time to assess your strengths and weaknesses, your ways of doing things. Remember that your operating style is an essential part of who you are—your design. When we discover and align ourselves with this design, we actually create energy for ourselves rather than let the tasks of Family Management drain us.

> "My business is not to remake myself, but make the absolute best of what God made."
> —Robert Browning

Decide what works for you. And use it, use it, use it. Have I emphasized that enough? Capitalize on your strengths. Know yourself and your family, and your management job will be about a thousand times easier.

The point of seeing yourself as a Family Manager is not to turn you into something you are not. I'm not suggesting that you alphabetize your soup cans—unless that gives you a sense of personal fulfillment.

Discovering Your Management Style

Most of us have a pretty good idea of who we are, what we're good at, and the areas in which we need help. And that's really what discovering our management style is all about. I can't count the number of different books and theories about management I've read in the past five years, and I won't bore you with them here.

Whichever side of the brain you are thinking with right now, it's important for you to stop and do some careful, strategic evaluation. If you don't, the pressures of responsibility that fall on every Family

Manager will invariably lead you away from managing your family in a way that can bring you joy and energy.

(1) **Recognize the energy boosters and drainers in your life.** There are some things that we love to do—that actually energize us. Sometimes I can work on a project for hours at a time—through meals and late into the night—and feel invigorated. On the other hand, there are some activities that drain me—five minutes seems like five hours. There are certain things each of us likes to work with. Certain results we like to achieve. Certain ways we like to work with (or without) people. Certain ways we like to be rewarded.

So how do you discover your own unique style?

One of the best ways is to follow the scent of joy in your life. I've found it helps to make a list of the things you really love to do. Do that now.

Next, ask yourself this question about each item on your list: "What is the best part of this thing I love?" Think about who or what you are working with—people, numbers, tools, animals, concepts, systems, colors. Is there a common element that runs through your experience?

Think about what you are doing, crafting, designing, organizing, etc. What are you doing that is so invigorating? Think about the payoff. Does someone admire your work or do you just sit back and pat yourself on the back for a job well done? How about people? Do you have an audience, or are you alone? Does anyone else help? What is the other person's role?

> "Before we can move into a new *ar—rangement,* we must first go through a period of *de—rangement.*"
> —M. C. Richards

As you begin to answer these questions and see patterns repeated in your life, you'll see why you hate to clean up the kitchen by yourself, but don't mind cleaning up when you have a team of people helping you. Or maybe you're like my friend who doesn't like help in the kitchen. She has an exact way she likes the kitchen to be cleaned, and she would rather do it herself so she can do it "right." My husband loves teamwork; he can go for hours at an unpleasant task if someone else is doing it with him. He bogs down in no time, sometimes even at things he likes, if no one's around. I am the opposite. I can get tons more accomplished if I'm by myself. (I found these principles in *Finding a Job You Can Love* by Ralph Mattson and Arthur Miller, Thomas Nelson, 1982.)

(2) Spend as much time as possible on what you love and what you're good at. When we operate in the realm of our capabilities, we will excel, be energized, and receive a great deal of satisfaction from what we do. On the other hand, when we're working at tasks where we lack skills and abilities, there is a predictable scenario of mediocrity, burnout, and frustration.

Unfortunately, this is the real world and none of us gets to do what we love to do 100 percent of the time, neither can we always do what we're good at. This being the case, at least we can be smart about it. To me that means finding ways to spend more time on what I love and feel like I'm good at.

What do you love to do? What skills or abilities do you have that you feel good about? What tasks give you pleasure when you've finished because you've enjoyed most of the process and you know you've done a good job?

(3) Whenever possible, delegate the stuff you hate to do to someone else. Realize that your nightmare can be someone else's dream. Two women told me how they used this principle to lighten their loads. Katy hates housework but loves yard work. Lori hates to get dirt under her fingernails but gets a great deal of satisfaction from cleaning her home. So, by mutual agreement, they decided to trade out tasks. One day a week

> "Do what you can, with what you have, where you are"
> —Theodore Roosevelt

74

Katy takes care of all the yard work for both homes, while Lori does the housecleaning. It's a win/win proposition.

What do you hate to do? What skills or abilities do you lack but feel you need to accomplish some jobs? What tasks do you perform that fall into the category of pure drudgery—you experience little joy in the process and the only thing you feel good about when they're finished is the fact that they're finished. What distasteful jobs can you delegate—to family members or someone else?

When I call a family workday at our house, I delegate the organizational jobs to left-brained Joel—bringing order to a chaotic garage, organizing the pantry, putting the videotapes in logical order. When I need a flower bed designed and planted, or if I need paint touched up, I ask John. The artist in him loves doing those types of things.

S t r e t C H YOUR MIND:
The fact is that great family management demands a set of skills
that no one person has. There will always be jobs you hate.
The trick is learning to work with your strengths,
work around areas where you are not gifted,
and through people who are.

Chances are, under your own roof, a whole stable of gifts are ready to be put on the right track. Discover what family members are good at, and put them to work in that area. When they're working at something they're gifted at, they'll usually work harder and faster, and you'll have less griping—which is a big plus in my mind.

(4) **Divide fairly the stuff no one likes to do, and try to figure out ways to pump joy into the experience.** I found it helps to reward your team, as well as yourself, with something you like after you've finished an unpleasant task. When there are distasteful jobs we have to do as a family (our pre-summer garage cleanout and yard cleanup is an all-day affair and, to the boys, ranks someplace between getting a tooth filled

and breaking a leg), we divide up the tasks, work really hard, then reward ourselves by eating out at a favorite restaurant.

"Speak softly and carry a
big carrot."—Howard C. Lauer

THINK ABOUT IT

(5) **Work as a team on some projects.** Teams are what "nineties management" is all about—breaking a project up into parts, then delegating the parts according to talent and skills. I've learned that no one is good at everything. I am good at some things, and I try to pour most of my energy into those things. That way, I'll be able to be excellent in something. Otherwise, I'll be poor to mediocre in everything. That's exactly what focusing on your weaknesses will do. If you spend all your energy trying to make up for what you don't have, you're pouring energy down a black hole. How much more productive to invest your energy in what you're good at. I used to think that I had to be Betty Crocker every time we had guests. I spent so much time trying to cook a memorable meal that I wasn't much fun to be around, before, during, or after the occasion. I'm afraid the occasion was all too memorable, but not for the reasons I'd hoped. Now, I usually let someone else do the things that are not my strong suit. I spend time focusing on the atmosphere and the people rather than food, and for the most part people leave our home with fond memories— not indigestion.

10 Benefits of Discovering Your Own Management Style

1. It will help you focus your time and energy.

Situation: The homeroom mother calls and asks you to be in charge of organizing field games for the May Day celebration at your child's school.

The old you: Although you are not a detail person, and you hate to administrate, coordinate, and orchestrate anything, you say "yes." You don't want people to think you aren't a good mother. The day of the event arrives, and you, your family, and most everyone working with you are somewhere between frustrated and miserable.

The new you: You understand that you are not good at organizing, but this doesn't make you feel inferior. You know you are skilled at other things—like painting. You graciously answer that you cannot accept the position of Field-day organizer, but you would love to provide special personalized plastic cups for all the children in your child's class to use at Field Day then take home as a souvenir.

2. It will help you make selective decisions when you are overloaded with options.

Situation: It's time to spring clean—a huge job. Your options are: Do it all by yourself—one day at a time until it's done, hire a cleaning service to do it all, do the major cleaning yourself and have family members clean their own rooms at designated times, get mad at your husband because he doesn't see the need to spring clean—he'd rather you plan something for the family to do together.

The old you: You're overwhelmed because you don't know which way to turn. You dread cleaning by yourself, you can't afford to hire a service, and you don't want to start an argument with your husband. You end up putting it off until next spring, or the next. You get angry every time you open up a closet and something falls on your head.

The new you: You understand that you work best under deadlines and with a team. You set aside one Saturday and make a list of everything that needs to be done. You gather your team (a.k.a. family members) and make a "Beat the Clock" game to get the cleaning done. When finished you do something fun as a family.

3. It will help you maintain balance.

Situation: Your older sister and her husband are coming to visit next month. You have a major deadline at work, and you feel like you can't cope.

The old you: Every day your personality goes from bad to worse. You're dreading your sister's visit because her house always looks like a maga-zine spread. You're down on yourself for being such a slob. Your office deadline looms and you can't imagine putting aside a few days to do nothing but clean the house to your sister's standards. Finally you're so distraught, you feel like you can't do anything right and you throw yourself across the bed and cry in desperation.

The new you: You acknowledge that you've let your housekeeping go while you spent more time at work. And you acknowledge that this is neither the worst thing that could happen to you nor a permanent situation. You choose not to be down on yourself, but to concentrate on some other things you've accomplished. And you set aside half a day to "party clean" the bathroom and the guest room for your sister's visit.

4. It will help you maintain your motivation.

Situation: You hate to clean up the kitchen after dinner.

The old you: You don't like doing it by yourself, so you grumble and complain that you're the only one who cares that the family has a clean kitchen and clean dishes to eat off of. You let them know that you're tired of feeling like everyone's maid, and you'd like to feel appreciated.

The new you: You acknowledge that no one in your family likes to clean up the kitchen. You call a family meeting to talk about the problem. Without blaming or complaining, you simply list the tasks that must be done and you all create a chore system that lists each family member's tasks—clearing the table, doing the dishes, putting up left-overs, cleaning the counters, sink, and floor, taking out the garbage— then for ten to fifteen minutes each night, all family members work together and get the kitchen cleaned up (Maybe not to your standards, but at least it's cleaned up). You also promise to let the kids order in pizza (or something else that's easy to clean up) one night a week and use paper plates and cups that night.

5. It will help you focus on your priorities.

Situation: A community service organization has asked you to be chairperson of a citywide project. It's an honor to be chosen for this position, and there will be a lot of publicity.

The old you: You accept, not thinking through the ramifications of your commitment. Not until it's too late do you realize that you'll be tied up working on the project every Saturday morning for two months, which means you have to miss your son's soccer games. You're miserable on Saturdays while working on the project because you'd rather be at your son's games. It's a lose/lose situation.

The new you: You recognize that you enjoy leadership positions, and some day you'd like to run for public office. But now's not the time because of your son's age and activities. You offer your leadership skills, though, by volunteering to head up the soccer league photo session. You get to use your organizational and leadership skills, get to know a lot of new people, and most importantly, you get to do this with your son.

6. It will allow you to plan events that suit you.

Situation: Each year you celebrate Thanksgiving with your sister and her family. You love to cook, and your sister hates to cook. But she loves to decorate and make things festive.

The old you: When you'd go to your sister's house, the occasion was festive. You played fun games, the kids won prizes, the decorations were fabulous, the music was just right, but the meal left a lot to be desired—like antacids. At your house the meal was always gourmet, but the festivities were a flop.

The new you: You still trade houses each year, but now you do the cooking, and your sister takes care of the decorating and activities. Everyone, including you, enjoys themselves immensely.

7. It will allow you, your husband, and your children to practice problem-solving and planning skills.

Situation: It's time to clean out the basement to get ready for your annual garage sale. Everyone knows it's coming and dreads the event.

The old you: You nag your husband and pull rank on the kids to get the job done. No one likes you for six weeks.

The new you: You sit down with the whole family and lay out all the tasks that need to be done. You begin by letting everyone know that they are important to the proper functioning of the family and then move to how you can get the job done as painlessly as possible. Let individuals pick the jobs they want to do and describe how they want to do them. Then divide the remaining jobs fairly and discuss what can be done to make these as painless as possible. Offer to split up the proceeds.

8. It will affect the quality of your life for the better.

Situation: You were asked by the principal at your daughter's school to be chairman of a fund-raising drive to buy computers for the school. It is a three-month commitment.

The old you: You used to say "yes" to anyone who asked you to volunteer for anything. In trying to meet everyone else's needs, you neglected your own. Because you had so many meetings, you didn't have time to work out at the gym, take that class that was offered during the fall semester, or spend any quiet time alone reading. You ended up empty and miserable, and to tell the truth, you made everyone around you miserable too.

The new you: You've learned to say "No" and you've limited the activities you are involved in to those that are really important to you. You're taking time to fill up yourself, so you have more to give to others.

9. It will affect the quality of your family's life for the better.

Situation: You hate to do the laundry, but it has to be done.

The old you: You did it because you thought it was your job since you were the mom. You know all the technical stuff — when to wash in cold or hot, what to bleach, what not to wash together—but were always receiving complaints because something wasn't clean and ironed.

The new you: You take time to teach each person how to do their own laundry and iron. Now each family member will take responsibility for his or her own clothes and won't blame anyone else if there is a problem.

10. It will give you increased opportunities to spend time doing fun things together as a family.

Situation: Everyone wants to go camping, but next week your brother is coming with his family for a week. You have a lot of work to catch up on from the office in addition to getting your house guest-ready.

The old you: Either you resentfully send your family camping without you, or you go, feeling guilty about all you have to do. You can't have a good time while you are there knowing what lies ahead when you get back.

81

The new you: You make a list of what needs to be done to get the house ready and what has to be packed for the trip. You delegate the tasks in age and skill-appropriate ways to get the house cleaned. You have time to get your office work done and head to the hills by Saturday noon.

The Bottom-Line Don't

"Don't let what you can't do interfere with what you can do."

—*John Wooden*

The Bottom-Line Do

"Build on your strengths and your weaknesses will be irrelevant."

—*Peter Drucker*

chapter 4

Time Management

"I must govern the clock, not be governed by it."
—Golda Meir

N o two of us are alike. We have different tastes, different political persuasions, different views about parenting, different ways to make dressing at Thanksgiving. We're each uniquely gifted. But it seems to me there's at least one thing we all have in common. We'd all like to accomplish more in less time and with less stress.

As I write this chapter, I can't see the top of my desk. For the past two weeks, we've eaten take-out for dinner more times than I care to confess. The final stages of writing a book are like that—all the more ironic because it's a book about family management and this is a chapter about time management. But this is real life.

A lot is happening in my family's life right now. We're redecorating a bathroom, such a small room, you'd think it wouldn't make that much

difference. Our twenty-one year old, although he's away at college, needs help from our end setting up an intern job for next summer. Our seventeen-year-old is researching colleges and scholarships. He needs some extra time from both his parents. Our fifth-grader needs to get to scouts, choir practice, and ball games on time. Bill is writing a book, so I'm proofreading for him each day. And, I'm trying to figure out how the five of us can take a trip together over spring break.

In other words, we have a pretty typical, busy American family. I spent years, one way and another, looking for the perfect time-management system that would straighten out all the bumps in the road, beep when

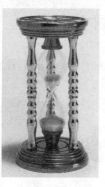

I'd forgotten an appointment, whir when it was time to turn the oven on, remind me that if I didn't start planning for the school Christmas pageant in October, I'd be dead in the water in December. The first basic truth of the matter is, with apologies to time gurus and the companies who manufacture elaborate notebooks and systems, and despite the fact that many of them have good ideas that are based on sound principles, no one way of handling time or one system works for everyone.

The second basic truth is this: How you manage each twenty-four-hour day can make the difference between a household in constant uproar and one that hums along smoothly. The reason you, the Family Manager, need to manage time in your family is so you all can have less stress and have more time to spend on the things that really matter to you.

The third basic truth is that all corporations, all families, all people have unexpected crises and opportunities that can't be planned for ahead of time. But if you're practicing some simple fundamentals of time management, you can make the best of these unexpected glitches.

Truth be known, if I didn't have some time-management strategies in place and some daily routines in operation, I would no doubt qualify for the Alice in Wonderland "White Rabbit of the Year" award. There's no way I could do what I do and maintain a sense of harmony and order in my family. And I think I can say the same for you. If you don't have some time-management strategies in place and some daily routines in operation, there's no way you can do what you do and maintain a sense of harmony and order in your family. Am I right?

> "My days ran away so fast. I simply ran after my days."
>
> —Leah Morton

Our families are different shapes and sizes, and we deal with different issues daily. But in varying degrees and slightly modified circumstances, we all know what it feels like when a child walks into our bedroom complaining of a sore throat thirty minutes before we're supposed to give a speech at a PTA meeting or leave on a business trip. Any toilet that has a propensity to overflow will do so when we have houseguests. We all have spur-of-the-moment opportunities to go on outings or trips and must do some last-minute arranging and juggling. We all have baby-sitters who cancel at the last minute, relatives and friends who have emergencies and need us—now. We have children who get pushed around on the playground and need to sit in our lap and be loved—ten minutes before our husband's boss arrives.

"The future is purchased by the present."—Samuel Johnson

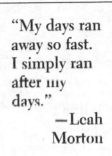

First Things First

Ten years ago I had a radical, life-altering experience. When our boys were aged eleven, seven, and six months, my life was chaotic. It's not that it had been smooth sailing up to that point. It's just that the older boys were all of a sudden in the sign-up-for-every-sport-and-activity-offered years, and we were getting used to having a baby around again. I was so busy, running from meetings, to appointments, to ball games, to events, to luncheons, and nursing the baby in between, that I was starting to forget important things—like depositing paychecks in the bank. Like making sure we had milk for breakfast. Like picking up the carpool after school. I felt like a charter member of the Always Hurried, Forever Worried Time Mismanagement Club. I was overwhelmed, exhausted, and ultimately I landed in the hospital.

After undergoing numerous medical tests, I was diagnosed with chronic mononucleosis syndrome. (Today this is called Chronic Fatigue Syndrome.) I was completely drained of energy and unable to think clearly or function without pain. During the six hours a day I managed to hold my eyes open, I did a lot of thinking. I thought about how I got myself into this miserable state. Was it because my calendar was booked to eternity? Was it because I had said "yes" to everyone who asked me to do anything? Was it because I got up at the crack of dawn and tried to cram too many things into each day—especially things I didn't enjoy but had committed to do—so that each night I fell into bed exhausted without doing many things I enjoyed? All of the above were true. Maybe my doing so much wasn't the cause of my illness, but I got sicker because I ignored the warning signs and didn't take care of myself. I continued to push myself harder and harder.

> "I didn't bite off more than I can chew—it just grew in my mouth."
> —Dr. Robert Ballard on his search for the *Titanic*

I closed my eyes and relived the day prior to my crash. In addition to the responsibilities of running my own home, I had attended two community-service meetings, cooked and delivered dinner to two new mothers, helped a friend frost her hair so she could save fifty dollars, and met another friend at a store to help her pick out clothes for a trip—all with my six-month-old in tow. I suppose everyone has a day like that every once in a while, but for me, that was typical.

STretCH YOUR MIND:
"Don't let your mouth write a check
your body can't cash."—Flip Wilson as Geraldine

Unfortunately that wasn't even the half of it. I realized that when I hadn't committed to attending meetings or helping friends, I had been wasting a lot of time—watching purposeless TV, chatting for long periods of time on the phone about nothing, shopping when I didn't need to shop. I was spending a lot of time on things that really weren't important.

As I lay in bed, I also thought about how I would spend the hours of the day if the gift of time were given back to me. I decided I would not merely spend time—doing this or that, I would use time for things I felt were important. Thankfully, my health and my time eventually were restored. Since then, I've never been the same. I see each day as a gift, undeservedly given to me to use as best I know how, and I've learned to manage my time pretty well.

WINSTON CHURCHILL SAID:

"Time is one thing that can never be retrieved. One may lose and regain friends. One may lose and regain money. Opportunity, once spurned, may come again. But the hours that are lost in idleness can never be brought back to be used in gainful pursuits."

If you in any way relate to this story, I'd like to suggest that you close your eyes and imagine how much more pleasant day-to-day life would be if you had your time under control—not always feeling at the mercy of the clock, not always wishing you could gracefully bow out of the countless projects you've committed to, not always feeling like you don't have enough time to do what you want to do, not always feeling like you're giving everyone but your family your best—being a good manager of your time and your family's time. If this sounds appealing then keep reading.

Getting Control of Time

Through my illness, two simple principles became clear to me and helped me get control of my time.

1. Let first things be first.

I began to understand that managing my time is a matter of priorities, deciding what really matters to me—who I want to be, what I want to do, where I want to go in life, the quality of life I desire for myself and my family, what kind of relationship I want with my husband, the values I want my children to leave home with, what kinds of memories I want them to take away—and learning to say no to requests that do not fall into my priorities. At that point in my life, I realized I was not giving many things in my life the time, emphasis, and care I really wanted to give them.

> "I have so much to do that I am going to bed."
> —Savoyard proverb

I made a list of my priorities and matched up each new request for my time to the list. When someone called to ask me to volunteer for something, no matter how worthy the cause, unless it fit into my priorities, I said "no." It was so freeing to be able so say that simple word without worrying what

What Really Counts

When the sink is piled with dishes and the ironing basket is overflowing, it's easy to forget that there could be more important things on which we should spend our time.

It might be more important to talk with my husband about a problem he's having at work than to mop the kitchen floor, even if we can't walk across it barefoot without sticking to the tiles.

It might be better use of my time to listen to my teenager practice an oral book report than finish stripping an antique trunk that I can't wait to make into a coffee table.

It could be more important for me to help my fifth-grader find the perfect moth for his bug collection than finish a magazine article.

people would say. Maybe for the first time in my life I felt as though I was doing the right things for the right reasons, and that's what mattered. I realized that projects and meetings could happen without me. That friends would understand if I said I couldn't help them save money right now. When Bill and I received an invitation to an event, unless we deemed it important enough to spend time away from our family, we said "no." Life was beginning to change for the better.

2. Learn to use, not just spend, time.

I started looking at time as a commodity—like money. I decided that since it's a good idea to break down each month's salary and decide how much money I can use on things such as groceries, clothing, and entertainment, then this might be a smart way to look at time as well. It's helpful to evaluate the end result of what I spend the money on each month and ask, "Did I spend too much in one area? Are we eating out too much? Can we spend less on entertainment? Is there something more significant I should spend it on?" So, I decided instead of letting another month go by and saying, "Where did the time go? I meant to do this or that," I would evaluate how I was using my time weekly, daily, even hourly. This helped immensely. I cultivated the habit of regularly asking myself, "Am I using this time—right now—well? What difference will it make if I do this or don't do that, and whose life will it affect? Is what I'm doing really what I think I should be doing or what I want to be doing?"

Now I'm not saying that every minute of every day should be a party, unfortunately. All of us have numerous responsibilities—some fun and fulfilling, some mundane and monotonous. I am saying that the priorities I decided beforehand—what's really important to me, my goals for myself and my family, and thinking of time in terms of using it instead of spending it—help me answer questions and make decisions.

Here and Now

I suggest you begin right now making your time your own. Put down this book and take this time, using the tool with which you are most comfortable—a yellow pad, notebook paper, a pretty blank book, a daily and long-range planner, a computer program—to list your own priorities. What are your "first things?" What do you wish you were doing that you aren't? What are you doing that you hate? What complaints do your children and/or spouse have about the family schedule? What do you as an individual and as a family wish you had more time for?

> "You will never 'find' time for anything. If you want time, you must make it."
> —Charles Burton

Make your list. Share it with your family. For the next month or so, when demands on any of your time come up, match the demand against the list. See if it doesn't make at least some of your difficult time-decisions easier.

Charity, as the old precept goes, begins at home. In order to manage your family's time well, and teach family members to manage their own time well, it follows that you need to manage your own time well. If you're tired, cranky, overworked, overextended, headed for burnout, and unclear about what you want to accomplish given the time you've got, how can things run smoothly?

Take it from the former Queen of Yes, all of us are constantly making trade-offs with our time and energy—balancing the competing demands of our family, work, friends, community, and our own personal needs. If we say "yes" too many times to too many requests, the result will be imbalance, frustration, and ultimately burnout.

Are there days when you fear you're headed for burnout? Are you experiencing any of these burnout indicators: fatigue, insomnia, mental lapses, headaches, irritability, rashes, loss of sexual interest, ulcers, regular

10 THINGS I COULD DO IF I MANAGED TIME BETTER
1. Read a book that I enjoyed as a child aloud to my own child
2. Enjoy a leisurely lunch with a friend
3. Putter in my yard, plant a small flower garden
4. Spend a romantic weekend with my husband
5. Take more bubble baths
6. Be in a better mood when I pick up my kids at school
7. Enroll in the ballet class I've always wanted to take
8. Swim three times a week at the YMCA
9. Finish the needlepoint pillow I started five years ago
10. Curl up with a cup of tea and read a book for pure enjoyment

illness? Lest this describe you and me, it's critically important that we learn to say "yes" and "no" with skill. Each of us has a limited amount of time, talent, and resources. So, in order to say "yes" to the things that we should be involved in, we must first create the time and energy by saying "no" to other things. When I'm presented with an opportunity, I try to ask myself, *Where does this activity fall on my priority list? and Is this the best possible use of my time?*

If I feel myself getting stressed out because I have too much to do, I stop and evaluate. I make a list of everything I'm responsible to do. Then I mark the things that absolutely must be done with a check. I mark the things that need to be done with a star. I consider which items on my list I can drop and which ones I can delegate. Then I take action and do so. I don't want to end up in the hospital again.

Time Management Is Really Self Management.

I learned that the real challenge in learning to use my time well is not only managing the hours in my day, but managing myself. To me, this meant getting to know myself better. What makes me feel energetic? What drains my energy? What time of day do I feel I'm at my best? What motivates me? What frustrates me? What skills and talents do I have? What brings me joy? Answering these questions helped me understand how I tick, which helped me get control of the clock.

> "One never notices what has been done; one can only see what remains to be done."
> —Madame Curie

Some of my answers confirmed feelings and tendencies that I knew were part of me, but I had never stopped long enough to figure out how to use the feelings and harness the energy of the tendencies for my benefit. I confirmed to myself that I have a lot of energy in the morning. (Finally I could quit beating myself up for feeling lazy at night.) If you want me to do anything or think about something significant, don't ask me after 10:00 P.M. If I have the choice about when to schedule a meeting, I'll choose a morning time slot, when I'm at my best. On my daily to-do sheets, I start my activities and chores a good while before breakfast, and I try not to schedule anything after dinner.

I also realized that I get frustrated if I'm only accomplishing one thing at a time. My family teases me because I like to work on a number of things at once. But the way I figure it, there will never be more

92

than twenty-four hours in a day, and it's a pretty sure bet there will never be less to do in those twenty-four hours. Ergo, I am constantly looking for ways to mesh chores. By combining two tasks at once, I accomplish more in less time, which to me, is a big incentive. When there's an article in a magazine I want to read, I read it while I'm on the step machine at the gym. When I need to catch up with a friend, I'll call her when I'm doing something else, like putting away groceries, straightening my desk, or painting my nails. There are a lot of advantages to doing two things at once, but the biggest benefit is the time I gain to do the things that require my focused attention with no distractions—like listening to James tell me about his hard day at school, helping Joel write a speech for a school campaign, enjoying an intimate rendezvous with Bill.

I've gotten my family into the two things-at-once mind-set as well. When everyone on the team is effective at two-timing, we have more time for family fun.

You may not be the type who likes to do two things at once. One friend gets frustrated trying to do more than one thing at a time. She is much more focused and thorough than I am and is meticulous about how she does a job. Another friend can't relate to my early morning hours. She is a night person. She does all of her housework from eleven at night until one in the morning (She makes me tired!) Still another friend invented the first daily planner specifically for women. Her days are scheduled in fifteen minute increments. She knows exactly when she's going to do what each day. When we get together and compare notes and ideas, we're amazed at how differently we all approach time management.

So who's the best time manager? Nobody's the best. We're all good time managers when we're getting to know ourselves better, learning to live each day in harmony with who we are, and always looking for new and better ways to manage our families.

"Dost thou love life? Then do not squander time, for that is the stuff life is made of."—Benjamin Franklin

THINK ABOUT IT

93

Double-Time Ideas

If getting into the habit of doing two things at once sounds interesting to you, pick a few of these ideas that fit your lifestyle. See if you don't begin to save five minutes here and ten minutes there. Then, before you know it, you've saved an hour here and two hours there.

 Get family members in the habit of never walking through the house empty-handed. Pick up and put up things as you go.

 Kids can fold clothes while watching cartoons. Have them stack complete sets of gym clothes or athletic uniforms together. Put directly into gym bag or in an easy-to-pick-up bundle.

 Have your child sweep the porch while you sweep the front walk.

 Ask teenagers to throw in a load of laundry while doing their homework.

 Young kids can strip beds and take dirty linens to washer while you put on the clean ones.

 Have young kids wash bicycles and patio furniture while older kids wash the car and the dog.

 Get everyone involved in cleaning out the attic, basement, and/or garage. Tag and price items for a garage sale as you go.

 The whole family can divide and conquer a trip to the mall or discount store with separate lists and assignments.

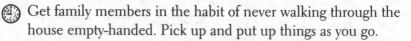 Accomplish a task while watching a young child in the bathtub—clean out the medicine cabinet, clean the mirror, straighten towels, shine fixtures.

Make a grocery list while cooking dinner. You're in the kitchen anyway, so it's easy to check on staples.

🕐 Start dinner preparations while putting away groceries.

🕐 Wash dishes or unload the dishwasher while waiting for water to boil.

🕐 Set the table as you unload the dishwasher.

🕐 Cook two, three, or four dinners at once. Clean carrots for tonight's pot roast, tomorrow's snacks, and tomorrow night's salad.

🕐 Make soup and stew at the same time. Double the recipes of both and you have tonight's dinner plus three more for the freezer.

At Your Desk . . .

When you call a number you've looked up in a phone book, use a highlighter pen to underline the number. It will be easier to refer to the next time you call. (If it's a number you might call often, add it to your personal phone and address book.)

Read the newspaper and magazines with scissors in hand for clipping coupons. Run a yellow highlighter over the expiration date. File coupons while you're on the phone.

Schedule some special "date nights" for you and your husband and write them down on your calendar. Secure baby-sitters at the same time.

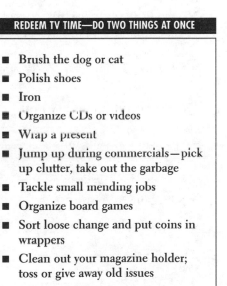

REDEEM TV TIME—DO TWO THINGS AT ONCE
■ Brush the dog or cat
■ Polish shoes
■ Iron
■ Organize CDs or videos
■ Wrap a present
■ Jump up during commercials—pick up clutter, take out the garbage
■ Tackle small mending jobs
■ Organize board games
■ Sort loose change and put coins in wrappers
■ Clean out your magazine holder; toss or give away old issues

Double-Duty Exercises

✚ Take a child with you on a brisk walk or bike ride. Spend quality time together and exercise too.

✚ Wear ankle weights around the house while doing housework.

✚ Do leg lunges while drying your hair.

✚ Do sit-ups while watching the news.

✚ Take long strides and tighten your thigh and hip muscles when walking through a mall or airport.

✚ Don't look for the closest parking place when shopping. Work some extra exercise into your day.

✚ Take the stairs whenever possible when going to an appointment.

✚ Catch up on magazine articles while you're on the step machine or exercise bicycle.

Don't Let the 3 Biggest Time-Wasters Waste Your Time

 When you're on hold on the phone . . .

- Clean out your purse.

- Purge your coupon file tossing the ones that have expired.

- Organize a drawer.

- Straighten your desk.

- Dust the closest piece of furniture.

- Put a coat of polish on your nails.

- Clean your glasses.

- Organize your wallet.

- Clean out your jewelry box and untangle necklaces.

- Tidy up your sewing box.

2 **When you're in your car—running from place to place, stuck in traffic, or parked and waiting . . .**

- Listen to cassette tapes. Catch up on the latest bestseller or learn something new.

- Drop off film at a one-hour processor or clothes at a one-hour dry cleaners on your way to run errands. Pick up on your way home.

- Go through review questions with school-age child for upcoming test. Teach a young child new facts.

- Moisturize your skin. (Keep a small-size lotion in your car.)

- Read the magazine articles you cut out beforehand, put in a self-sealing bag, and stored in the door-well of your car to pull out while waiting.

- Organize your glove compartment.

- Dust your dashboard and console.

- Wipe off rearview and sideview mirrors.

- Gather coins that have fallen in between seats.

- Read your mail. Use a highlighter pen to note important items.

- Look through mail-order catalogs to get gift ideas and plan purchases.

3 When you're waiting for an appointment . . .

- Start a leisure list in a small spiral notebook. Write recommended restaurants, movies to see, videos to rent, books to read, and places you want to go.

- Write out next week's menus.

- Plan a party. Jot down possible dates, invitation list, food and decoration ideas.

- Read part of a book.

- Write down tomorrow's to-do list.

- Balance your checkbook.

- Update your Christmas card list.

- Start your Christmas gift list. Watch for items any time of year.

- Plan a weekend outing.

- Write down vacation ideas.

- Catch up on correspondence. (Take a pen, stationery, and stamps with you.).

Three Steps to Change

I have the privilege of speaking to groups of women in many parts of the country. It doesn't matter where I am, there are always women who approach me after my speech and tell me they are frustrated, that they can't find the time to do all they need to do and want to do. After they hear my story, they comment that they don't understand how I accomplish all that I do. I honestly respond by telling them that I used to feel the same way. I explain to them that it helped me immensely to ask myself some difficult questions about where my time was going.

> "Everything becomes different when we choose to take control rather than be controlled. We experience a new sense of freedom, growth, and energy."
> —Dr. Eric Allenbaugh, *Wake-up Calls*

Then I adjusted my life according to my priorities. During most of these conversations, the women tell me that they feel the need to do the same. If they're serious about the issue, I give them this three-part assignment:

1. Track your time in a time journal. Keep a time journal for one week. Each day, from morning to night, in thirty-minute increments, record what you do and how much time you spend doing it. Be specific, and make sure you include the following:

- What time you get out of bed

- What you do when the kids leave for school

- What you do while commuting to and from work

- Small tasks and large projects—how long do they take to finish

- Phone calls—how many, how long, and what they're about

- Shopping and errands—when you go, how long it takes

- Length of your breaks and lunchtime

- When and how long you watch TV

- When and how long you clean house and do the laundry

- What or who interrupts you

- How much time you spend searching for misplaced items

- What and when you read

Did you know? If you get up thirty minutes earlier for a year, you add seven and one-half days of "awake" time to your schedule.

2. Analyze your time journal. Identify time robbers. You may have spent unnecessary time on the phone, watched more TV than you thought you did, shopped when you really didn't need to, or spent of lot of time in the car, stuck in traffic, trying to get to where you need to go. Lost minutes add up to lost hours; lost hours add up to lost days.

Identify priority pirates. Who or what got you sidetracked from where you really want to go? What did you read and was it helpful in helping you become who you want to be? Did you spend enough time with your children making the positive memories you want them to leave home with? Did keeping your house spotless keep you from enjoying time with your husband?

Don't get me wrong. Every minute of every day does not need to be filled with purposeful activities. Relaxation is important. Downtime is non-optional, if we want to be at our best at other times. What I am saying is this: Look at each day, each hour, and each minute as a gift to be

> "I'm constantly amazed by the number of people who can't seem to control their own schedules. Over the years, I've had many executives come to me and say with pride: 'Boy, last year I worked so hard that I didn't take any vacation.' It's actually nothing to be proud of. I always feel like responding, 'You dummy. You mean to tell me that you can take responsibility for an eighty million dollar project and you can't plan two weeks out of the year to go off with your family and have some fun?"
> —Lee Iacocca, *Iacocca, An Autobiography*

used wisely. Work smart. Make sure your rest is really restful. When you take time off to have fun, make sure it's something you enjoy.

3. Recognize procrastination for what it is and decide to do something about it. Procrastination is many things to many people: the easy way out of a distasteful situation; a trendy excuse for a job left undone; an indefinite escape from that persistent to-do list. Actually, procrastination is a thief that robs you of time, money, and peace of mind. The sooner you tackle that difficult task the sooner it's behind you—and you can use your calendar, checkbook, and brain cells for better things.

Sometimes we have a tendency to blame our children, husband, friends, neighbors, or coworkers for wasting our time. The truth is, no one wastes our time more than we do ourselves—especially when we procrastinate.

Procrastination is every Family Manager's enemy, and it's nothing more than a bad habit. But it's a habit with far reaching consequences. An unwillingness to tackle an unpleasant household maintenance project when you first detect a problem—peeling paint, a leaky pipe—may cost you a lot more time in the long run. Postponing decisions about your family's activities—such as how to spend your weekend—can cause unnecessary strain and frustration in family relationships. Putting off a financial job—paying bills, balancing your checkbook, renewing an insurance policy—can be costly. Simply put, when we procrastinate we're not doing what's best for our family or ourselves.

I've pinpointed three circumstances where I find it easy to procrastinate:

1. When I have a distasteful task to do

2. When I feel a task is too hard to do

3. When I have a difficult decision to make

Are there areas in your life where you are procrastinating right now? Acknowledging these things is the first step to victory. Write down the things you want to get behind you.

Over the years I've discovered some tricks that have helped me stop procrastinating and wasting time. You might apply some of these ideas to your own procrastination list. Then, when you complete the task, check it off. It will feel so good! Use this process any time you feel yourself getting buried under demands because you've been procrastinating.

"Hard work is often the easy work you did not do at the proper time." — Bernard Meltzer

How to Get Out from Under the Pile

1. Set a date and a time very soon to tackle an unpleasant task. Write this on your calendar as you would an appointment. Unless there's an emergency, don't let anything stop you from getting this task out of the way. I have to do this when it's time to gather information to file our income tax.

2. If it's a big task you're dreading, do it in little pieces. If you have piles of papers you need to organize and file, do it in seven- to ten-minute segments. If you need to clean out all your kitchen cabinets, do it one a day until you're

> "Nothing is particularly hard if you divide it into small jobs."
> —Henry Ford

finished. Nothing is so distasteful that you can't grit your teeth and do it for a short stretch of time! Pretty soon you'll find that you are well on your way to finishing.

3. Tell a friend that you have to accomplish your distasteful task by a certain time. I've found that it's easy to procrastinate when the only person I'm letting down is myself. Once I've announced that I am going to act, the task itself seems better than facing embarrassment.

4. Delegate the task to someone else. Maybe you, like me, have some things in your life that you don't want to do because you can't find the time to do them well—organize closets, catch up on ironing, coordinate a school fund-raising project. In many cases, it's better to let someone else do it, even less competently, than for the task to be left undone.

5. If you feel overwhelmed by a task that seems too complex, treat it like a jigsaw puzzle and work on the "edges" of the problem. Do the pieces that you understand. The more you do, the less complex and overwhelming the rest of the project will seem.

When we moved into our house, most of it needed remodeling. This seemed like such an enormous job that I found myself putting it all off. But this made me even more frustrated because I hated to walk through the ugly rooms. Finally Bill and I decided to start making small changes, one weekend at a time—a little paint and wallpaper, some new hardware, new light fixtures—and, a little bit at a time, we've almost remodeled the entire house. It became immediately more livable as we made small changes, and now I love it!

6. If a task is hard to do for emotional rather than technical reasons—like you need to talk to a neighbor about her child's misbehavior—remember that you're only going to feel worse the longer the task hangs over your head. Understand that being decisive will not only make you feel better faster, but that you are really helping the other person.

    When our boys were young, there was a child in our neighborhood who called other kids names, cheated at games, and broke toys and lied about it. His mother seemed to feel her son could do no wrong. It took me weeks to get up my nerve to talk to her about her son. In the meantime, his behavior got worse, and so did the knot in my stomach. When I finally made up my mind to talk to her, she responded very graciously. She told me she appreciated my honesty and now that she was aware of the problem, she could work on it with him. Boy was I sorry I waited so long to tell her!

7. Sometimes we procrastinate about making a decision because we want so desperately to be right. In this case it's fear that is holding us back. But the fact is, by procrastinating we are actually making a decision—a decision not to act at all. The best way to overcome the fear of making the wrong decision is to understand that there's nothing wrong with making mistakes—in fact, many times it's the way we learn.

    Don't let this petty thief steal your best resources. Let tasks become speed bumps rather than roadblocks in your daily journey.

All of the departments you oversee as a Family Manager are affected by how well you're handling your time.

THINK ABOUT IT

Routines: One Route to What Really Counts

Routines didn't come about overnight in our family. It was a process—getting a morning routine established, then afternoon and evening routines, even weekend routines. I started by making a list of the consistent stress points in our family—bedtime on school nights, how much and what TV we watch, how we divide up chores.

Then, one at a time, I inaugurated various routines. To my amazement our home started to run more smoothly. Even more amazingly, my family responded positively. The boys like not having to rush around in the morning. They like knowing what usually happens in the afternoon and evening. They like knowing who's responsible for what chore and not having to fight over whose turn it is to do the dishes or take out the garbage. And, since we relieved a lot of bickering and stress, they like seeing me more cheerful.

Routines make it easier to stick to our priorities. Deciding what we want to do, and then establishing a routine to do it helps us follow through on what is truly important to us. Routines give our children a sense of security because they know what to expect.

It's likely you already have some routines, even if you don't call them that. The trick is to identify your routines and take them a step further to make them work harder for you and your family. Maybe it's your practice to wash the bedsheets once a week. To turn this practice into a time-saving routine, set a specific day of the week for your family to take their sheets off their beds and put them in the laundry room before they leave the house. Then after school, one of the kids' chores can be to put the clean sheets back on his or her bed.

I think you'll find it helpful to look at each family management department and pinpoint areas where you can create time- and stress-saving routines. Start by establishing one routine in each department, and slowly add more that make sense for you and your family.

Morning and Evening Routines

Mornings

Recently I read an article in a popular parenting magazine about how to survive mornings. The article suggested that if mornings are too hectic at your house, then let family members grab a bite of breakfast at their own pace, at whatever time works for them. I bristled because I believe that the goal is not just to get the kids, your husband, and yourself (if you have another job) out the

> "The morning hour has gold in its hand."
> —Benjamin Franklin

door. Mornings are the launching pad for your family's day, and they need a positive boost.

How mornings go at your house can make a huge difference in your child's day. It's important to organize your schedule so that you don't have to rush around, creating stress as you go. Your kids will have enough stress when they walk into school. As I've talked to moms from all over the country, they named these problems as their top stress-producers in the morning.

1. Too much to do in too little time

2. Indecision and bickering about school clothes

3. Kids waiting until it's time to leave to give you papers to sign or school mail to read

4. Lunchboxes not ready or lunch money not on hand

5. Playing hide-and-seek at the last minute—looking for an important item to put in a backpack

Routines are what can help you turn chaos into order. Who you, your husband, and your kids are will determine what your morning routine is like. Here are some ideas to help you create routines for your family. Pick and choose the ones that seem like they'd work for your family, then adapt them to fit your specific needs.

 Give each child an alarm clock—it will motivate him or her to be responsible for his or her own schedule.

Make a rotating schedule for the bathroom and assign each child a time. Put a timer in the bathroom so they'll know when their time is up. (Have teenagers get up fifteen minutes earlier than younger siblings since they need extra time in the bathroom. Put a makeup mirror in girls' bedrooms to free up more bathroom time for others.)

 Make a "Sunshine Jar" for young children who move slowly in the morning. Drop a quarter in the jar each day they make progress toward adhering to the family schedule. Let them spend their money on a treat at the end of the week.

 Use your time around the breakfast table in the morning to encourage your children and show interest in their worlds. Talk about their day, what's going on, what tests they have. (Or if you're the kind of family who needs to stare at the cereal box for half an hour without talking, then do that. Chances are you're more inclined to spend time talking before bed.)

 Create a morning chore chart. Post it at kids' eye level on the refrigerator or on a kitchen bulletin board—no more arguing over whose turn it is to feed the dog or take out the garbage. Allow younger children to put a star or scratch-and-sniff sticker beside a task when completed.

 Eliminate distractions. Don't turn on the TV unless a child needs to watch a news report for a class.

 Make a work-before-play rule and stick by it. Buy a special game or toy to be played with only when the child is ready to leave for school a few minutes early.

 When your kids walk out the door, say "I love you. Have a great day—you're a great kid!"

Evenings

 When your kids arrive home from school or you arrive home after work, don't underestimate the importance of transition time. Everyone needs to relax and acclimate before beginning end-of-the-day activities. Change into comfortable clothes, turn on music, and don't take any phone calls.

 If you can't be there, make sure the caretaker is someone who will give the children the message that they are cared about, especially by listening to them individually talk about their day and asking questions that draw them out. You can also leave notes for your children that reinforce your care for them. Write a week's worth at a time. Put them in the same place for your child each day. For kids who aren't old enough to read, the baby-sitter/nanny/older sibling can read them your special note.

 Show-and-tell time. Create a chance for everybody to talk about what happened during the day. Try to make this a time when you don't take phone calls or allow any other distractions that would draw your attention away from the kids. You could be, for instance, mending or hemming something while you talk to a kid, but not vacuuming or working on a budget. Do that some time when the kids don't need your attention.

 Share dinner responsibilities. One parent can cook while the other spends time with the kids. Let the older kids take turns helping in the kitchen. Simplify dinner preparations. Schedule certain dinners for certain nights. Plan an order-in night as well.

 After dinner share kitchen cleanup chores. Load lunchboxes for tomorrow with nonperishables. Make sandwiches and store them in refrigerator. (Add lettuce to sandwiches in the morning to retain crispness.) Place frozen juice in refrigerator to thaw.

Schedule some time each evening to do something fun as a family. Play a board game or a hand of cards, read part of a book aloud, take the dog for a walk, or work on a jigsaw puzzle.

 Create a homework-friendly environment. Mom and Dad should do "homework" as well. Sort the mail, read, or work on a project. Don't turn on the TV, and keep other distractions to a minimum. Be available to help with kids' homework when needed.

 Prepare for tomorrow morning. Make a checklist for yourself, noting appointments for the next day and items to take (cleaning, library books, show-and-tell items, etc.). Lay out your clothes and accessories. Establish a specific place for keys, glasses, purse, and briefcase.

 Ask kids to decide what they'll wear and set clothes out at night. (Pack away all clothing that doesn't fit and put away out-of-season items to simplify choices.)

 Kids should load backpacks with school gear before bed. Have them check the weather report to see if they need to locate rain gear, coats, hats, gloves, etc. Put by the exit door.

 Anticipate bedtime distractions. Make sure the younger kids go to the bathroom before going to bed. Put a glass of water by the bed of a child who frequently needs a drink. Provide a night-light or flashlight if they tend to be frightened in the dark.

Take Time to Make Time for Fun

Routines aren't just about saving time and reducing chaos, they're about family fun as well. As you think about establishing routines for your family, create some that include spending time together doing something fun every weekend. Realistically, there will be some weekends, because of soccer games, housework, yard work, and car-care chores, you won't be able to schedule a daylong or even a half-day outing. Maybe you can only fit in an hour and a half for a picnic and kite flying at a nearby park, or maybe an hour of roller blading in your neighborhood. And that's okay. At least you're establishing a routine of doing something fun every weekend as a family.

Spend some time as a family making a list of fun things to do on the weekend. (This is one family meeting your kids will definitely want to participate in.) Then organize your ideas by how much time the activity takes—one hour, two hours, a half day, all day, and all-weekend outings. Keep your list easily accessible and refer to it as you plan each week. Make it your routine to pick one thing to do from it each weekend.

"There is a time for everything, and a season for every activity under heaven."—Ecclesiastes 3:1

E-Z Time Savers

I used to feel like a circus lady performing a plate-spinning act. One by one I spun my good china plates on the ends of broomsticks. Just when I got plate number ten spinning, I had to run across the room to rescue number one, which was about to fall. I could do it if I kept running really fast. But Ecclesiastes doesn't say anything about running really fast.

In my quest to slow down and still keep the plates spinning that have to keep spinning, I started collecting ideas that could help me save time. Now I have a file full of them. Some of the ideas I've incorporated into my life and managing my family. Some didn't work for me exactly as they were written, so I adapted them to meet my needs. Some I still need to work on.

Here's a list of random time-saving ideas that have helped me. Pick a few that speak to you and see if you don't begin to save five minutes here and ten minutes there. Then, before you know it, you've saved an

> "If a man insisted always on being serious, and never allowed himself a bit of fun and relaxation, he would go mad or become unstable without knowing it."
> —Herodotus
>
> "Don't put off for tomorrow what you can do today, because if you enjoy it today you can do it again tomorrow."
> —James A. Michener
>
> "Saving time, it seems, has a primacy that's too rarely examined."
> —Ellen Goodman

hour here, and two hours there. And surprisingly, after a while, you will have added a day here and two days there—days to spend in meaningful ways with your family.

- Don't waste time beating yourself up when you make bad decisions. Learn from your mistakes and move on.

- If you have a speaker phone, use it, so your hands will be free to work and do other things while you're talking.

- When you need to phone someone you know is longwinded, call just before lunch or at the end of the day.

- When you end a meeting or a phone conversation, always verify who will get back to whom and when. You can save literally hours trying to chase down busy people.

- Invest the time it takes to learn to use new computers or software efficiently. You'll save time in the long run.

- With your priorities in mind, make a checklist of things you want to accomplish every day. Create ten blank spaces for variable tasks. Photocopy your list, and fill one page out each morning. Glance over your goals each day, then prioritize tasks. Work on the most important things first.

- Take your calendar of birthdays and other special occasions to the store and buy cards for the year.

- Add sixty hours to your year! Resolve to put away everything you get out—where it belongs. (Ten minutes a day looking for misplaced items wastes sixty hours a year.)

- Make a master list of things family members can do when they have an extra five, fifteen, or thirty minutes: water plants, brush the dog, sew on a button, straighten the board games, sort through a pile of papers. When someone has a short block of time, they can refer to the list and accomplish a "quickie."

- Whenever you're dealing with kids, expect the unexpected. Realize that almost everything takes longer than you expect; plan accordingly.

- If you turn off the television, as an "average" American adult you will add thirty hours to your week.

- Get visits to the dentist or doctor out of the way fast by scheduling family members' appointments back to back. Have each person take something to accomplish while waiting. Write a list of questions and concerns before appointments. You won't have to call back to get answers to questions you forgot to ask.

- Avoid doing things at times when everyone else tends to do them. Don't go to the bank at lunchtime, on Fridays, or the day before a holiday. Go out to lunch a half hour before or after the general population. Go to the movies on a weeknight or early on weekends.

- Determine the value of your time when considering the cost of a project. Hire others—mechanics, housekeepers, tax preparers—to do jobs that can be done more efficiently and less expensively by them than by you.

- Organize your family with color. Identify each person's possessions with an assigned color, and mark children's toys and equipment—lunchboxes, rain boots, sports gear—with colored tape or markers. Put colored tape around the neck of hangers to identify whose clothes are hung on them.

- Make a personal source guide. When you discover a store that has products you like, make a note and write down the phone number. This will save you time later.

Welcome to Control Central

Every business manager has a base of operation—a place from which he or she carries out management responsibilities. It's no different for a Family Manager. We need a place to organize and administrate the countless daily details we oversee that have to do with managing not only our family's time—schedules, appointments, invitations, phone numbers, school papers—but the other countless details pertaining to the other departments. Control Central is my own base from which I manage our family.

Setting up Control Central in your home can help you manage your family more efficiently and effectively. First, choose a smart location. A desk by the phone in the kitchen or family room is ideal, but the corner of a bedroom or hallway, or under a staircase will do. (One friend turned a centrally located closet into her Control Central. She had a phone jack installed, created a desk from an old door and two filing cabinets and made a giant bulletin board to hang on the wall above the desk.)

Next, stock your desk. You'll want to have all the necessary office supplies on hand, but also some things to personalize your space. I have some pretty desk accessories, lots of photographs, and a favorite lamp. I've found that if my desk is attractive, I'm motivated to spend more time there organizing and working on details. Here's a list of what I keep at my Control Central.

- A big calendar on which everyone writes their activities, appointments, and important dates
- A stand-up tickler file
- A filing cabinet
- A pretty file box
- Colorful file folders
- A bulletin board
- Push pins
- Note paper and envelopes
- Stamps
- Transparent tape
- Pens, pencils, and markers
- Rubber bands
- Sticky-back notes
- Paper clips
- Ruler
- Stapler
- Phone directories
- School directories
- Family address book

Of course, there's more to Control Central than just setting it up. It's important that family members get involved. They need to understand, first and foremost, that everyone, not just Mom, has responsibility for managing schedules and activities. At our house, we had a family meeting to discuss actions and procedures that would help us all do a better job of managing our time and schedules. We came up with some guidelines that everyone (at least those old enough) agreed to abide by. After the start-up period, you'll find that it helps to have regular family meetings to see how things are going and to refine your place and your process. Don't give up just because there are one or two glitches. All new systems take time to learn and implement. Besides, nobody's perfect. That's why we need Control Centrals.

Go over these Control Central guidelines with your family. Write your own to fit your family.

☎ Do write down your commitments on the calendar — parties, appointments, etc. Do let Mom know about details — if you need a ride, if you need to take a gift, if you need to pick up anyone else — by writing a note, if you're old enough.

☎ Do put all phone messages on the bulletin board. Don't throw them on top of the desk.

☎ Do post invitations and other pertinent items on the bulletin board.

☎ Do put your important papers in your special folder [assign one to each child] in the stand-up tickler file so I'll know where to find them.

☎ Don't remove supplies from this area.

☎ Do let your Family Manager (a.k.a. Mom) know if you see you're running low on something.

☎ Don't commit anyone's time for anything without checking with Control Central and a parent first.

☎ Don't make Control Central what it is not. It's not a substitute for talking to each other, especially about conflicts in schedules or preferences in activities—especially for Mom and Dad and older kids.

☎ Do post jokes or cartoons or other items the whole family will enjoy or laugh at.

☎ Do make a family commitment to keep the control center as neat as possible.

Set Up Time-saving Work Centers

Gift-wrapping/mailing center:

A drawer, cabinet, or closet where you can store everything you need for wrapping and mailing.

What you need: A few generic adult gifts—picture frames, pretty writing pens, favorite books, some age-appropriate birthday gifts for your children's friends, wrapping paper for different occasions, ribbon, various sizes of gift sacks, gift tags, colored pens and markers, tissue paper, scissors, transparent tape, packing tape, various sizes of padded envelopes and flattened boxes, mailing labels, a small postal scale, various denominations of stamps.

Sewing center:

A special place for family members to use sewing supplies or put to-be-mended clothes.

What you need: Scissors, needles, straight pins and pin cushion, safety pins, assorted colors of thread, tape measure, fabric glue, iron-on patches, different size and color buttons, safety snaps, hooks and eyes, elastic for waistbands and Velcro strips.

Stretch your mind:

Time Management Goal:
Spend less time on the things you have to do
and find more time for things you want to do.

c h a 5 t e r

Food Management

". . . A mother stirs a little bit of herself into
everything she cooks for her family."
—Marjorie Holmes

"You don't get over hating to cook,
any more than you get over having big feet."
—Peg Bracken

Marjorie Holmes and Peg Bracken reflect two pretty different attitudes toward food in these brief quotations. And I've included them both because I believe they are both true, and maybe not as antithetical as they seem at first glance.

Our attitudes toward food and food preparation say a lot about our family culture. And the little bit of myself I put into most of my cooking for my family often has to do with humor. I would venture to guess that my family has laughed more at some of my cooking attempts than at any other single category of our family life together. I simply don't like to cook, maybe because I'm not particularly good at it. (But that does not mean I don't like good food. Read on.)

I also don't think it's an accident that cookbooks, nutrition books, homemaking books of every kind, encyclopedias, and ethnographic tomes about food abound. I wonder how many millions of them have been written just in this century. Throughout history food has been a favorite subject for artists. Food, is of course, like air and water, necessary to life. It gives us nutrition and energy. And it gives us pleasure. Food feeds, if you will, all our senses. The sight of a piece of chocolate cake whets our appetite. The sound of sautéing onions in a frying pan is music to our ears. The smell of freshly brewed coffee helps us get going in the morning. A lick of smooth frozen yogurt delights our tongue on

a hot day. And what could taste better than a juicy hamburger with all the fixings right off the backyard grill.

But food is far, far more. For one thing, it's a key part of any country's culture. Our identity as people is built around the kinds of food we eat—a real "meat and potatoes" type, the Pepsi generation, junk-food junkies, health-food nuts. It's also built around who we eat it with, when, and where, whether we stand in the kitchen and wolf down a sandwich or sit down at a perfectly laid table.

We usually don't stop to think about what food means in deeper ways to our families. Actually food has a lot to do with the culture of our homes. How we talk about food, how we act around it, as well as what we serve and when and under what circumstances we eat, say a lot about our family and give our children attitudes for life.

*"The most remarkable thing about my mother is that
for thirty years she served the family nothing but leftovers.
The original meal has never been found."—Calvin Trillin*

I have one friend, who despite the fact that she knows fresh fruit is
good for her and loves it when she does eat it, has to force herself to
remember to eat it. In the back of her head, she can hear her mother,
who pushed fresh fruit on her as a child repeating variations on the
theme: "You should be thankful you have this. When I was a child
during the Depression we were lucky to get one orange at Christmas."
It's important to think not only about what we serve and how we serve
it, but about what we say regarding food and how we act around it.
What attitudes are we giving our children? Again, volumes have been
written: how we can "cause" obesity by insisting children eat everything on their plates; how we can "instill" guilt by reminding our children of others less fortunate to try to influence their eating habits; how
we can "foster" eating disorders by consistently pointing out how food
can make a person fat.

I have another friend who tries to have a savory aroma coming
from the kitchen when her children come home from school
because she has fond memories from her own childhood of walking
into the house to a good smell after school. Sitting at the table, eating warm cookies or popcorn, and talking about her schoolday with
her mom is a wonderful memory for her, and she wants to pass on
the same memory to her children. I admire this friend and think this
kind of gesture is wonderful, within reason. First of all, I wouldn't
recommend it to anyone like me, who would consider it pretty much
torture to come up with a different homemade snack on a daily basis.
Secondly, I wouldn't recommend it to anyone who would resent
having to be in the kitchen every day at 3:00 P.M. Third, I wouldn't
recommend that anyone go on ad nauseum, even with the best of
intentions, about how my mother did this for me and I'm going to do
it for you. Kids pick up on those things.

When we think about food management, and believe me, whether we consider this category to be among our stronger or weaker points, there's a lot to think about. There's food, what we eat. Then there's how we buy and prepare it; who does it? On what schedule? Then there's where we eat and with whom and what goes on at mealtimes. Make no mistake. This is an important department of Family Management. So let's start with the food itself.

Healthy and Wise

In the last twenty years or so, we have, as a society, become more and more aware of eating healthy diets. At the same time, it seems we have an increasing array of wonderful ethnic foods to choose from in our grocery stores and restaurants. To me, as a Family Manager who is concerned not only about the physical health of my family, and myself, but also about our growth in various ways, food is a major opportunity, as well as a major challenge.

"Millions of our children—the majority of them in middle- and upper-middle-class homes—face the prospect of serious diseases and shortened life spans because of sedentary living and poor nutrition."
—Dr. Kenneth Cooper, Kid Fitness

In my kids' early elementary school years, I went on a nutritional binge. I decided with fervor, "Not a granule of white sugar or refined flour will pass our threshold again." I drove to a farm to buy honey straight from the hive, bought undefiled peanut butter at the health food store, and baked homemade bread which we could have used for a doorstop.

> "The person who decides what shall be the food and drink of a family, and the modes of its preparation, is the one who decides, to a greater or less extent, what shall be the health of that family."
>
> —Catherine E. Beecher and Harriet Beecher Stowe, *American Woman's Home,* 1869

Every morning I self-righteously prepared a healthy lunch for my first-grader: a sandwich built from the spoils of my health-food acquisitions and some stone-ground wheat cookies. I turned up my nose at less conscientious mothers who actually put chips and cupcakes in their children's lunches. How irresponsible, I thought smugly.

When it came time for my parent-teacher conference, the teacher assured me that John was doing very well in school. But she questioned my attitude toward nutrition. "Did you know, Mrs. Peel, that your son eats donuts and candy bars every day for lunch?" It seems that by noon, John's sandwich had turned board stiff. (I guess I should be glad he wasn't eating them. A broken tooth is hard to fix.) And the kids used my cookies for Frisbees on the playground. The other children felt sorry for John, so they took turns donating their extras to him every day. My nutritional binge ended suddenly.

Today we try to be wise in our eating habits. We try to limit sweets and junk foods, and we've cut way back on our fat intake. We eat lots of fresh fruits and vegetables, complex carbohydrates—pasta, rice, and whole-grain breads—take vitamins daily, and try to drink a lot of water. All of us think about what we eat, but we're not rabid nutritionists. We eat pizza like the rest of the world. We have junk food in our pantry, although we tend more to popcorn and pretzels and granola bars than potato chips and candy bars. We're just more careful now. We read labels, we never fry anymore, we're more conscious about what goes into our bodies.

What Goes into the Mix?

When you're thinking about managing your family and food, you have to begin with who you are and who your family is. Are you the experimental type? Do you like to try new recipes and new foods? Do you balk at fixing, oh, let's say beef stew, once every two weeks, alternating with meat loaf? Does your husband like to cook? Do you have older children who can cook? What kind of special dietary needs does your family have? Discovering your family's "food personality" is the place to start.

No doubt you know the answer to most of these questions, and perhaps as you incorporate the concepts of Family Management into your life, food is something you'll put on the back burner because things are just fine in the kitchen, thank you very much. Even if that's the case, I suggest that you devote a family meeting to reassessing your family's food personality. Maybe you or other family members have been wanting to shed a few pounds. Maybe you're concerned about the amount of fat you're eating. The best way to change your eating habits is consciously and over time.

Even if you're entirely satisfied with what you eat and the way you eat it, maybe it's time to reassess who does what.

Attitude Is Almost as Important as Ingredients

I love to eat. I love to share meals with my family, friends, and strangers. I'm sort of like Will Rogers in that I've never met a strange dish I didn't like. I love to entertain and have people in our home.

There's just one slight problem. If you've gotten this far into the book, you are well aware that I'm not at my best in the kitchen.

It's not that I hate to be in the kitchen. I love the smell of a fragrant soup simmering away on the stove or an apple-cinnamon cake baking in the oven as much as anybody. I love the idea of elegant French cuisine. Maybe a little fresh fish in a delicate sauce, turned out onto a plate with baby carrots and steamed courgettes. The problem is simply that I lack skill. I've taken lessons. I've read books. I've endured my family's laughter. I've wrung my hands in despair over the fact that food management is, beyond a shadow of a doubt, one of my substandard departments.

Every Family Manager is going to have at least one department where she feels like a failure. So, as the kids say, "Deal with it."

The great news is that we can compen-sate for our weaknesses. No CEO worth his or her salary ever claimed to be able to do all things equally well, or even all things at all. Smart managers will tell you that they hire staff who aren't replicas of themselves. If they're weak on details, they hire people whose idea of fun is keeping track of hundreds of little things. If they know they're not good at systematizing and prioritizing, they hire people who are. The idea is to be smart—to use our skills, talents, and abilities to do what we do best, and let somebody else do what they do best.

But it's sometimes difficult for some Family Managers to delegate something we feel, for one reason or other, is "our job," especially something as integral to our family's welfare as food. Truthfully this was a problem for me for years. Attitude is important. When we let our feelings of inadequacy take over, we tend to crush the abilities we do have. We dig ourselves into "I can't" holes. And it's a well-known fact that it's harder to jump hurdles when you start in a hole.

This may sound like a small thing, but I felt indescribably free when I decided that it doesn't make me less of a woman to let someone else

> "It's so beautifully arranged on the plate—you know someone's fingers have been all over it."
>
> —Julia Child

create my children's birthday cakes. Each of my kids wants a special kind of cake—the same kind every year—so I order it from the bakery. They're happy, I'm relaxed and not crying over another cake I baked that looks like the Leaning Tower of Pisa. I'm also calmer now when we have dinner parties. I know it doesn't make me less of a hostess if I delegate some of the food preparation for a big dinner party to Bill and my local wholesale food club.

Bill's mom was a whiz in the kitchen. As a young boy he sat on a stool in the kitchen and watched her cook. He inadvertently picked up a lot of her know-how and techniques. After years of blackened chicken (and I don't mean the kind New Orleans cuisine made famous) and tears, Bill said, "Let's be smart about this." Our family's solution is that he cooks approximately half the time, and I cook half the time. And I practice a precept I've found effective in many areas: Keep it simple.

Periodically we have a Cook Day together; I gather all the ingredients and put them on the counter along with the recipe books, the right pots and pans, utensils, and everything we're going to need. (I'm a great planner. Execution is my weak point.) I give Bill his apron and put on some music. Then I sit on a stool and wait for orders. In one big pot we might stew chicken breasts for making chicken enchiladas, chicken spaghetti, chicken divan, and chicken-noodle soup. In another big pot we might brown lean ground beef for chili, sloppy Joe's, and meatballs. We put up six or eight meals in the freezer. I clean up. Not only do we have all those meals prepared ahead of time, but we've spent a leisurely

> "Where's the cook? Is supper ready, the house trimmed, rushes stewed, cobwebs swept?"
> —Shakespeare

day together, with time while we're chopping and sautéing and simmering and roasting, to talk about current events, vacation dreams, the kids, and a number of other topics we might not have time to cover in the hurry of our usual schedules. I like my husband a lot, and even though it still is true I don't much like to cook, spending a whole day working with him in the kitchen has its rewards. He enjoys doing something with me, and I don't have to cook. It's a win/win solution.

Food and Teamwork

Food and teamwork go hand in hand, perhaps more naturally than any other area of family management. Eating and cooking together build bonds. Even the youngest child can, with encouragement, participate in family conversations around the dinner table and carry flatware or dishes to or from the table, wash carrots (even if they have to be rewashed), or help Dad stir the Saturday morning pancake batter.

Corporate managers know that one of their roles is that of teacher. Good employees become better over time as they learn new skills and are able to assume more responsibility in an organization. Teaching and delegating in the kitchen may be difficult for some Family Managers. The kitchen may be your place to shine, or you may be a person who doesn't like clutter or has a hard time letting someone else do something you could do faster and better. On the other hand, consider the gift you are giving your children when you pass along to them on a daily basis the skills and knowledge you have about food. There's a lot of talk these days about teaching children lifelong sports, that is sports they can and will play as adults. Teaching them to cook and to work cooperatively with other team members in the kitchen is, in a very real way, a lifelong sport.

Teamwork can endure long past the time we live at home. My friend Michelle likes to cook. So does her sister, Ann. They're both good, if plain cooks, but with far different strengths. So over the years, for holiday celebrations and regular Sunday-night get togethers, they've combined their skills and talents. Michelle is a whiz at main courses. She's one of those people who can invent a magazine-worthy casserole with whatever happens to be in the refrigerator. She can stretch a pound of hamburger from here to thirteen people. Soup, well, you just throw in a little of this and a little of that, and pretty soon you've got something worth sitting down around the table for.

When Ann's kids were little, they threatened to leave home if she ever made another stew or casserole without following a recipe. And even when she followed the recipes exactly, well, strange things happened. But Ann can bake lovely cakes from scratch. And she makes the most elegant salads you're every likely to see outside a four-star restaurant. Not to mention, she can make a lovely centerpiece out of whatever Michelle leaves in the crisper drawer. She has the eye of an artist.

These women have been cooking together since they were very young. And they've discovered a way to do it, to the delight of the many they've fed over the years, that capitalizes on both their strengths, shelves their frustrations, and makes them both feel good.

Food for Body and Soul

Food is the center of most families' lives. Certainly it's the center of many of our celebrations and traditions. And, if it's not the center of everyday life, it probably should be. There's something about sitting down and eating together, especially when everybody has had a hand, no matter how small, in getting the meal on the table, that can soothe the savage beast within. So, along with making the food the best it can be, I see part of my job as Family Manager of the food department, to use the food to bring out the best of the diners, whether they're my own family or special guests we've invited to share our meal.

Food is the center of most meaningful celebrations because there is something about eating together that brings closeness. Effectively managing food can make celebrations—from the most festive to the everyday—more special and memorable. The effort you exert to plan and prepare food for your daughter's surprise sixteenth birthday party won't soon be forgotten. And when your son gets his braces off and you serve favorite foods he hasn't been able to eat in two years, you're making a wonderful memory.

> "Eighty-six percent of people polled in a *Los Angeles Times* survey called eating dinner with their families "very important.""

Food has a lot to do with traditions and our family legacy—making recipes familiar to generations of our family. There's just something about being able to say, "We always have Great Aunt Ada's homemade vanilla ice cream at family reunions," or "Christmas wouldn't be Christmas without Grandma's fudge." Whatever it is in your family, these kinds of traditions and family rituals bind a family together.

Good food keeps kids at home. When they know there's good food and enough of it to share, your kids will want to invite their friends to hang out at your house. I learned this from my friend and cooking expert Judie Byrd. When her kids were in high school, hardly a day went by when there wasn't a passel of kids at her house. It was definitely THE place to be. I decided I wanted the same thing to happen at my house when my kids got older. This afternoon I know that, as usual, Joel and three or four of his friends—very large friends I might add, Bill calls them Raiders of the Lost Fork—will come to our house between school and basketball practice, raid our refrigerator and pantry, and hang out for a while. (To some Family Managers this would be a mixed blessing. But I'd rather our grocery bill be a bit higher and the music a little louder and have the kids hanging out at our house. That way I know where they are and what they're doing.)

When our oldest son John hit adolescence, Bill and I worried—as many parents do—about where John and his friends would go and what they would do after football games and school dances. There weren't too many alcohol- and trouble-free places to hang out. We decided this problem might be an opportunity in disguise and hit on what has been for us a great idea. Now, after too many football games and dances to count, teenagers have congregated at our house. Bill dons his chef's apron and fixes his famous midnight pancake break-fasts. We serve pancakes with seasonal toppings, juice, sausage—all the fixings. Sometimes these are elaborate events, planned in advance with appropriate decorations. Sometimes they're more spur-of-the-moment. Sometimes we record the event for posterity with pictures. Our kids know that the fun place to be where's there's plenty of food is at home—with their friends always welcome.

Good food also plays a part in building friendships with other adults, like when we host a party or invite a few couples over for dinner.

> "Food, glorious food . . ."
> —Orphans in the movie *Oliver*

Entertaining, this way in which we share ourselves with other people, can be done by anyone, on any budget. Whether you live in a five-bedroom home or a tiny apartment in a new city, who you are—yourself, your family, your imagination, your inter-est in others—in short, your hospitality—is the same. And entertaining doesn't always have to be for a meal in the evening, which may be a hard time for you. You can have friends over for an after-work tea party or pancakes on Saturday morning. Or you can invite three families to each bring a salad, dessert, or bread for Sunday lunch. You provide the main dish. It's getting together that's important, not that you do it all yourself.

One of our fondest memories as a young couple is organizing a Gourmet Club with seven other couples, who, by the way, are still good friends fifteen years later. (Note: It should be obvious since I was a member of the club that you didn't have to be a gourmet cook to belong.) We met once every seven weeks and took turns hosting a dinner party for the other couples. We only had to "do it up big" once a year, which was doable—and enjoyable.

Getting Organized

I've learned through trial and error (mostly error) that if you effectively manage food, it makes a lot of things run smoother. You eliminate time-robbing, last-minute trips to the store and you save money by cutting back on fast-food outlets because you need food fast. When meals are planned in advance, with all the food and ingredients on hand, everyone tends to feel calmer and a sense of order pervades. When your husband calls home extemporaneously to tell you that he's bringing his boss by in twenty minutes, you simply shift into emergency-guest-plan mode and pull out the hors d'oeuvres—the ones that you keep hidden from your kids for just such an occasion as this. Mornings are much calmer because you have breakfast foods on hand. On a daily basis, the transition from afternoon to evening in your home will be less stressful if you're managing food well.

Make Your Kitchen Work for You

It's helpful to have the right tools, no matter what department we're talking about, but it especially helps in the kitchen. I'm not talking about fancy, expensive equipment. I'm talking about basics. And truthfully, the better I get as a Family Manager, the more I'm seeing the importance of simplifying. Many times, extra equipment just means more to clean up and maintain.

Maybe you need to take inventory in your kitchen. Do you find yourself frequently wishing you had a bigger or smaller pan? Needing a strainer that you can't find? Do you have to move a serving dish you use maybe once a year every time you go for the Dutch oven you use once a week? A detailed inventory of what you have can help you reevaluate what is currently useful. Just as we periodically need to weed out old clothes from our closet, we need to do the same with our cookware. Our eating and cooking patterns change over time, and there's no need to keep the mini-deep-fat fryer if you've eliminated fried foods from your diet.

If you don't have the right tools handily available, that's the place to begin. Enlist your family's help. (If they help you get the kitchen in order, they'll be more likely to help keep it that way.) You might plan a family workday to give your kitchen a facelift.

Think about what goes on in your kitchen. And what you'd like to happen there. For most families the kitchen isn't just for cooking. It's a social center where people eat, entertain, work, relax, and communicate. Kids, neighbors, guests, grandparents, and caregivers gather in this room to cook, snack, and chat—so organization is essential.

> "What you eat standing up doesn't count."
> —Beth Barnes

To get your kitchen in good working order, first think of it as a coffee shop—a gathering place for food, fun, and conversation. Is your kitchen a place where you like to spend time? Does your family congregate there? Are there good traffic patterns, both for the cook(s) and the spectators? Do people work and visit together easily in there or get in each other's way? Is it light enough for you to work there at night? Is there adequate storage space? Do you have easy access to spices? Do your young kids have easy access to nonbreakable cups and dishes? Is there enough workspace? Are the people who use your kitchen left- or right-handed? Does anyone have a special physical condition that limits his or her ability to bend or stretch? Analyze your answers to these questions and brainstorm as a family about possible solutions to problem areas.

Then rethink your kitchen in terms of work centers—where you perform specific tasks like cleaning, chopping, cooking, and making lunches. Each center revolves around a major appliance, some storage space, and a work surface. Think of how you can store equipment and food near the center where they'll be used—pots and pans near the stove, baking goods and utensils near the mixer, dishes near the dishwasher. This will save steps.

Begin reorganizing with the cupboard closest to the sink and work your way methodically around the kitchen. Take everything out of each cupboard. Wipe the shelves and repaper if necessary. (Use a warm iron to remove old contact paper.) Put duplicate items or items you seldom use in an "extras box." Place items used daily on the most accessible shelves nearest the work center where they'll be used. Store items used several times a week in space accessible with a small stretch. Continue in this manner until items used least frequently are stored in the least-accessible space.

Move things like the huge roasting pan you use three times a year for holiday meals to storage in the garage or basement. Donate that punch bowl you got for a wedding present and have never used to somebody who can use it. Make a wish list for kitchen utensils and dishes that you can buy as your budget allows. Keep it handy so when your favorite kitchen store has a sale or your sister asks what you want for your birthday, you're ready.

Okay, so you've got the kitchen ready. Now it's time to think about menus.

"What's for Dinner?"

Meal planning has been the subject of many of those millions of books about food and nutrition. I have become—

133

not only out of desperation, but because I think it's a smart thing to do—a big believer in having three weeks' worth of dinner menus. Unless you have a lot of extra time to kill, keep them simple. You can adapt, enhance, and alter them to fit your schedule or need at the moment, but at least you know you have some basic things you are prepared to fix. After three (or four or six, whatever works for you) weeks, recycle your hard work by reusing the weekly menus again and again. You don't have to have roast chicken every third Thursday. Have it on Monday in the fourth week instead. It is my experience that this basic meal plan can carry you throughout a year, making allowances and changes for seasons—consider what fresh fruits and vegetables are available and what foods your family especially likes to eat at various times of the year—without anybody ever even figuring out you're eating the same basic foods in a rotating schedule. In fact, summer foods don't always have to be summer foods. Consider having a winter picnic one Sunday night in front of the fireplace or on the den floor. Serve just what you would at a picnic supper. Or, if it's an unseasonably cold and rainy summer day, be flexible and serve a favorite "winter" soup.

> "In general my children refused to eat anything that hadn't danced on TV."
> —Erma Bombeck

Making this basic rotating meal planner should involve your whole family, their tastes, and your and their ideas about what they need to eat. Some small children hate variety. They'd eat the same thing every day if they could. Consider them when you plan your meals. If you're serving pasta with a rich sauce, for instance, you may want to set some plain pasta aside for your toddler, to serve with a little butter and/or parmesan cheese. Keep carrot sticks and other raw vegetables your smaller children do like to eat on hand. Then if they taste the spinach soufflé and gag, you have an alternate vegetable to offer them.

An aside about children and introducing new foods. I belong to the

"Don't hit them over the head, but introduce them to new experiences," school of thought. We have a rule in our house. "Try it, you might like it." Nobody is ever forced to eat something they can't stand the taste of. All we ask is that they taste it. And, without becoming a short-order cook, you can offer alternatives.

If you're the mother of a finicky eater, don't despair. There are things you can do. My children have always been finicky eaters. I tend to look at this as sort of a chicken and egg sort of thing. Maybe they were born that way. Or maybe it's my cooking. Or maybe, most young children are conservative creatures of habit and thereby labeled finicky eaters. Whatever the reason, these simple ideas have helped tremendously at our house. Feel free to try them yourself.

One way to involve everybody in menu planning is to hold a brainstorming meeting. I recommend this periodically even if you're not dealing with finicky eaters. Get some paper and a pencil to take notes, then have everybody call out their favorite foods, what they'd like to eat that you haven't fixed for a while, maybe something you've never served but a child had at a friend's house. You can organize the brainstorming list as you go by meal—breakfast, lunch, dinner or by category—fruit, vegetable, etc. Or you can simply list everything and organize it later.

Remind everybody of the basic ground rules of brainstorming before you start. 1) There are no stupid or wrong ideas. Every food

TEN COMMANDMENTS FOR FEEDING FINICKY EATERS

Thou shalt:

1. Keep it simple!
2. Refrain from feeding them lots of fats and sugar.
3. Sneak in the four food groups every day.
4. Never guilt a child into the clean-plate club.
5. Find ways to make mealtime fun.
6. Involve even the youngest finicky eater as sous chef.
7. Never use food as punishment or reward for other behaviors.
8. Stock proven favorites even if you get bored.
9. Keep trying to find pleasing foods.
10. Let the finicky eaters help with menu planning.

mentioned goes on the list. 2) No commenting on another person's suggestions. No "aarghs" when shrimp is mentioned, for example. 3) As with any other meeting, only one person talks at a time.

Once the meeting is over, all you, the Family Manager, have to do is to organize the foods into reasonable menus. If family members mention foods that are unavailable or totally outside the realm of your ability to afford or prepare, you can explain that later. I suggest, depending on the age of your children, you share the brainstormed list as it has been organized into menus with everyone. It will be a revelation, and maybe the next time, someone else would like to volunteer to help or organize the menus.

Keep in mind that you are making sure your family eats three meals a day, 365 days a year. That's 1,095 different meals. Since coming up with that many different menus will tax the brain of even the most creative person, it's a good idea to simplify and create the following:

 1 week of different breakfast menus

 2 weeks of different lunch menus

 3 weeks of different dinner menus

 2 or 3 simple company menus

If you feel like you want or need more input to make this basic plan, you might consider inviting three or four women to lunch for a menu-planning meeting. (This is the equivalent of corporate executives from the same or related industries who get together at trade organizations to share information, look at new developments, or work on causes of common concern. And, as in corporate meetings, you don't have to give away all your trade secrets, like the recipe for Aunt Mary's one-pan killer brownies.) Depending on you and your friends, this could be a more "visionary" meeting, talking about how you each plan menus and look at food. You'd all come away with strategies to apply. Or it could be a more nitty-gritty meeting in which you share menu plans and recipes and talk about specific problems, like nine-year-olds and vegetables or teenagers and junk food.

My personal opinion is that there is such a thing as too many cookbooks and too many food magazines. Too much input in this category sidetracks and frustrates me. I begin to think I can make the mile-high meringue pie that looks so easy on the cover of a woman's magazine. I believe the food editor who says any twelve-year-old can julienne perfect vegetables. And I get overwhelmed looking through seven cookbooks for menu ideas of things I can't cook and my family probably wouldn't eat. My advice here, once again, is this: Unless food is your thing and your family is willing to go along with the program, keep it simple. Choose a few favorite cookbooks you know you can rely on. Save only the simplest or most intriguing of magazine menus and recipes. And keep it all in one place.

Shopping Survival Skills

I'm a big believer in planning your grocery-store strategy around where you are in life. Maybe you're an "I want some help" kind of shopper. If so, take an older child along to help fetch items for the cart to cut your shopping time down and to help carry groceries to the car and to the house. I have a friend whose regular routine is to head out every Saturday morning with her grocery list, menus and coupons, and sit in the coffee bar of her grocery store. Here she enjoys her coffee and coordinates coupons, reads about store specials and finishes her shopping list. She loves having this special time to think and plan, and then shop. This routine has worked so well for her, now other women meet at the store on Saturday morning to do the same thing. They share ideas and recipes, and have turned grocery shopping into one of the highlights of their week.

When my boys were young, I went to the grocery store every Wednesday morning at 5:30 A.M. This may sound ludicrous at first, but think about it—peacefully shopping without traffic, kids, and long checkout lines. It was wonderful! As our family has grown, I've adopted a new grocery-store strategy: delegation. Since cooking and grocery shopping are not my favorite pastimes, we've resolved this problem by having Bill or an older boy go to a wholesale club once a month and buy in quantity: frozen foods, nonperishables, paper goods, and cleaning supplies. I go to the grocery store once a week for fresh foods, dairy products, items on special, and if we need something in the meantime, we take turns.

It helps to have a permanent shopping list of everything we use in our home. If you have a computer, it can be well worth the time and effort to enter such a list on it. Then you can print it out for whoever is doing the monthly or weekly shopping and check off the items you need that time. (The more specific you are about brands and sizes, the easier it will be to delegate the shopping task.) Categorize the list according to the way things are arranged in your store—Meat, Produce, Dry Goods, Paper Products, Canned Goods, Drinks, Toiletries, Cleaning Supplies. If you don't have a computer, make a master list and then photocopy it for repeated use.

Coupons and store specials can help you shop wisely and save money, but only if the special is something you would have purchased anyway. Depending on how much pantry and freezer space you have, you can use these specials to stock a long-range supply of staples. But don't fall into the trap I did. After eating what I thought were divine salmon croquettes at a friend's house, I was inspired to make them for my family. Boy was I in luck that very week. Canned salmon was on sale! In my excitement I decided to stock up on salmon. A lot of salmon. Too bad I forgot to ask Bill and the boys if they liked salmon. (At least John won the canned-goods-drive prize that month at school.)

"Dining is and always was a great artistic opportunity."—Frank Lloyd Wright

The Art of Eating Well

There is far more to eating than good food. The ambiance—where and how you set you table or trays or organize your picnic—has a lot to do with whether your meal is a pleasant experience and will help define your family culture. Ever since Bill and I were married twenty-five years ago I've kept my table set all the time with colorful placemats, coordinating cloth napkins in napkin rings, pretty dishes, glasses, and silverware. There are candlesticks on the table because we like to eat dinner by candlelight, and most days there is a vase of fresh flowers as a centerpiece. I realize this is a little extreme and not everyone, maybe not anyone, is going to want to do this. But I do it since the kitchen is not a place I by nature want to hang out, and it helps me want to be in there if I have a pretty table set.

There are added benefits as well. It saves me time to always keep the table set. We set it straight from the dishwasher and put out fresh napkins every other day. I keep pretty placemats on bamboo trays we sometimes use to eat in the den while we watch a video.

Plus, if my family has to endure my cooking, I feel the least I can do is create a pleasant atmosphere. If I can't serve pasta with yummy homemade sauce, the least I can do is serve what I do have on a silver platter, in a beautiful setting and try to orchestrate meaningful, fun conversation at the table. Maybe my family doesn't eat as well as our neighbors who live with Betty Crocker, but we're having a good time, because along with the pasta, I serve ambiance.

> "Meals are small acts of great importance, moments set aside for conversation, reflection, and communion"
> —Alexandra Stoddard

I like to acknowledge the different seasons and holidays during the year as part of our family traditions. I don't have a lot of extra time to do this, so I keep seasonal paper goods on hand. (When I'm in a big hurry and just don't want to deal with dishes, I can use my love of traditions as an excuse for using paper goods.)

I want my boys to grow up to be gentlemen—to practice good manners and to be just as comfortable eating at the governor's mansion as a hole-in-the-wall truck stop. It's easy to teach them which utensils to use at home since we use them on a daily basis.

S t r e t C H YOUR MIND:

"The dinner table is the center for the teaching and practicing not just of table manners but of conversation, consideration, tolerance, family feeling, and just about all the other accomplishments of polite society except for the minuet." —Judith Martin, *Miss Manners' Guide for the Turn-of-the-Millennium*

What Makes for Good Eating Besides the Food

My bottom line is this: As the Family Manager, you are creating a place where food can bring out  the best in the diners. When you think about your family meals and what you'd like to change (if anything), take the same approach I suggested for the kitchen. Think of the place you eat—whether the kitchen, a breakfast nook, or the dining room—as a coffee shop or restaurant that promotes an enjoyable experience. What do you have on hand that does that? What dishes and serving pieces will you use sometime in the next century only if everything else in the house falls off the shelves and breaks? Break down and use them to set a pretty table. How can you arrange your food preparation schedule so as to be in good spirits when you serve it?

The Daily Dozen for Pleasant Dining

1. Plan your dinner by 10 A.M. Use your menu plans.

2. Prepare everything you can early in the day. Involve your children in the planning and preparation—like creating an interesting centerpiece for the table from fresh flowers, greens, fruits, or vegetables.

3. If you work outside your home, make good use of your Crockpot and microwave. Wherever you work, if you're especially harried, pick up some take-out and serve it on pretty dishes.

4. Unplug the telephone during meals or let the answering machine take charge of calls.

5. Design a fun reward system for good manners. Everyone will enjoy the meal more, and your children will learn to feel comfortable in any setting.

6. Eat by candlelight often. Your children will love this. (Store candles in the refrigerator; they'll burn longer.)

7. Collect pretty placemats, napkins, dishes, etc. Watch for white sales, and you can usually find very nice, but inexpensive linens at flea markets and estate sales.

8. Turn off the TV and turn on pleasant background music.

9. Ban critical words and arguing at the table.

10. Consider making one night a week, or whatever works for your family, an "assigned topic" night. Take turns picking a topic to discuss at the dinner table. I'm not going to suggest topics since family cultures vary so widely on what's appropriate and what's not. But do remind everyone of the ninth rule in this list.

11. Learn to laugh at your flops. My family still laughs about the time I burned at least one part of dinner every night for a week.

12. Compliment everyone who helped with the meal every night.

"Life is too short to stuff a mushroom."—Shirley Conran

 THINK ABOUT IT

Beat the Clock or It Will Beat You

Of course there's a whole department and chapter devoted to time management. But we would all do well to remind ourselves again of the importance of working smarter, not harder. This applies to fixing dinner just as much as it applies to washing windows. It applies not only to preparation, cooking ahead, short-cut recipes and the like, but being smart about your circumstances in life as well. This means if you're the mother of three children under six, be smart. This is not your time in life to fix recipes that call for seventeen ingredients and take a minimum of two hours and lots of supervision to prepare. It means if you're a single mom with another full-time job besides being a Family Manager and you have two teenage boys to feed, be smart. Buy in bulk, and buy things they can fix themselves.

Wherever you are in life, there are some smart things you can do to manage this department. (Once again, use the ideas on this list that work for you and discard the rest. Feel free to improvise and adapt.)

1 Every week's menu should have at least one or two quick-as-a-wink dinners for those days when the kids have ballet, soccer, and piano lessons all at the same time, the dog escaped from your yard and came home at 5:00 wearing your neighbor's garbage, or you have a headache that won't quit. I keep angel-hair pasta, which cooks in five minutes and a jar of interesting spaghetti sauce in the pantry, pre-washed lettuce in the refrigerator, and pre-sliced, pre-buttered French bread in the freezer, ready to pop in the oven, for days like these.

② Cut up carrot and celery sticks for lunches and snacks when you bring the veggies home from the store.

③ If you buy bigger quantities of chicken breasts, wrap and freeze in the amount you need for your family. Make ground beef into patties before you freeze.

④ Grate a large block of cheese and store it in self-sealing plastic bags. It freezes well and is easy to get in and out when a dish calls for grated cheese.

⑤ Cook larger quantities of soup stock, stew, casseroles and freeze them for future use.

⑥ Enlist help. Four hands are faster than two when it comes to getting dinner on the table.

⑦ Buy a cookbook specifically devoted to simple meals that can be made in a hurry.

⑧ Keep as many staples—pickles, olives, beans, canned and frozen foods—on hand as you have storage room for. You're less likely to be out of the crucial ingredient for tonight's dinner.

⑨ Keep a running shopping list posted, ideally at your Control Central, or on the refrigerator or some other in-the-way place.

⑩ If you're especially harried, take ten minutes before you begin to cook or while the soup is simmering. Run a hot bath and soak for just a few minutes. Sit down with a cup of tea. Or, if you have small children around and can't do anything else, take ten deep relaxing breaths. Do some bending and stretching with your overactive toddler.

What's a Meal?

Sometimes it helps to broaden your definition of what a meal is. I have a friend who instituted a Friday-night tradition when her children were small. In addition to being a Family Manager, she worked outside the home. Her husband worked full-time plus went to school. This was a busy household. She told me that by most Friday nights nearly everybody was in meltdown. So this was her solution. Friday nights for dinner they had carrot and celery sticks, sometimes raw broccoli or zucchini, whatever was available, cheese slices, cut up apples and popcorn. You read that right—popcorn. This Friday fun meal was easy to fix, quick, and fun. Sometimes they popped in a video when they got to the popcorn part. Sometimes they just sat around and told stories about their week.

If you think this meal is a nutritional travesty, please think again. It contains all the major food groups. Raw vegetables and fruits are arguably more nutritional than cooked ones. Cheese is protein. Popcorn is a grain. It has less fat (even with butter on it) than just about any fast-food alternative I can think of. It takes less time and costs less than ordering and waiting for a pizza, which, really is the whole point—disregarding old definitions to make way for new, fun, creative alternatives that feed your family in more ways than one.

S T R E T C H YOUR MIND:
"We are indeed much more than what we eat,
but what we eat can nevertheless help us to be much more
than what we are."—Adele Davis, *Let's Get Well*

chapter 6

Managing Home and Property

"We shape our houses,
then our houses shape us."
—Winston Churchill

H ave you ever stopped to think about the fact that we shape our houses—the place where we sleep, eat, play, relax, recuperate from the day's stresses, raise our children, make our lives, and sometimes run a business? The atmosphere of our homes is important to the development, or shaping, of the people who live there.

One way to say we shape our houses is to say we're in charge of what shape they're in. The whole point of this chapter is to help you make your house—the physical building and everything that's in it and around it—a place that reflects and facilitates who you and your family want to be. Some people choose to live in apartments in the city because that's where they work, that's where their interests lie. Some people choose to live in farmhouses, country cabins, or modern houses in the suburbs near schools, malls, etc. Where we choose to live, in what kind of house and how, is often a compromise—a balancing act between time, money, careers, and schools. The point is, wherever you live, you can make daily choices of how you live there that will enhance your life.

"Think of what you can do with what there is."—Ernest Hemingway

THINK ABOUT IT

Managing your family's tangible resources is a big job—a huge job. We're talking about your house, yard, furniture, accessories, decor, appliances, tools, electronic equipment, books, clothing, toys and sports equipment, to name a few. We're talking about cleaning, storing, maintaining, organizing, redoing, decorating, and using for daily living. We're talking about living rooms and workrooms and garages and cars and closets and basements and attics and order and clutter and the stuff of daily living.

We're talking about a variety of tasks and skills, from the simplest, like picking up toys after toddlers, to the most repetitive—I don't think anyone has yet invented a self-cleaning toilet, to those which draw on our creative and technical skills, like redecorating the living room or rebuilding the engine of a second car so it will run another 100,000 miles. And, of course, managing home and property draws on planning, organization, and delegation skills, because no matter who you are, there are some jobs and tasks in this department you will want or need to delegate to others, either hiring an expert or relying on one of your family member's expertise.

> "Housework can't kill you, but why take the risk?"
> —Phyllis Diller

First, Shape a Plan

Of course, I can't tell you exactly how to manage this department in your home. A lot of how you manage it has to do with the uniquenesses of your family—how much laundry you do weekly, what kinds of furniture you have, the age of your appliances, how many cars you own and how old they are, the size of your house and yard, your schedule, the amount of clutter you can tolerate, your standards of cleanliness, whether you live in a city or the country, whether you work outside the home.

But I can tell you this: Time spent thinking about what it means to you to make your house a home, having an overall plan, creating some standard operating procedures for caring for your belongings, will help save you time, money, and energy. Don't get me wrong. I'm not talking about rigid rules written in stone that say you must clean your

bathroom floor on Tuesday and sweep down the front stairs with a wet broom every second Thursday.

Our families and circumstances are constantly changing, and we have to be flexible—or else lose our minds. Babies turn into toddlers. The people who couldn't tolerate a fingerprint on their glass door now can hardly see through the bottom third of it. Maybe you decide to go back to a career outside the home

after a few years off, and now you need more help with the basics, like weekly cleaning and laundry. Change is inevitable. But the basic issues are the same. And unless you have some idea of your bottom line about them, you're likely to be adrift when it comes to managing this area.

"The best things in life aren't things."
—Art Buchwald

THINK ABOUT IT

Using Things and Loving People, not Vice Versa

Art Buchwald says it all, as far as I'm concerned. The number one tenet in my philosophy of Home and Property is that things aren't as important as people. And people don't need a lot of things to be creative, content, fulfilled, and growing into the best they can be. So, my philosophy about the things we live with is to make sure they serve us, that we need them, use them, and realize their relative importance in the grand scheme of life.

Another thing about things: Unless you have the luxury of a full-time housekeeper, handyman, mechanic, groundskeeper, and laundress, the job of overseeing the acquisition, usage, storage and maintenance of your home and property can be more than a full-time job. Many of our belongings need some type of routine care and maintenance,

> "I have only one life and it is short enough. Why waste it on things I don't want most?"
> — Louis Brandeis

and some need periodic repairs and improvements. How well we care for and maintain them has a lot to do with how much money we end up spending on repairs and improvements. And, if given the choice, which I am, I'd rather go to lunch with a friend or take my kids to the park than have to scrub my kitchen floor on my hands and knees because I haven't taken the time to mop it regu-larly like the instructions suggested and now it's marred. Or, if I have the choice of whether to spend our money on a family mini-vacation or pay a handyman to replace the rotted wood trim on the house because we didn't take the time to paint it when the paint started to look weathered, I'll choose the trip. So, it's part of my Home and Property philosophy that once we've determined the things we need to live a happy and fulfilled life, we make a shared commitment to take care of them.

STRETCH YOUR MIND:

"Go home, and take care of what you have. Provide places for all your things." — Mother Ann, Shaker Founder

People, Places, Things: Five Essential Questions

There's nothing magic about these questions. They're certainly not the only five. But they are things you need to think about as you formulate your philosophy and some standard operating procedures for managing your home and property. They're meant to be food for thought, grist for your family meetings, and for ongoing discussions about how you'll manage your home and property on a daily basis. I urge you to take some time to envision what your house would look like in your ideal scenario. What would it feel like to live there? What would happen on a daily and weekly basis?

ONE. What is the stage and age of your family?

Who lives at your house? How old are they? What are their interests? What can they do to contribute to your family's general well-being? When you think about the stage and age of your family, children and their needs come to

mind. However, you also need to think about your own and your husband's needs and available time. How much time do you have to invest in ongoing care and cleaning? Do you want to do that cleaning during the week or on the weekends? Who is good at what? Who likes to do what? How will you negotiate?

Every home has a certain personality, which helps define the culture of the family that lives there. You can walk into one home and it will be so crisp and clean, you wonder if anyone actually lives there. Then maybe you realize that the children are grown and live away from home. Or you can walk into another home where three preschoolers live and you have to be careful not to trip over the toys. Still another home may just seem comfortable—there's some mess here and there, but it seems to be a somewhat controlled mess—a

> "Cleaning your house while your kids are still growing is like shoveling the walk before it stops snowing."
> —Phyllis Diller

model airplane half-way finished on a card table, stacks of folded laundry waiting for the designated courier to put it away, a salt map of South America drying on the kitchen counter. A great deal of your home's personality depends on where you are in life and the ages of your children.

Many children discover their life's work through creative, playful activities—which, for some Family Managers who have neat-as-a-pin standards, means you need to put up with some creative mess and give up your dreams of winning the House Beautiful award. I heard a story recently about the late Jim Henson, the creator of the Muppets and Sesame Street. It seems when he was a young boy, his mother let him make puppets from her drapes. Inventive pursuits often produce creative messes. And those creative messes can have far-reaching effects in our children's lives.

"The art of being wise is the art of knowing what to overlook."—William James

As you define for your own purposes the stage and age of your family, remember this will have a lot to do with the standards and procedures you create to care for your home and property.

TWO. How do you spell clean?

What's spick-and-span to one person may be filthy to another. Everyone has a different tolerance level for dirt. I think  there's a lot of truth in the old adage "Home should be clean enough to be healthy, and dirty enough to be happy." In other words, I don't know of anyone who likes bugs crawling on their countertops. But on the other hand, who cares if they can eat off of the kitchen floor if Mom's always playing chief nag? It's important that you find a clean comfort level that's built on common ground. This means everyone will probably have to give a little (and maybe in some cases a lot), but that's what being a family and a team is all about.

The idea here is like a scale from -5 to +5 with 0 in the middle. Filthy is a -5 and super-clean is a +5 and somewhere in between is your family's comfort zone.

"Cleanliness is not next to godliness. It isn't even in the same neighborhood. No one has ever gotten a religious experience out of removing burned-on cheese from the grill of the toaster oven."—Erma Bombeck

As you and your family are coming up with your family definition of "clean," be specific and let everyone have a say. Have everyone describe what each room looks like if it's "clean." It has been my experience that this is an eye-opening exercise, mainly because you, the Family Manager, will "see" things that others take for granted. For example, maybe your teenager will give a general description of how he likes the bathroom: clean. Maybe he's never thought about why there is or isn't mildew in the shower or what that funny little brush is in the container behind the toilet. Coming up with a definition of "clean" is a good springboard for discussion and a good way to start the process of delegating the chores it takes to maintain your shared definition of "clean."

"Women, for hormonal reasons, can see individual dirt molecules, whereas men tend not to notice them until they join together into clumps large enough to support commercial agriculture."
—Dave Barry

THREE. How do you define "order"?

I have two very different friends. One friend's definition of order is not being hit on the head with a falling object when she opens her closet door. The other friend's blouses, skirts, and dresses are all categorized by color and hung in graduated lengths, all facing the same direction on the same kind of hanger. Her belts are stored in perfect rows in graduated sizes. It probably goes without saying that the first friend craves more order in her life. She'd love to be able to find the belt that goes with a certain pair of pants when she needs it. The orderly friend confessed to me that she would like to learn to relax her standards a little, be more spontaneous. She'd like to go for coffee with a friend or go for a spur-of-the-moment walk, but never feels the freedom to until everything is in its place.

As with cleaning the principle is: Find some middle ground. You'll waste precious emotional energy if you hope your insurance policy is up to date every time you open your high kitchen cabinets. And, quite frankly, life's too short to spend it organizing three children's drawers into color-coordinated outfits.

> "The strength of a nation, especially of a republican nation, is in the intelligent and well-ordered homes of the people."
> —Lydia Huntly Sigourney

I like order, but it doesn't come naturally for me. I'm always searching for ways to bring more order to my home. I like opening a closet or cupboard without fear of what I might find there—or what I won't. For me, order relates closely to eliminating what we don't need and concentrating on caring for what's important to us. I've made it my motto: "Eliminate and Concentrate." Sometimes I even find myself repeating it softly as I dig into the layers of papers on my office floor at the end of a project, eliminate and concentrate, eliminate and concentrate. . . .

The last portion of this chapter provides specific ideas and suggestions for cleaning, making order, maintaining your home and property, and the "equipment" therein, and decorating. But first, let's finish off the five questions.

FOUR. How do you maintain and fix your belongings?

Whether you're a do-it-yourselfer or like to have help because you're a danger to yourself and others with a hammer in your hand, you need to survey the situation and figure out your family's best way of keeping things going for the long haul. How do you balance time off with money? How do you decide when to invest dollars and when to invest sweat into repairs or remodeling? What's your bottom line?

No house lasts forever, but some last longer than others. The difference between Andrew Jackson's Hermitage and the thousands of other houses that were built around 1820 but didn't survive is not how much it cost to build them. It's how they were maintained.

I've found that a calendar-based maintenance plan works best for our family. So that's what begins on p. 173. You may find a room-by-room system works best for you. What's in your kitchen, garage, family room, etc., that needs regular care and maintenance? Where are the related warranties and other documentation you might need? Or, perhaps a person-based system will work best for you. Whatever system you use, you need to begin with a clear idea of the task. What are the regular maintenance jobs? Who will do them? How will you keep track?

FIVE. What is your taste and style?

It seems like yesterday we were stripping varnish from an estate-sale "find," while our preschoolers painted the side of the house with a clean brush and a bucket of water. Actually, it was seventeen years ago when Judie Byrd and I moved into adjoining older neighborhoods. We both had small children, small houses, and small budgets. But there was something else we shared—a desire to turn our houses into attractive homes that had a warm and welcoming atmosphere for both family members and friends. Over coffee and time, Judie and I became fast friends as we shared ideas about decorating and remodeling on a shoestring.

Depending on the age and stage of your family, you may no longer be on a shoestring, or your budget may be thin as a thread. I'm a big believer in making the most of what you have whether it's a mansion, a farmhouse, or a small apartment. I've met a lot of women who are waiting for their dream home, discontent and nonmotivated to improve where they are. It's important that we all remember that wherever we are, that place is our home.

Creating Atmosphere with Common Senses

It's important to me that when a child walks in the door from school or Bill comes home from a meeting or I get back from a trip, that we say, "It's good to be home!" There's not one certain element that makes home a good place to be, but a number of things working together, producing a pleasant environment.

As human beings we interpret our environment through our five senses. I use the five senses as a guide to help me create a "good place"

for all of us. You might find it helpful, as I do, to ask yourself some questions about what your family "senses" as they walk into your house: *Do you sense order or clutter?*

Mess causes stress. Our house is not the neatest house on the

154

block, or even close. But we've found that we're all happier when we're living within our definitions of *clean* and *order*. It's not pleasant to walk into a kitchen with a sink filled with two days of dirty dishes and not be able to find a clean glass to get a drink of water.

Do the rooms seem dark and enclosed or light and airy?

Dark rooms can be depressing, as well as hard on your eyes if it's where you read or work on projects. You might need to replace existing overhead light fixtures with ones that give off more light or add reading lamps beside seating.

Too much furniture and clutter in a room can make it visually shrink in size. Evaluate what's taking up space. Does it really need to be there?

Are there things — art, photos, mementos — in each room that bring to mind good memories?

I love to walk into a room and remember how excited Bill and I were to find an oak buffet for seventy-five dollars on a Saturday outing when our kids were young. As a matter of fact, almost everything in our house has a story behind it—items we've brought back from vacations, gifts from family and friends, something we scrimped and saved for and finally bought.

How do your things feel to the touch? Is your furniture comfortable?

We bought a sofa once that was the right style, the right size, the right color, but we didn't think about the fact that the fabric was scratchy and uncomfortable to exposed skin.

What do you hear as you walk through your house? Is the television blaring? Are family members yelling?

Noise pollution can ruin a home's environment. Our "No yelling in the house" rule has been in force for umpteen years now, and I can testify that it makes a difference in the atmosphere in a very positive way. We only turn on the television to watch specific programs. And every morning I put on soothing classical music to be the background for our breakfast conversation and the rest of our day.

What does your home smell like?

Every home has a certain scent. Good smells in a home create an immediate sense of a pleasant environment. On the other hand, a home with bad odors can seem unwelcoming—even offensive. I have potpourri in most every room, and each day I put a drop or two of fragrance oil on a lightbulb ring to give our home a fresh scent.

Is there anything in your home that conjures up pleasant thoughts about food—your sense of taste?

Try a big bowl of shiny apples on your family room coffee table, warm cookies cooling on the kitchen counter, or favorite mints or candy in a pretty dish.

Dream and Plan

Along with the five senses, I've found "dream and plan" to be important watchwords when it comes to creating a "good place." Creative vision is a wonderful thing. It births more creative vision. A friend told me the story of her living-room drapes. When she and her family moved across the country, they found a new home that fit their needs, but the asking price stretched their budget. They wouldn't have anything left over for decorating. The house was in good shape and, for the most part, decorated in colors she could live with. In fact, ten years later, the same wallpaper hangs in the dining room. But the living room was another story. One wall was papered in dark burgundy that matched the heavy drapes hanging over beautiful French doors. She lived in the dark but envisioned light, so, even though she knew she probably couldn't afford it, she got quotes from a designer friend on white window treatments. She was right. She couldn't afford it. But she had a vision. Then one day, walking through the mall, she happened to see a freestanding white screen, the kind people use as room dividers. Trembling, she walked into the store, and checked the price. They were fifty dollars apiece. She would need two of them, one for each set of French doors. That was about one fifth the price of window treatments. She bought them and loves the way she can stand them in front of the doors at night for privacy, then fold them up to let light stream in during the day.

On page 180 I'll introduce you to another friend, professional interior designer Peggy Zadina. I'll share with you strategies and tips she's shared with me over the years. She taught me that it doesn't take a lot of money to turn a cold, mundane room into one that is warm and charming. It's the simple, personal touches that can turn the ordinary into something that reflects you and your family.

Remember . . .

No one starts with an empty slate when it comes to Home and Property, any more than in any other department. As you begin to make changes, remember, transformation happens slowly. So dream and plan. Keep your family's stage and age in mind as you make your changes. Construct your own definitions of cleanliness and order. Determine what you have and how it needs to be maintained and cared for. And always be on the alert for the small personal touches that will help your home reflect who you are.

The rest of this chapter is about the nitty-gritty. It's a buffet table of ideas, and like a buffet table is roughly organized from the beginning to the end: from salads and soups through desserts and coffee, or in this case from catching up and keeping up through decorating tips. Of course, since life is short, sometimes we might eat dessert first. And sometimes we might be more motivated to keep up with the daily stuff in a newly decorated room. So pick and choose what appeals for you. And enjoy making your home a good place to be!

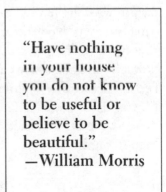

"Have nothing in your house you do not know to be useful or believe to be beautiful."
—William Morris

Remember the Motto:
Eliminate and Concentrate

Moving cross-country can be a real eye-opener about how big this job of managing home and property really is. Two years ago when we moved from Texas to Tennessee I realized this was a perfect opportunity to take stock of our family's changing needs and priorities, and to fine-tune my philosophy and plan for managing our home and property.

I live with three boys who grieve when they're asked to throw away their old toothbrushes. Imagine their responses when I suggest they might want to donate their tricycles and children's books to a good cause. I think they take after their father, otherwise known as Mr. It-Might-Come-in-Handy-One-Day. You never know when you're going to need a part from a broken doorknob.

As I contemplated cleaning, sorting, and packing twenty-five years worth of clutter one more time, my motto kept coming to mind: eliminate and concentrate. Why, I wondered, couldn't five reasonably intelligent human beings learn to eliminate what they don't need, use, or enjoy? Why couldn't we see that would free up space? If we don't own it, we don't have to take care of it, and we have more time to do what we want. Now, there's a trick phrase in this paragraph, and it's twenty-five years. Since accomplishing a major overhaul on our time, property, and possessions, I've vowed to do it on a regular basis. That's become part of my philosophy and plan for home and property. Moving gave me a perfect opportunity to work with the aforementioned hoarders to decide what we really want, need, use, and would keep in our lives.

Five Little Questions

Use this simple evaluation/action plan any way it works for you. You can do this over time, or when you move. You can do it on a room-by-room basis, once or twice a year. You can do it on a regular basis, maybe as you contemplate a new purchase.

1. When is the last time I/we used it? Saw it? Wore it? Fixed it? Played with it?

2. Where do I/we keep it? And if I/we didn't have it, what would I/we store there instead?

3. What is my/our emotional attachment to it?

4. What do I/we want to do with this thing—from the table lamp to the bassinet? (Note: It's at this point that realism enters the picture. You might want to throw out your washing machine and install a mini-gym. Unfortunately, you wouldn't have any-where to wash your gym clothes.

5. How will I take action—use, fix, sell, restore, or donate?

"How many things I can do without!"—*Socrates*

THINK ABOUT IT

Catch Up Before You Can Keep Up

Okay, maybe you've purged your home of unnecessary clutter. And maybe your family has come up with your definition of clean. But you still fear the mayor may put your house on his Clean-Up-the-City hit list. Maybe you see the need to catch up before you can stay caught up with your idea of a clean house.

If it has been a while since your house has had a good, deep clean-ing; that's a good place to start. Make this a family affair. Remember, if they help clean, they'll be more likely to follow the procedures you've established to keep it clean.

1. Try to schedule a big cleanup when you can do it two days in a row. This way you save on start-up/knock-down time, you will be more serious and do a better job, and the results become visible more quickly—which will give everyone more momentum.

2. Start by surveying your home. Walk through each room with paper and pen. List the jobs to be accomplished in each room and what supplies and equipment you'll need. Decide which big, time-consuming jobs you might want to hire out or undertake during another session, such as cleaning windows and window coverings, shampooing carpets, stripping and waxing floors, and cleaning upholstery.

3. Take stock of your cleaning supplies and equipment. Make a list of the items you need to buy or rent to do the job right. Store everything in a central location until you're finished. Have plastic totes or buckets to hold small items so family members can easily carry them from room to room. Also have a basket for one person to pick up misplaced items and redistribute them to the proper room.

4. Have Clean Team members dress so they can put all their energy into the job. Wear comfortable clothes you don't care about soiling, tennis shoes, and have work gloves available.

5. "Do what you are doing." Make this old adage your motto. Don't allow nonemergencies to interrupt your cleanup time. Eliminate all distractions. Turn on your answering machine, and turn off the TV.

6. Encourage your team to be motion-minded. Work around the room instead of crisscrossing it, so you won't have to carry your supplies and equipment back and forth. And use both hands whenever you can. While finishing one task with one hand, start the next task with the other.

7. Keep in mind that deep-cleaning your home has a bigger purpose than just getting rid of dirt. It will help you and your family live more efficiently and effectively.

Your Cleaning Task Force

In business a task force is a group of people working on a common project. Common and project. Important words. Cleaning is common all right. Common in the sense that it has to be done regularly. And it serves the common good. And it's a project which, like all projects, is accomplished one task at a time, for the common good of all.

Once you've given your house a good deep cleaning, you need a plan to keep it clean. The following ideas and tips are meant to help you formulate a plan for caring for your home and property that's compatible with who your family is. You'll read some ideas that may not be a good fit for your family, but hopefully some of them will help you come up with some standard operating procedures, and give you some practical ways to find a clean comfort level that everyone agrees to.

> "A perfect summer day is playing eighteen holes of golf, two sets of tennis, lying by the pool for a couple of hours—and knowing that the lawn mower is broken."
> —Joel Peel, age 18

Start with the list of cleaning tasks you made for your big cleanup. Add anything you need to clean in your garage, basement, or yard. Categorize the cleaning tasks for each room and area by how often they need to be performed—daily, every other day, weekly, every two weeks, monthly, quarterly, semiannually, or annually.

SOPs for Your Task Force

Have a family meeting and create some SOPs (Standard Operating Procedures) for the cleaning tasks on your list. The procedures should include what you're cleaning, what you use to clean it, how often you clean it, and what special precautions you need to take. Assign cleaning tasks according to age and skill level, and available time. This way family members will always know whose turn it is to do what, how they're supposed to do it, and when they're expected to do it. And remember, the idea is to keep your home and property clean in the least amount of time, so you'll have more time for fun.

Easy as One, Two, Three

My friend, author, and home-management expert Rosemary Brown, created a cleaning plan for her family. We adapted parts of it to fit our own family's needs. If your team can incorporate ninety minutes of concentrated cleaning time into your weekly schedule, you may never have to give up a whole day to clean again. The secret's in being faithful to follow the plan every week.

First, do the chores in each room's speed-clean list every week. Then pick one chore from lists 1, 2, and 3 to stay on top of the heavy-duty cleaning. It's a sure way to spend less time cleaning and more time having fun.

Assign each capable family member a certain area of the house to speed-clean. Then give each person their own copy of the checklist. This is a good way to help him or her complete the job.

Speed-clean living areas:

❑ Pick up clutter

❑ Clean glass, mirrors, tabletops

❑ Dust furniture, lamps, windowsills, pictures, mantel

❑ Empty wastebaskets

❑ Vacuum carpets, damp-mop floors

❑ Pick one job to do from List 1

Speed-clean bedrooms:

❑ Pick up clutter

❑ Straighten closet and hang clothes

❑ Sort laundry for mending and dry-cleaning

- ❑ Clean mirrors, glass, tabletops
- ❑ Dust furniture, windowsills, pictures
- ❑ Empty wastebaskets
- ❑ Vacuum or dust-mop floors/carpets
- ❑ Pick one job to do from List 1

Speed-clean the bathrooms:

- ❑ Pick up clutter
- ❑ Collect dirty towels and take to laundry area
- ❑ Spray and wipe mirror with glass cleaner
- ❑ Clean sink
- ❑ Use glass cleaner on faucets and chrome
- ❑ Spray tub/shower walls with heavy-duty cleaner
- ❑ Squirt cleaner in toilet and swish around bowl;
  wipe outside of bowl
- ❑ Wipe off windowsills and scale
- ❑ Empty wastebasket
- ❑ Sweep or vacuum floor, and damp-mop
- ❑ Pick one job to do from List 2

Speed-clean your kitchen:

- ❑ Pick up clutter
- ❑ Clean outside of large appliances with glass cleaner
- ❑ Shine outside of small appliances with glass cleaner
- ❑ Wipe off windowsills
- ❑ Wipe off countertops
- ❑ Wash and disinfect trash can; replace liner
- ❑ Sweep or vacuum floor, then damp-mop
- ❑ Pick one job to do from List 3

List 1

- ❏ Polish wood furniture
- ❏ Use attachments to vacuum baseboards, moldings, lampshades and behind furniture
- ❏ Vacuum upholstered furniture and drapes
- ❏ Toss or recycle magazines and newspapers
- ❏ Dust knickknacks
- ❏ Polish silver
- ❏ Clean inside cabinets and drawers

List 2

- ❏ Wash throw rugs
- ❏ Scrub tile and grout
- ❏ Vacuum baseboards and moldings
- ❏ Clean woodwork and exposed storage areas
- ❏ Clean inside of medicine cabinet and other concealed storage areas
- ❏ Wash shower curtain and/or liner
- ❏ Scrub floor

List 3

- ❏ Clean stovetop and replace burner bibs
- ❏ Vacuum vent hood and coils
- ❏ Clean oven
- ❏ Clean woodwork
- ❏ Polish chrome
- ❏ Clean out pantry
- ❏ Wipe out drawers
- ❏ Clean out cabinets
- ❏ Scrub and wax floor
- ❏ Clean out refrigerator; wipe off interior walls and shelves
- ❏ Defrost or clean out freezer and take inventory

Motivating Your Team

Like I said, stay flexible, families do change. Today at our house, we've become a little less structured. Our habit is to work together as a team on Saturday following our list to get our chores done. We do some daily chores and laundry during the week, and catch up with the rest of it on the weekend. Unfortunately, no one in my family was born with a natural love for housework, so, over the years I've had to be creative in motivating my family, as well as myself. Here are some ways to get your team moving:

- Make a simple "Laundry Man" cape and mask for a younger child who's in charge of folding laundry.

- Give older kids a "Cash-and-Carry" incentive for large jobs. Offer a small cash reward for carrying all the boxes to the attic, or hauling the mounds of garbage outside.

- Play "Beat the Clock" while working on a particular job. Set the kitchen timer and see who can finish his or her task before the buzzer rings.

- If you're doing a major cleaning, station laundry baskets, boxes, clothes hampers, and trash cans in strategic locations around the house. Label each receptacle according to what you want to end up in it, and let the kids gently toss in clothes they've outgrown, unbreakable items and trash into their respective containers.

- Designate one person to be in charge of sorting through and folding the clothing items that will be stored or given away. Unusable clothing can be cut up for rags, and the buttons can be cut off for crafts.

- Put on some peppy music while doing chores to keep everybody moving and energized.

- Go out for a treat together after you finish all your chores.

STRETCH YOUR MIND:

"It is my belief that no one (except infants and individuals who are ill or physically disabled) should have a free ride when it comes to the work of the house. This does not mean that everyone should share equally; circumstances may dictate otherwise. But neither does it mean that one person should become the sacrificial household lamb."
—Marjorie Hansen Shaevitz, *The Superwoman Syndrome*

What Kids Can Do

Establish "Room Rules" for kids, such as:

1. Do not take food in your bedroom

2. Keep all dirty clothes in basket or hamper

3. Do not leave dangerous items on floor—balls, sharp plastic building pieces, roller skates

4. Put away toys you're finished playing with before getting out something new

5. Clean up room before going to bed

Preschoolers can . . .

- Make bed (A comforter is easier for them to handle)
- Fold towels and washcloths
- Put away clothes in drawers
- Pick up toys
- Wipe off baseboards, window sills, and wooden shutters wearing an old pair of socks on their hands
- Wipe off the front of large appliances using spray bottle of water and sponge

Kindergarteners can . . .
- Vacuum small areas with lightweight, hand-held vacuum
- Sweep porch
- Clean bathroom sinks
- Straighten plastic dishes in a lower cabinet
- Dust furniture
- Wipe windows that you've washed with a clean blackboard eraser to keep them shining

Younger elementary kids can . . .
- Take out garbage
- Sweep stairs and walks
- Clean out car
- Vacuum own room
- Sort and straighten toys
- Empty dishwasher
- Sort clothes for washing
- Clean off outdoor furniture

Older elementary kids can . . .
- Clean bathroom mirrors
- Vacuum most rooms
- Clean toilets
- Clean countertops and kitchen sink
- Mop small-area floors
- Fold most laundry and put away
- Pull weeds
- Clean pet areas

- Clean cobwebs and dust in high places with a cobweb pole
  (Put one thick cotton sock inside another and slip them over
  the end of a yardstick, securing with a rubber band.)

Middle school kids can . . .
- Wash windows
- Mend clothes
- Mow yard
- Wash car
- Change sheets on bed
- Do own laundry
- Clean bathtub

High school kids can . . .
- Clean out refrigerator
- Defrost freezer
- Clean out and organize attic, basement, garage
- Heavy yard work
- Clean light fixtures
- Wax car
- Learn to repair and maintain car

A Word about Laundry

The old adage is that nothing is sure in this life except death and
taxes. Well, I'd add a few things to that list, and laundry would probably be at the top. My personal opinion is that anyone who is old

"Man's best friend, aside from the dog

enough to dress themselves is old enough to help in some way with laundry. At least they can put clothes they take off in a hamper instead of on the floor. Learning this simple task may take time. But it will be time well spent. And when family members start doing their own laundry, or at least helping, it's amazing how kids think twice before changing outfits three times a day,

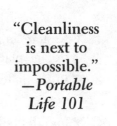

"Cleanliness is next to impossible."
—*Portable Life 101*

towels get used for more than one shower, and hampers that were once filled with dirty as well as clean clothes (because the wearers were too lazy to hang or put them up) now have only dirty clothes. Miracles do happen!

Keeping Order

The following two-step strategy offers ideas and suggestions to help you get to that middle ground, to find order, reduce chaos, and enjoy the feeling of actually knowing where something is when you need it.

Step One:

Analyze how existing storage space is being used. Ask three questions about each item in storage: Has it been worn or used in the past year? Does it have personal/monetary value? Will it be worn or used again someday?

If you answered no to one or two of the questions, don't store it in a prime storage space. If you answered no to all three questions, give it or throw it away.

Step Two:

Maximize available space. Identify non-traditional storage areas in your home.

s the wastebasket." —*Business Week*

Living Areas

▼ Restore an antique trunk or hope chest to double as a table and storage place.

▼ Build shelves under stairwells; build in corner shelves and cabinets.

▼ Jut tall bookcases into a room to create a nook and storage shelves.

▼ Build a window seat with underneath storage for deep-set windows.

▼ Hide clutter in a corner behind a pretty screen.

▼ Convert an old armoire into a cabinet for your TV and electronic equipment.

▼ Hang speakers on a wall to free up floor space.

▼ Look for dead space on top of a cabinet or hutch to store attractive items.

▼ Install a towel rack on the inside of linen-closet door to hang tablecloths.

Bedroom

▼ Put mattresses on platforms with built-in drawers, or attach coasters to plastic storage boxes and slide under beds.

▼ Stack attractive storage cubes to use as nightstands.

▼ Nest luggage or use seldom-used pieces to store out-of-season clothes.

▼ Use ice-cube trays or egg carton bottoms to organize small items in drawers.

▼ Store sports equipment in large plastic garbage cans in the garage or basement.

Children's Bedrooms

▼ Have colorful plastic containers of all sizes and shapes to hold children's belongings—baseball card collection, Legos, rock collection, beads for stringing, doll clothes.

▼ Buy a chest or use a footlocker to store odd-sized toys. These items do double-duty when it's time to pack your child for camp or leave for college.

▼ Use comforters instead of bedspreads on the beds. They'll be easier to make up.

▼ Make sure your children's books are easily accessible. Help them arrange their books by topic or author so they'll have a sense of pride and ownership in a growing library.

▼ Install some shelves for your child to display personal treasures.

Kitchen

▼ Build a high border-shelf around perimeter of kitchen to store baskets, decorative dishes, and seldom-used cookware.

▼ Free up drawer space by installing a magnetic strip on the back of a cabinet door to store small knives. Display wire whisks, spatulas, and other large cooking utensils in a pretty crock on kitchen counter.

▼ Use bar soap to wax the runners of drawers without rollers.

▼ Place a shelf across the back of a deep cabinet to elevate some items and store others underneath.

▼ Use a plastic utensil divider to separate kitchen-junk drawer items.

▼ Put a lazy Susan in your refrigerator for easier access to small jars and containers.

Bathroom

▼ Hang a shoe bag on the back of bathroom door to store rollers, brushes, etc.

▼ Attach a magnetic strip to back of medicine chest door to hold tweezers, clippers, and other small metal objects.

▼ Build shelves in the sink cabinet to store tissue, soap, and cleaning supplies.

▼ Hang a wine rack on wall to hold rolled towels; provide a wall hook for each family member to hang wet towels.

Maximize Closet Space

▼ Clean out closets twice a year. Box or toss unnecessary items.

▼ Hang work clothes, play clothes, and dressy clothes in their respective category, giving prime placement to the kind of clothes you wear most often. Group the same types of clothing within each category.

▼ Don't keep wrong-size clothes in your closet.

▼ Keep clothes to be mended in a designated place.

▼ Store out-of-season clothes in another closet or trunk, or put a sheet around them and hang in the back of your closet.

▼ Put hooks on the inside of closet wall to hang nightgowns, robes, shoulder bags, or other items with straps.

▼ Hang a mug rack on closet wall for small hats and purses.

▼ Install two to four, sixteen-inch kitchen hand-towel racks on back of closet door for hanging scarves.

▼ Store shoes in transparent boxes on a shelf above rod. Roll up magazines and put them in boots to store in an upright position.

▼ Use a clear, shoe-organizer hanger to store socks and hosiery.

▼ Hang a mesh laundry bag with a tie for dirty hose and delicate lingerie. Toss it into the washer with other clothes. Keep a laundry bag in your closet for clothes to go to the dry-cleaners.

▼ Install a men's tie or belt rack to hang leotards and lingerie.

Clutter-free Kids' Closets

Kids' closets should be functional and orderly, so they can reach often-used items without asking for help. Here's how:

Divide the closet into two parts: one for hanging clothes and one for shelves. Have two rods on hanging side, a high rod for out-of-season and seldom-worn clothes and a child-level rod. Buy adjustable plastic or metal shelving to fit in closet, or build wood shelves low enough for kids to reach. Make sure shelves are splinter-free. For easier cleaning, paint wood shelves with polyurethane or cover with washable contact paper.

For shoes, buy or build a simple shelf that runs across the bottom or along the side of the closet. Keep a small stepstool in the closet for kids to reach higher shelves.

Have a small laundry basket for easy cleanup of dirty clothes.

Beat the Repairman Blues:
A Month-by-Month Maintenance Checklist

Use this list as a start for your own. Cross off jobs that don't apply to your home and property. Add things you do need to take care of.

Mark the jobs that you or your team members can do. Decide who will be responsible. Also decide what jobs you'd like to learn to do.

Brainstorm about how you'll learn—check out household-repair books from the library, watch a how-to video, ask a friend to teach you, take a course at a community college. Then decide which jobs you'll hire someone else to do. Start now collecting names from friends or neighbors who have been satisfied with the work of an electrician, an auto mechanic, a plumber—whatever you don't want to do. You don't want to start guessing when your water heater springs a leak and you don't know a reliable plumber.

First Quarter—January, February, March

❑ Check plumbing system for leaks.

❑ Unscrew aerator from end of each faucet, wash carefully, then replace.

❑ Inspect ceramic tile grout around tub or shower. Caulk as needed.

❑ Insulate any exposed water pipes.

❑ Clean mineral deposits inside dishwasher. Pour a gallon of white vinegar into dishwasher and run through a wash cycle.

❑ Tackle indoor painting jobs.

❑ Use a tiny artist's brush to apply spackle to hairline cracks in walls.

❑ Repair or replace wallpaper as needed.

❑ Check hot-water heater pressure-release valve. (See your owner's manual.)

❑ Vacuum coils beneath refrigerator.

❑ Do an attic/basement safety check—make sure there's no accumulation of trash or dirty rags, look for evidence of faulty wiring, see that circuit breaker box is well-marked, and check that no paint or flammable liquids are stored in same area as furnace or hot water heater.

❏ Treat septic system.

Second Quarter—April, May, June

❏ Plan any major remodeling or repair projects. Get bids from contractors.

❏ Check your attic for roof leaks. On a rainy day use a flashlight to locate water drips and spots. On a sunny day stand in your yard and use binoculars. Repair or replace any broken, bent, or missing shingles or tiles.

❏ Moth-proof and store winter clothes.

❏ Clean outdoor furniture, repair as needed.

❏ Have car serviced for vacation.

❏ Service and clean lawn mower and garden tools.

❏ Clean gutters and downspouts.

❏ Check for carpenter ants and watch for termites swarming. Call an exterminator if necessary.

❏ Remove wasp nests on or around your house in early morning when it's cool.

❏ Open foundation vents.

❏ Hire a chimney sweep to remove creosote buildup before it hardens, clean soot and check for birds' nests from flue, and inspect for cracks.

❏ Shut off furnace pilot light for the summer.

❏ Change air-conditioner filters now and several other times during cooling season. (If your filter is permanent, soak it in warm, soapy water, and rinse.) Vacuum evaporator coils behind front grille of window units. For central units, have a professional wash the condensing coils, oil the fan motor if required, and vacuum evaporator coils located in ducting.

❑ Check the grading of your yard and landscaping for settling or erosion.

❑ Move surplus fireplace wood away from foundation of house.

❑ Trim any branches near a heat pump or air-conditioner condenser so they don't obstruct airflow or tangle the fan.

❑ Make sure windows open smoothly. Give the garage-door hardware a squirt of lightweight oil.

❑ Check for damage to exterior wood trim. Look for water stains, new cracks, blistering paint, warping, and soft places—which can mean dry rot. Repair as needed.

❑ Check fences and decks for damage and repair as needed.

Third Quarter—July, August, September

❑ Pressure-wash driveways, walkways, and house exterior.

❑ Saturate grease and oil spots on driveway and garage floor with paint thinner. Cover soiled area with cat litter or sawdust, then sweep away the next day.

❑ Caulk all joints and cracks around posts and columns, doors, and windows. Touch up any other areas that show signs of weathering.

❑ Drain water heater to remove sediment. Check owner's manual or consult with a plumbing do-it-yourself shop.

❑ Have carpets cleaned by a professional or rent a steam cleaner and do it yourself.

- ❏ Trim back any branches or shrubs two feet from the roof.
- ❏ Clean clothes-dryer exhaust vent. Check the flapper door on the outside exhaust vent and remove any lint buildup with a vacuum. If vent is flexible, check for kinks and patch any small holes with duct tape.
- ❏ Replace washing-machine hoses if you didn't do so last year.
- ❏ Clean out and organize garage.
- ❏ Get school clothing ready.

4th Quarter—October, November, December

- ❏ Take out window air conditioners or cover outside of unit to prevent rusting. Cover central air conditioner outdoor unit with a waterproof tarp

- ❏ Replace heating-system filters; have system professionally serviced if necessary.

- ❏ Drain outdoor plumbing; store hoses.

- ❏ Rake leaves.

- ❏ Clean gutters, downspouts, and window wells of leaves and debris

- ❏ Close or cover foundation vents before first freeze.

- ❏ Cover attic turbine vents and outside faucets.

- ❏ Winterize your lawn mower: clean, change the oil, and drain the gasoline.

- ❏ Weather-strip leaky windows and doors or put on storm windows.

- ❏ Check electrical system. Be sure bathroom, garage, and outdoor circuits are grounded and protected by ground-fault breakers.

- ❏ Add insulation to your attic.

❏ Install a carbon-monoxide alarm; change smoke-detector batteries and battery-powered emergency radios and flashlights; recharge fire extinguishers.

❏ Store summer clothes; get out winter clothes. Replace outgrown items.

❏ Clean out and organize toy and sports-equipment storage places.

❏ Cover any delicate plants before hard freezes.

If you're not a handy person . . .

Be aware that professional repair people and home-improvement contractors rank high on the complaint list of the Better Business Bureau and the U.S. Council of Consumer Affairs. Use the following ideas and questions to help you find the right professional for your need:

1. Ask friends or your local builders' association for recommendations. Check with the Better Business Bureau about their reputations.

2. Interview and get estimates from at least three contractors. Ask:

   ■ Do they have a current license? (Not all states require licensing.)

   ■ Do they have liability insurance and workman's compensation? (If not, you could be sued if he or she is injured on the job.)

   ■ What projects have they recently completed that are comparable to yours? Ask if they would mind if you called former customers.

3. When you receive the work-order form or contract, make sure it includes:

- A good definition of the job to be performed

- Starting and completion dates

- A detailed list of services and materials or parts that will be used

- And an itemized estimate and total price

- Payment schedule (Ideally, you should pay one-third at the beginning, one-third when half done, and one-third when the job is satisfactorily completed. Never pay cash.)

S t r e t C H your mind:

It's not just about taking care of your stuff.
It's about teaching your kids about life.
You are doing your kids a favor when you let them participate
in the maintenance of your home and property.
Do your children know how to do the laundry,
rewire a lamp, chop wood, and start a fire?
Do they know the difference between
a crescent wrench and a pipe wrench?
Do they know how to use a plumb line?
Are they able to change the oil, replace the air filter,
and fix a flat tire on a car?

A Home That Reflects Your Family

First and foremost, don't forget that you're enhancing your home for your family to use seven days a week, not for occasional guests. Also, remember that decorating is a process. Take your time and think things through. If you rush decorating, trying to finish so you can begin to live, there's a good chance you'll make some decisions you'll be sorry about.

Start by creating an idea file. Cut pictures from magazines of rooms you like. Try to identify themes, colors, or looks that are the same in each picture. You may find that you keep choosing rooms that are light and airy, dark and cozy, dramatic, colorful, or soft and subtle.

Then before you start remodeling or decorating, ask yourself the following questions about the room or area you're working on.

How much comfortable seating do you need? Or, if it's a bedroom, how many people sleep in there?

What kind of tables would be helpful or enhancing—end tables, coffee table, nightstands, a game table for board games, cards, puzzles, hobbies?

How much electronic equipment—TV, CD player, speakers, video games—is in the room? How can you place these things in the room for maximum enjoyment when in use, and can you store them out of sight?

Do you have a lot of books or collectibles? How many bookcases do you need?

Does anyone study or do office work in the room? If so, plan a space for it. Is this where you keep your home computer? Can it be built into a cabinet?

"An interesting room is often the product of a well-furnished mind."—Unknown   THINK ABOUT IT

Over the years, I've collected ideas from books and magazines, and tips from Peggy Zadina. Here are a few room-by-room ideas to help you enhance your home:

Kitchen

- Add warmth to your kitchen by using as many organic materials as possible—wood, tile, cork, baskets, terra-cotta.

- Use personal treasures to decorate—frame a restaurant menu to remind you of a memorable meal, hang your Grandmother's plates on the wall, buy an old wooden highchair at a flea market and set a favorite teddy bear in it.

- Promote conversations in your kitchen by having at least one stool in there. A 30-inch-high stool is a comfortable height for sitting at a counter.

- Recover the seats of your kitchen chairs or make thin seat pillows that tie to the backs of the chairs. Sew napkins from coordinating fabric. This will be a pleasant change for little time and money spent.

- Store small appliances that you don't use every day. Decluttering countertops will make your kitchen seem more spacious.

- White paint reflects light and gives a clean, fresh look to the dreariest of kitchens. Lighter colors are good choices for walls as any dirt will show immediately and can be wiped away.

- Use hearty green plants; they add life to any room.

Living Room/Family Room

- Stenciled or wallpaper borders around the door and window frames are a quick way to enliven a dull room.

- When considering furniture arrangement, start with the focal point of your room—like a fireplace or tall piece of furniture—and plan seating from that point.

- One of the most important pieces of furniture is a sofa. If your room is large, an 84-inch sofa that seats three people is ideal.

- Choose a kid-friendly color and fabric for your sofa—something that wears well and doesn't show dirt. It's a good idea to have furniture sprayed with a professional protective coating that repels spills.

- If the room you're decorating is small, a few pieces of normal-sized furniture will look better than cluttering the space with more pieces of smaller-scaled furniture.

- For each chair and sofa, there should be a table or surface to put down a book or drink.

- If you have a coffee table in front of your sofa, place it about thirteen inches in front of the sofa and allow approximately nineteen inches at either end so people can move easily around it. If you have small children, avoid a glass coffee table or one with sharp corners.

- End tables don't have to match, but they should be about the same height—from 26-30 inches. A one-inch difference is okay. A skirted table is nice at one end of a sofa or by a chair and is a great place to display family pictures.

- Keep your room from showing too many legs by striking a balance between upholstered pieces and wood pieces.

- When displaying collections, avoid a cluttered look by grouping like objects together.

- Paint is usually better than wallpaper for a family room. You can hang paintings, photographs, and quilts without a distracting background.

- To find out how intense a color will look in a room, look at the inside of the paint can. The shadows inside the can will give a similar appearance as in a room.

- Try to make your floor darker than your walls if you have low ceilings. This will make your room feel grounded.

- Be consistent with the treatment of all four walls in the room. A rich color painted on one wall will give a dramatic effect, but will tend to make the room look smaller.

- Don't crowd a room with too much clutter. Let the space "breathe"—especially the corners.

- To lighten a dark wood-paneled room, consider painting it a light color or putting a light wash on it. (A paint store will have instructions on how to do this.)

- Arrange lighting so you can read in all seating areas in your family room. Use three-way bulbs and install dimmer switches for flexible lighting.

- If you need curtains, extend them approximately 8 inches out on each side of your window so you won't block out light when they're open.

- Hang a mirror between two windows to add light and space to a room.

- Hang pictures at eye level when people are standing. Sixty inches from the floor to the center of the picture is about right.

Entry Way

- The front door is the first and last thing your family and friends see going in and out. The paint should be high gloss—white on the interior to match the trim. The exterior can be a pretty color— taupe, French blue, daffodil yellow, barn red, hunter green.

- Hang a pretty wreath on your door. Place seasonal potted plants on either side of the entrance.

- Use a colorful rug as a welcome mat inside your front door.

Make sure the background is a medium color so dirt won't show.

- Consider painting your entrance hall yellow. It brings the sunny cheerfulness of the out-of-doors into a space where there aren't as many windows as other rooms of the house.

- Natural things will add warmth to a room—fresh flowers in your grandmother's vase, a hearty plant in a terra-cotta pot, a basket of apples, or some lemons in a pretty bowl.

- Hang a favorite painting or mirror in your entrance hall so you and everyone else can enjoy it coming and going. Be sure to double hang (use two hooks instead of one) your picture or mirror so it will remain stable when the door is slammed.

- A collection of small pictures all matted and framed in the same matter is a nice way to warm up a blank wall.

- A small lamp on a table will create a warm atmosphere in your entrance hall.

- Install a dimmer on your overhead entry-hall light to control the ambiance of the room.

- Place something surprising in your hall—an antique child's wooden rocking horse, an old steamer trunk, a group of old dolls.

- Wallpaper with vertical stripes will make the ceiling seem higher.

Think "Process"

Moving cross-country afforded us an opportunity to think and talk about what kind of house we wanted to live in, to dream and plan. After days of discouraging house hunting, we drove by a house on a hill with a tiny For Sale sign nailed to a tree near the road. From a distance, it looked like a miniature Tara, white porch and all. I grabbed Bill and said, "This is our house. I just know it."

After a tour of the house and acreage, I gushed, "Just imagine it at Christmastime with hundreds of lights on the trees," I swooned. As it turns out, my dream was Bill's nightmare. And he was right.

"The living room floor has a 5 percent grade," he pronounced.

"We could have a garden—grow our own vegetables," I said optimistically.

"There are enough rodent droppings in the basement to fertilize it," he answered.

I don't like mice. I know when to give in.

Within a few days we found another fixer-upper—a house with "good bones," but little charm. "Oh well," I rationalized, "some paint, some paper, some lumber, some new appliances, some home-improvement money from the bank—it'll be fine. And think of all the fun we'll have working on it together as a family." I pictured happy weekend workdays, with Bill and the boys merrily installing shelves and sanding floors, while I wielded a roller on the newly patched walls. At lunchtime, we'd stop for an elegant picnic on the dining-room floor. I'd lay a bright, freshly ironed picnic cloth and we'd eat cold roasted chicken and sundry delicacies. We'd smile and joke and then one of the boys would say, "C'mon, it's time to go back to work. We can get in another five hours before dark." Sometimes dreams die hard.

What really happened is that two years after we started, we're still filling in around our home's "good bones." Our bathrooms work—most of the time, we have an almost-finished kitchen, and our ten-year-old finally has light in his bedroom. We're still in process—and that's okay. As a matter of fact, I doubt there will ever be a time when we're not in process, because that's really what managing Home and Property is all about. Process.

chapter 7

Financial Management

"About the time we think we can make ends meet,
someone moves the ends."
Herbert Hoover

"Make all you can; save all you can; give all you can."
—John Wesley

There's a foundational truth of the Family Management System: No Family Manager is equally proficient in all of the seven departments she oversees. I know I've said it before.

I say it again here because we have just entered the uncharted, frightening territory of Financial Management, my second least-skilled area, (Second only to the Food Department). I have made a lot of progress though. And I can confidently say that you don't have to be a Wall Street wizard to do a good job of managing the finance department of your home.

For years I felt threatened, stupid, and unqualified when it came to managing money. Banking information seemed to be written in a foreign language, a language I was sure every other adult in the world was conversant in. "I'm not a numbers person," I used to say. But in the early years of my career as a Family

> "I am not afraid of storms for I am learning how to sail my ship."
> —Louisa May Alcott

Manager, when Bill was taking a full load in graduate school plus working, I became the numbers person in our family by default. And that's how I made decisions too, by default. I didn't plan ahead because I didn't know how to plan ahead. We rarely had enough money in those days to meet monthly expenses, not to mention saving for the future, so I thought setting priorities was not important. I was not doing a good job. I made mistakes. Bill got angry because I made mistakes—like forgetting to pay the utility bills or the mortgage. I got angry because all the responsibility ended up with me. I was beginning to understand how marriages end up on the rocks as a result of money issues.

I saw that many of our money problems arose because I tended to procrastinate over things about which I knew little and felt overwhelmed by. Sometimes my unwillingness to tackle a financial task or make a timely decision cost us a lot more money—and time—in the long run, causing even more strain on our budget and our relationship.

One of the tasks I felt especially insecure about was balancing our checkbook. Believe it or not, before we married, although I'd had a checking account since high school, I had never balanced it. I didn't know how, and at that point in my life, I didn't feel the need to learn. When my balance would get low in college, our family banker would call my mother and she would deposit money into my account. (Boy, talk about the good ol' days!) Now, the bank didn't call my mother. It merely sent my checks back to the parties to whom they were written.

After running up over two hundred dollars worth of returned check charges one month, I decided it was time to ask for help. A man in the customer-service department of the bank spent two hours with me, getting my account straightened out and teaching me to balance my checkbook. It was a humiliating, but worthwhile experience.

After that incident I decided that for my own sanity and the ongoing well-being of my family, I had to be as much of a financial manager as I could be. I also realized that I couldn't afford not to be prepared for the worst case scenario—if Bill dies before I do and I am left alone to deal with my family's finances. That meant both learning all I could and, as any good manager does, involving the rest of my team in planning and decisions.

"An investment in knowledge always pays the best interest." Benjamin Franklin THINK ABOUT IT

If you, like me, are not a numbers person, or, if you're tempted to think of your position as Family Manager as unimportant and non-professional, I'd like to take a minute to remind you of some of the financial concerns a Family Manager must deal with:

$ Establishing and periodically reviewing your family's financial priorities

$ Stretching limited dollars

$ Preparing tax forms and keeping records

$ Selecting appropriate investments

$ Selecting appropriate charities

$ Calculating correct amounts of insurance

$ Setting up a retirement plan

$ Dealing with sensitive issues such as wills and after-death decisions

$ Getting ready to send kids to college

$ Shopping smart for a car

$ Stretching your childcare budget

$ Shopping smart for groceries, clothing, furniture, gifts, and appliances

$ Establishing credit

$ Teaching your kids the value of a dollar

This covers the basics. But, given your family situation, there will always be something else. Maybe it will be creating a crisis plan to weather a financial storm. Needless to say, that will be easier to do if you already know how to shop smart, have a monthly budget (so you know where cuts will hurt the least), and are living by the priorities your family has agreed to. Maybe it will be setting up a home-based business.

As I tried to feel more competent and comfortable with managing our family finances, it dawned on me that we weren't talking about the Federal budget here. We were talking about one family and how they make, save, and spend their money while living on planet Earth. One family, one budget. It could, I told myself, be done.

Blazing New Frontiers

When I need to do something I don't know how to do, I generally look at it as a challenge. I research by asking people I know and admire, who have expertise in the area I'm interested in. I read books and clip magazine articles. And, maybe most important of all, I cast around for a way of looking at the task or problem that is familiar to me.

So, instead of looking at finances as this complex, intimidating area of our life, I decided to look at it like a jigsaw puzzle—that same strategy I employ when I've got a hard project staring me in the face.

To treat the task of financial management like a jigsaw puzzle, I began to work on the "edges" of the problem. I tackled the pieces that I understood—getting the most for our money at the grocery store, watching for sales before purchasing items, setting up a simple filing system, gathering and reading information about saving and investing. I found that the more I did, the less complex and overwhelming the rest of the department seemed. I became comfortable asking questions, learning a little at a time and getting the department in order, a little at a time—which, by the way, until someone invents whiffle dust and finds a good fairy to dispense it, is the best way to approach any department in your home that's out of order.

> "Simplify, simplify."
> —Henry David Thoreau

Something else that seemed logical as I was trying to get a handle on our finances was to simplify—figure out the core issues in this department. Bill and I together came up with four very basic, but very important issues we needed to deal with. We needed to: (1) determine our philosophy of finances, (2) identify our priorities, (3) come up with a plan, and (4) create procedures to carry out our plan.

"Most people don't know what they really want—but they're sure they haven't got it."—Alfred E. Newman

THINK ABOUT IT

Philosophy

Philosophy means a particular system of principles for the conduct of life. It's a word we seldom use in our day-to-day dealings with family-management issues. But whether we're aware of it or not, we live out our philosophies of life all day, every day. It's important that we understand what our philosophy of money is, because this will influence our priorities, our plans, and our procedures.

All of us were influenced to some extent by the way our parents handled finances and what they valued. So when two people unite in marriage, they bring with them a philosophy of money and a lot of standards they think are perfectly normal. Bill and I came from drastically different backgrounds, and we had very different views about money.

Early in our marriage, some of the decisions we had to make when setting up our home brought our differences to a head—deciding how much we were willing to spend on an item, different ways of measuring quality, conflicting definitions of needs and wants. But when we had children, our backgrounds really started to clash.

I was raised in an upper-middle-class environment. I thought all responsible American parents signed their four-year-olds up for private swimming lessons in the summer, took their kids to the dentist twice a year and had braces put on their teeth when deemed necessary, and sent their kids to camp for two weeks, starting at age seven. In the world I came from, I, along with many of my friends, expected a car of my own the day I got my driver's license. And our parents automatically paid for our college of choice. To me, these were guaranteed.

> "Fools can make money. It takes a wise man to tell how to spend it."
> —English Proverb

Boy, did I have a rude awakening!

Bill was raised in a home which was much more conservative with money. He never lacked necessities, but there weren't a lot of extras. He didn't get the latest toy or bike. He took swimming lessons at the public pool. As a teenager he worked for his spending money and didn't have a car of his own until he was a junior in college. His college choices were limited to those where he could get scholarships and financial aid. Bill never thought of this as especially hard or unreasonable, because it's all he ever knew.

We got married before our senior year in college, and our first year of marriage was great. Mom and Dad paid my tuition and continued to send my monthly allowance. Coupled with Bill's financial-aid package and his part-time job, we had everything a young couple needs to get started.

When we graduated from college and my parents cut the apron strings (as well as my allowance), I resigned myself to live with less. But the realities of life out on our own brought problems I'd never dreamed of. After we paid the bills, we had barely enough left for a movie and a hamburger out. Bill had a lot fewer expectations about our lifestyle than I did and was fairly content living in what felt to me like real deprivation. He couldn't understand my frustration when I couldn't go out and buy a new winter wardrobe and why I was so depressed about something so frivolous.

We realized that if we didn't talk openly about our differences and come up with a common philosophy about money, we were in for a lot of stress and strife. It didn't happen immediately, but as we got to know each other better, as we laid our expectations and preconceived notions out on the table one by one, we gained a new respect for each other and saw that we stood to learn a lot from each other. Instead of butting heads trying to get our own way and make sure our personal point of view prevailed, we decided to accept each other "as is," appreciate our differences, and look for what we had in common. We discovered that we both agreed on six principles that have become the foundation of our philosophy of finances. We continue to strive to live by these principles. As you read, think about what principles form your own philosophy of finances.

1. Be responsible.

We need to take care of our money and our belongings, as well as anyone else's we're responsible for. I had to learn that it was important to change the oil in my car every three thousand miles so our vehicles would last longer. Bill had to learn that an investment in a quality item of clothing was better than a cheap one and, when taken care of, was less expensive in the long run.

2. Be productive.

This is something that Bill and I were together on from the beginning. Both of our parents had a strong work ethic, and they passed it on to us. In our early married years we tried to seize every opportunity to make extra money. I was constantly looking for jobs I could do and stay home with my kids—tutoring, direct sales, taking care of pets and plants for people when they were out of town.

When there was something we wanted but couldn't afford, we brainstormed about ways to make extra money. Whenever our family moved, we looked for do-it-yourself options. When we needed new furniture, we shopped for used furniture and refinished or reupholstered it ourselves. If we needed to make home repairs, we bought home-repair books and tried to figure out how to repair it ourselves. We've saved a lot of money and learned a lot this way.

> **"Opportunity is missed by most people because it is dressed in overalls."**
> **—Thomas A. Edison**

3. Be honest.

Again, this is a principle that both Bill and I brought with us from our respective homes—that honesty is not only the best policy, it is the only policy. We felt that if we had to be dishonest to get something or had the opportunity to pilfer or steal it was wrong. This is a financial principle we live by, but it pervades more than our philosophy about finances.

4. Be generous.

Winston Churchill said, "We make a living by what we get, but we make a life by what we give." Bill taught me the joy of generosity early in our relationship. I saw that extra money was not always for buying something I wanted, but sometimes for helping out someone who was worse off than we were or giving to a cause about which we felt passionate. We found that it helped to brainstorm about how we could live generously, how we could become a family of givers. We wanted to experience the true satisfaction of giving to someone else that we might truly "make a life."

5. Be yourself.

We need to understand that we are not what we own, wear, or drive. Each of us is valuable as a unique human being. If the latest fads, fashions, or activities are a "must" for us, this is a problem. This is a sure sign that we are seeking our identity in material things, not quality of character and personal relationships. It's important that we remind ourselves regularly of our worth as individuals.

6. Be realistic.

None of us always gets what we want or what we think we deserve. That's a fact of life. Sometimes we get more, sometimes less. But most of the time, we will have more than we need. The goal is to be content and thankful for what we have.

Not too long ago we experienced unexpected circumstances which caused financial peril and family stress. As the Family Manager I had to ask myself some tough questions. Was I going to let hard times make me bitter or better? What was going to be the tone of our home while we went through this? I decided that my attitude might be the key as to whether something positive could come from this difficult situation. We pulled together as a family and we got creative. We decided not to concentrate on all the things we couldn't buy or do, or places we couldn't go. Instead we made a list of things we could buy or do or places we could go—lots of which were free—or at least less expensive. Maybe we couldn't go see a new movie right when it opened; but we could rent a video, pop some popcorn, and watch it as a family. Or we could go to a matinee.

Our philosophy is something we began talking about early in our marriage, and it's something we continue to talk about, both to teach it to our kids, and to reaffirm it for ourselves for daily living. It hasn't changed too much over the years.

"Money can be translated into the beauty of living, a support in misfortune, an education, or future security. It also can be translated into a source of bitterness." —Sylvia Porter ☜

THINK ABOUT

Priorities

Once we had our philosophy pretty well nailed down, we could set our priorities. Over the years, we decided that we would try to make enough to take care of our family, but not so much that the quality of our life suffered from one or both parents being driven into the ground because of hard work or working at a hated job. We made a mutual decision when we started our family that I would stay home. This was not an easy decision. I had a new degree from a major university, and my friends that I'd graduated with were landing nice jobs, going out for business lunches at nice restaurants, and bringing home nice salaries. But I was at peace with my decision. I wanted to be home with my kids, and if that meant raising them on linoleum rather than carpet, so be it.

Every woman must be true to her gifts and talents and pursue those as she feels called. She must, at the same time, balance her family-management responsibilities and her own personal development. Each of our situations is very different, and every family is unique. And some women don't have the "luxury" I had of choosing linoleum over carpet. Not until our kids were thirteen, ten, and three, and Bill moved his office home, did I begin a career in writing.

If you're ever going to get the financial department of your family under control, then you must decide what's important to you. Some

"You never know what is enough unless you kno

people value education, image, a beautiful home—or maybe more than one home, social status, recreation, travel, nice cars, building large savings for the future. None of these things is wrong in and of themselves; you just have to decide where they fit in to your priorities and your lifestyle.

We live in a day of information anxiety. Every day we're bombarded with data—data intended to help us form our priorities and move us to make decisions. Television and glossy magazine ads make real life seem gray in comparison to their make-believe spotless kitchens, beautifully appointed family rooms, and professionally engineered closets. They show us how our homes are really supposed to look. They remind us that we would feel better about ourselves and about life if only we had this or that. Redo and be happy. Bigger is better. Newest and latest is best. Trade in, trade up. Invention becomes the mother of necessity. Excess becomes ideal.

> "The use of money is all the advantage there is in having it."
> —Benjamin Franklin

Unless we've made some decisions about our priorities, it's easy to lose perspective about what's really important to us. We end up making impulsive decisions and spending money we shouldn't spend, which makes us feel worse than we did before we tried to make ourselves feel better. Or if we can't spend any money, unless we've decided what we value in life, we can easily feel insecure, discontent, and unable to enjoy the blessings of life we do have.

Have you ever stopped to think about financial priorities for your family? Now is probably as good a time as any. Do it by yourself or together with your spouse. Include older children if it's appropriate—however seems best for you. Use these questions and fill in the blanks to guide you in developing your priorities.

hat is more than enough." —William Blake

1. List five things that you value most about your life today.
   _____

   _____

2. List five things you want that money can buy.
   _____

   _____

3. List five things you want that money can't buy.
   _____

   _____

4. How much is enough? I'll feel okay about money when we have _____ amount in the bank. I'll be content when we have _____.

5. List the causes you'd like to give money to. How much would you like to give?
   _____

   _____

6. Where would you like to be financially in twelve months? in five years? in twenty years?
   _____

   _____

7. How do you feel about going into debt? About getting out of debt?
   _____

   _____

8. Given the choice between a job you'd love for less money and the job you have now and dislike at your current income,

which would you choose? If you want a job you love, what can you do to either cut expenses or increase income in other ways?

_____

_____

9. Ask yourself this question: "If I had more money, I would spend it on . . ." (Sometimes looking at what we want to spend money on and where we actually spend money can help us do some shifting without increasing the amount of money we spend.)

_____

_____

10. Fill in the blank: "If we suddenly found ourselves in a financial crisis, I could do without_____."

11. If you were suddenly blessed with wealth, do you know how you would react? How would your priorities change?

_____

_____

S T R E T C H YOUR MIND:

Financial management, like any other kind of management—
and cleaning bathrooms—is really a process rather than a goal
to be once achieved and then it's done. Although your basic
philosophy will probably stay the same, priorities change
as families grow. Feeding a family of five costs more
than feeding a family of three. Automobile insurance
for a teenager is more expensive than a tricycle.
College costs more than preschool.

Priorities are a point of reference.

They are standards when you're considering a purchase. When you say "yes" to one thing, you say "no" to another.

Ask yourself if you bought the item now, how many of your priorities would the purchase fulfill? What other ones would it fly in the face of?

Priorities make decisions easier.

If you begin checking the items you want or need to purchase against your priorities, pretty soon it becomes second nature to you. You won't lose sleep or waste time weighing the pros and cons. You've already decided where things fall on your list of what's important to you.

Priorities help you understand how you operate.

In business, they say each person has a particular modus operandi — a certain way he or she does things. This is very helpful information when it comes to family finances. One friend said that when she and her husband worked on their priorities, they decided they both liked some sense of spontaneity and wanted to build room in their budget so they could have some. So, for example, when they bought a car, they could do it on the spur-of-the-moment — and they were both comfortable with that.

Priorities can eliminate a lot of arguments with your spouse.

When you've established some financial priorities and your husband says you have to postpone buying a new sofa in order to pay the orthodontist, nobody's to blame. When your husband goes to the boat show and comes home with a boatload of brochures about the boat he wants to buy, he can't get mad at you for reminding him that college tuition is just around the corner.

Priorities encourage creativity.

When you put something you want high on your priority list, but can't afford it, this will motivate you to think creatively about how to get it. Remember I said that I came into marriage thinking summer camp for kids is a guarantee? Well, although I learned that camp was not a "given" in most families, especially those who didn't have a lot of discretionary income, I still wanted my kids to go to camp. Thus, I had to think of creative ways to make the extra money to send them. So, we had a family brainstorming session about possible income-producing jobs. We came up with the idea to start a flower-bulb business for the boys (then ages six and nine). We ordered bulbs wholesale from Florida and they went door to door, under my supervision, and took orders for the bulbs. They sold enough to pay for most of their camp and each year their business grew.

A friend shared with me how lack of funds forced her to think creatively about vacationing. She said that she and her husband wanted to go on a much-needed vacation, but didn't have any money to spend on a trip. So, for a few of the days they sent their small daughter to day care and explored the city they lived in on their own, going to museums, historical sights, and afternoon matinees. The other days they took their daughter and had fun going on kid-friendly outings—to the zoo, on a picnic at a park, on a nature hike. They ate out most nights, like they would have on vacation, but slept in their own beds, announced to their friends that they were on vacation, did as few regular chores as possible. She reports that they had a great vacation for very little money.

Priorities help you have discipline.

Restraint is something not many of us enjoy. But if we ever want to make progress financially, we must learn to live within our means. Establishing priorities helps us do this. I've found that it helps to begin to think of purchases as trade-offs. Is a new house really worth the extra financial pressure the larger payments will put on our family? Is a new car really worth not being as free to go out to eat or not being able to buy a new outfit? It's easier to make choices based on the lifestyle we've decided on beforehand, not on an impulse to have the newest, latest, or best.

A Personal Priority

Early in our marriage we decided that we felt it would be a good investment to spend money on making memories with our children. When we had the choice of whether to take a family trip or put more money into savings, we decided we'd go for the trip and deposit memories in our kids' mental and emotional savings accounts. Twenty-five years later, our savings account at the bank is nothing to write home about, but we have a huge account of great family memories. Plus we have a wonderful relationship with each of our children. To us, this is worth millions.

Less monthly financial commitment means more freedom and flexibility to spend money in more ways.

The Passing Pleasure of Purchases

Think about your last major purchase—a new car, new sofa, a deck added on to your house. If we were honest, I think most all of us would confess that sometimes we fall into the trap of thinking that if we get whatever it is, it will bring us satisfaction. Have you noticed how long that rush of joy over a new purchase lasts? I have. Not very long. It's not long before I want something else. If you in any way relate, recognize this temptation and refuse to be sucked into the excitement of always getting something new. Remember that the joy will probably not last as long as the payments.

Money Is a Tool

Some people who have money don't enjoy their money. We've all heard stories, seen movies, and may even know people who become self-absorbed, greedy, and ultimately miserable. Attitude is important all the time. Character is tested in two dramatic ways: in adversity and in prosperity. Thomas Carlyle warned us, "Adversity is sometimes hard on a man; but for every one man that can stand prosperity, there are a hundred men that will stand adversity." There is something about success that tends to promote prideful self-sufficiency, rather than humble gratitude and a giving spirit.

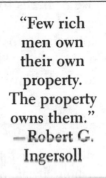

> "Few rich men own their own property. The property owns them."
> —Robert G. Ingersoll

We shouldn't feel arrogant about prosperity, but neither should we feel guilty about enjoying the good things in life. In my experience, when we rest our security on our wealth, we will always become

TABLE TALK

It's never too early to introduce the idea of philosophy and priorities about money to kids. I've found these quotes to be good springboards for soliciting our kids' opinions and sharing ours. One night at dinner, read these quotes and talk about what they mean to your family.

"From everyone who has been given much, much will be demanded; and from the one who has been entrusted with much, much more will be asked." Luke 12:48 NIV

"Put in its proper place, money is not man's enemy, not his undoing, nor his master. It is his servant, and it must be made to serve him well."—Henry C. Alexander

"In this world, it is not what we take up but what we give up that makes us rich."—Henry Ward Beecher

entangled in preserving it—something we simply can't guarantee. Most people who strive after wealth, at the expense of family life, personal health, and healthy spousal relationships, eventually find that the wealth controls them rather than them controlling it. Attitude is important all the time.

> "The greatest use of life is to spend it for something that will outlast it." —William James

I've found that the attitude that prevents any of us from slipping into selfish indulgence and enjoying what money we have is compassion toward the needs in the world around us. In other words, we should not use wealth as a security blanket or a scorecard, but rather as a tool. According to *The Wall Street Journal*, 1% of the nation's households own one-third of the nations private wealth, 60% of the corporate stock, and 30% of interest-bearing assets and nearly 10% of its real estate (9/21/92). Interestingly, American households with incomes of less than $10,000 gave an average of 5.5% to charity, while those making more than $100,000 gave only 2.9% (*The Popcorn Report*, p.191).

Plan

Once you've decided on your philosophy and your priorities, you need a strategy to make those things happen. Because each of our situations is different, I can't tell you exactly how to create a financial plan for your family. I can

tell you, though, the issues we all need to deal with as we formulate a personalized strategy for our families' financial well-being.

You need a budget.

Budgeting is one of the most important parts of managing your family's finances. Having a budget will help you identify possible problems in spending patterns, discover ways to overcome these problems, and plan realistically how to balance your spending with your income. Books with budget strategies and worksheets come in a bewildering variety of formats and styles. I've found *The New Century Family Money Book* by Jonathan D. Pond (Dell Publishing, 1993) to be very user-friendly.

You need a savings plan.

If you're unsure about the different methods of saving and investing—savings accounts, CDs, mutual funds, stocks—begin your own quest for information. Call your bank, collect and read about various plans, look into a financial-planning service. Consider having money automatically deducted from your paycheck and deposited into a savings account. Whatever you do, do something.

You need an easy and organized way
to keep important records.

If papers, receipts, and important documents are filed in piles at your house, realize that the investment of time it takes to set up and maintain a good system of family files and records will pay off over and over again. You'll save time when you need to find an important document or piece of information. Never again will you have to spend two hours hunting for a canceled check or a child's social-security number.

Another important benefit of getting organized is all that you will learn about your family's finances. For example, in organizing your legal documents, you may discover that you have not updated your will since adding a child to the family. You may see that you could reduce your insurance costs by increasing the deductible.

Having a well-organized filing system eases the stress of family emergencies such as severe illness or an unexpected death when records about medical coverage, guardianship arrangements, and even burial-plot information is easy to find. A filing system will make tax time easier, too.

Your filing system doesn't have to be fancy. It just needs to be accessible or you will end up postponing filing items. You should try to file bills, warranties, bank statements, and other records as they come in, or collect them all together in one location and sort them periodically for filing.

If in debt, you need a strategy for reducing that debt.

Debt can be debilitating to you and your family. One of the best books I've read on getting out of debt is *The Cheapskate Monthly Money Makeover* by Mary Hunt (St. Martin's Paperbacks, 1995). The author tells her own story of how she ran up alarmingly high credit-card debts, putting her family in financial danger. She shares the strategy of how she paid off those debts and has learned to live debt-free.

"There is nothing so habit-forming as money."
—*Don Marquis.*

THINK ABOUT IT

Do you or your children have some bad spending habits that are causing your family financial stress? Shopping and spending money can become an addiction.

You need to know what your insurance covers—and what it doesn't.

Make sure your insurance is up to date and adequate.

Be sure that all foreseeable areas of risk for your family are covered by your policies. You should evaluate each of the policies you purchase to make sure you have the coverage you need. And keep in mind that although you may have adequate coverage now, your needs will undoubtedly change in the future. It's wise to review your insurance once a year, and if you have a big change in your life—birth of a child, job change, moving—you'll want to review immediately.

You need to have a plan for making major purchases.

Cars don't last forever, roofs need to be replaced, refrigerators die, and families need to take vacations. It's important to have a plan for how you'll make major purchases. Working on this now will help you when you experience an unexpected large-purchase moment. One friend shared what I think is a ingenious savings plan for their family vacation. She shops for groceries at a store where there is a small branch bank inside the store. An avid coupon clipper, each week at the checkout stand when she receives the refund (which can run as high as $20.00) for her coupons, she walks directly over to the in-store bank and deposits the money into their vacation savings account. If your store doesn't have a bank, you could make it your practice to always put your refund money in a designated place at home until you can get to the bank. And maybe you'd rather save for something else, like a new sofa or Christmas presents.

You need to file tax returns.

This means doing it on time and well. I, for one, believe in letting them who do it best do it. In this case it's letting a CPA handle our income tax. But a CPA is only as good as the information we provide. Good records are critical. Ask your CPA for an income tax worksheet. This way, you'll know what information you need to keep tabs on during the year. You can also buy computer software to help you take care of taxes yourself.

Plan a way to meet children's college-education costs.

With one in college and another starting next year, take it from one who knows. When you look at your kindergartner's sweet face and small hands, it's easy to think that college is a long way off. It's not. It will be here before you know it, and it's expensive. Start now putting aside money for education. And on the nights when you think you're too exhausted to help your child study for that math test, let one word spur you on: scholarship. Time spend studying now can pay off later.

Know when you'd like to retire and what you plan to live on when you do.

Again, when your kids are young and you're in your prime, retirement sounds like the distant future. The real distant future. But it's important to start now, putting aside a little at a time. Compound interest over the years adds up.

Make sure your will is updated and your estate is properly planned.

I don't know anyone who likes to talk about estate planning. But even though it's an unpleasant subject, it's important to have your affairs in order and to know that your heirs will be provided for. Chances are, your personal records will also be better organized once you get your estate in order. Whatever your situation—whether your estate is worth ten thousand dollars or ten million dollars—you need a will, a power of attorney, a living will, and a letter of instructions. If you don't have these documents, you will probably cause both yourself and your loved ones a lot of extra grief.

Procedure

Working as a team on family finances can ward off a host of misunderstandings and problems, maybe more than any other department. Although establishing our principles and priorities and creating a plan helped, we still had to decide who would implement the plan—or what would be our procedure. We decided to divide up responsibilities. At our house, since we both work, we split up who pays which bills. Bill pays the mortgage, insurance, utilities—the monthly stuff out of one account. I opened a special household checking account to pay for groceries, clothing, haircuts, school needs, etc. You may have a better way. I have one friend who uses what she calls her "envelope method." At the first of the month, she withdraws the cash she needs to pay for her family's household expenses (not bills) for a month. She puts budgeted amounts in labeled envelopes—groceries, drug-store items, entertainment, school supplies, clothing, baby-sitting, miscellaneous—and keeps them in a drawer. She pays cash for everything, and when the money is gone for the month, it's gone.

Decide to pay bills once a month, twice a month, weekly—whatever works for you. It helps to set up a bill-paying center—a specific place to keep bills, a calculator, pens, checkbook, extra envelopes, stamps, a return-address stamp or labels, a trash can, and a filing cabinet. (We open the bill the day it arrives, throw away the original envelope, tuck the bill inside the flap of the return envelope, write the due date on the spot where the stamp goes, then place the bills in chronological order according to due date in a stand-up tickler file on top of a chest which serves as our bill-paying center.)

You also need a way to account for how you're spending your money and if you're staying within your budget. If you have a home computer, you can install software that will not only write and print your checks, but it will categorize each amount that you spend according to budget categories. Or you can write your budget categories in columns on a spreadsheet and record by hand what you spend money on.

STRETCH YOUR MIND:

"Beware of little expenses.
A small leak will sink a great ship."
—Benjamin Franklin

Work as a family on your spending habits.
Identify any small leaks and plug the holes.

If you've been filing in piles and are ready to get your files in order, here's a step-by-step plan:

1. Gather together in one place all items to be filed. Have a waste-basket handy, along with file folders, labels, and pens.

2. Pick up the item on the top of the pile (or the first folder if you're revising an existing file) and decide whether it has any value to you. If it doesn't, throw it away. If it does, go on to the next step.

3. If it's worth retaining, choose a folder heading for it, label the folder, and slip in the piece of paper. Some potential file folder headings could be: household repairs, personal letters, medical records, tax deductions, warranties, and guarantees.

4. Pick up the next item in the stack and go through the same procedure, the only variation being that this may fit into an existing folder, rather than one with a new heading. Consolidate whenever possible.

5. Assemble your pile of folders and put them in alphabetical order.

6. Put your alphabetized folders into a file drawer or a carton that you have specifically set aside for files.

7. Each time you consult a folder, page through it quickly and identify and discard the deadwood. That way, your files won't become crowded.

What to Keep, What to Toss

You must keep records that support an item of income or a deduction on a tax return until the statute of limitations on the return runs out—usually three years from the filing or due date.

Keep receipts of home improvements you make to your house or rental property for as long as you own the property. Improvements made to property can change the basis for computing capital gain or loss for income-tax purposes.

Keep canceled checks (if your bank still returns them) in case you have a dispute about whether or not a bill has been paid. Some people keep canceled checks indefinitely, because they can be used to substantiate expenses long after other records have been discarded.

Store bills of sale, warranties, and guarantees in a separate file so that you can quickly locate exactly what you need when equipment requires repair or replacement.

Save all receipts and sales slips so that you're able to check the accuracy of your monthly bills and in case you need to return an item or get it repaired sometime during a warranty period.

Store all your owner's manuals in a file folder or punch holes in them and put them in a ring binder.

You can dispose of your personal tax records after six years. Tax returns are only subject to audit for up to three years after filing under normal circumstances, for up to six years if income has been understated by more than 25 percent.

Helping Your Kids Manage Money

One of the most important aspects of our children's education is a healthy perspective about money—and they won't learn that in school. Our homes must be the classrooms, and we are the teachers. But this is a hard lesson to learn—and to teach.

It's important to Bill and me that our boys have a healthy perspective about money and possessions. This means, first of all, that we, their parents, must have a healthy perspective. Kids won't buy a double standard. We must live out the values we want our kids to embrace.

"Children have never been very good at listening to their elders, but they have never failed to imitate them."—James Baldwin

THINK ABOUT IT

Second, we must look for natural opportunities in the course of everyday life to teach these values to our children. When our boys were young, our attempts at teaching them values about money and possessions left a lot to be desired. Why we thought over-energized little boys would sit still to listen to Mom and Dad lecture on a healthy perspective about money and possessions is a mystery.

We decided that no one in the family (including the parents) had the attention span, not to mention the time, for long, boring lectures. But we wanted to instill healthy values. We got smart and figured out if we wanted them to learn, we'd better make it simple and we'd better teach them at times when they didn't think they're being taught.

We took the principles we used to formulate our own philosophy of money and adapted and simplified them to a child's level. No, we don't teach them these principles perfectly every time an opportunity arises. But we believe in the old adage, "If you aim at nothing, you'll hit it every time."

You can adapt these principles to fit your own family's financial values, then purposefully begin to look for teachable moments in the course of daily life to instill your values into your children.

1. Be responsible.

Respect for their own possessions or someone else's is not something most kids come already-equipped with. When our boys were younger, they regularly left their bikes in the rain, toys in the yard, and coats at school. They had to learn, both from discipline and natural consequences, that items would not be replaced if they were broken, destroyed, or stolen because of someone's irresponsibility. They also had to learn the hard way that when they broke (even accidentally) another child's toy, as the responsible party, they had to help pay for a replacement.

> "If you want your children to keep their feet on the ground, put some responsibility on their shoulders."
> —Abigail Van Buren

As our boys grew older, we looked for other ways to teach them responsibility. When John turned seventeen, his job became to help pay the monthly bills. He wrote the payee and the amounts on the checks, then Bill or I would sign the check and record the amount. This was an eye-opening experience for John about the cost of living and the importance of being responsible with money.

2. Be productive.

As soon as children are able to help around the house, they need regular chores. Even a two-year-old can fold towels and pick up toys. Toddlers probably won't fold the towels as neatly as you'd like, but that's okay. It's more important that they learn to be productive. I know a wise mother who, even though she has a full-time housekeeper, requires her kids to do a lot of household chores. She understands the importance of her kids taking an active part in the work routine around the house. Children need to see themselves as productive contributors to the welfare of the home, since they benefit from living there.

As kids get older and getting an allowance becomes an attractive possibility, this is an excellent opportunity to teach them that getting money is related to working. They get paid for doing part of the family's work, and therefore get a portion of the family's money. If children choose not to do part of the family's work, they don't get a portion of the family's money. It's that simple.

We made the decision to never do anything or buy anything on a regular basis for our children that they are capable of doing or buying for themselves. Our role as a parent is to help them become independent, productive adults.

One way to do this is by creating opportunities for your children to earn their own money. Encourage them to work and save money for things they dream about.

3. Be honest.

This is not only the best policy, it is the only policy. In addition to being clear about not stealing from stores, from neighbors, or from anyone else, kids need to know that nonmaterial things can be stolen, such as time from an employer, credit for something someone else accomplished, someone's talent or services you use but don't pay for. Here is where a double standard is especially dangerous. We've found we need to ask ourselves regularly, "Is there anything in our home that we have, that we should be paying for, but we're not—extra cable channels that we might get by mistake or a neighbor's magazine or newspaper subscription that comes to our address?"

Children will learn a lot about being honest if they are with you at a store, a clerk gives you back too much change, and they see you point out the error and give back the extra money.

4. Be generous.

I've never met a mother who wanted her child to grow up to be greedy. Interestingly, children don't have to be taught to be selfish and greedy. It comes naturally to them. We've found that the best way to fight greed is by giving.

Even the youngest children can be taught to share. When toddlers have the opportunity to play with others, they can begin to understand how to share and be generous.

As kids get older, you can talk at the dinner table about specific ways you have been treated generously. Brainstorm about how you can live generously. Becoming a family of givers lets your children experience the true satisfaction of giving to someone else.

5. Be yourself.

Kids need to understand that they are not what they own, wear, or drive. Each of us is valuable as a unique human being. If the latest fads, fashions, or activities are a "must" for a child, this is a problem. This is a sure sign that the child is seeking identity in material things, not quality of character and personal relationships. It's important that we remind our children regularly of their worth as individuals.

The most powerful way we can show our kids that they are valuable is by spending time with them—enjoyable quality time and lots of it. Studies show that parents spend an average of twenty minutes a day communicating with their children, and nine of those minutes are spent in disciplinary situations. (Maybe this is why so many kids look to material things to determine their value.) If you feel you haven't been spending enough positive time with your children, don't get caught in the trap of spending money on them to ease your guilt.

6. Be realistic.

Kids need to know that it's a fact of life that none of us always gets what we deserve. Sometimes we get more, sometimes less. But most of the time, we will have more than we need. The goal is to be content and thankful for what we have.

Our kids need to see an attitude of contentment in us. When there is not enough money for what we want, do our children see us griping? Are we

> "Go on in fortune and misfortune like a clock in a thunderstorm."
> —Robert Louis Stevenson

able to be content with what we have, or are we always wanting more? It's important that we model what it means to be content—even with the little things of life. We can be content with a good meal, a comfortable bed, a warm bath, shared family time, or pleased that our day went according to plan.

Maybe you'll find, like we did, that living out the values we want our children to embrace is sometimes difficult. Very difficult. When we fail, it doesn't help to wallow in guilt. We simply need to acknowledge our mistake, ask our children to forgive us for setting a bad example, and get back on track. Our honesty, coupled with a sincere desire to live out what we say we believe, goes a long way toward teaching our children what we want them to know.

chapter 8

Special Projects

"Special events are the exclamation points of life."
—Anonymous

*"If you make children happy now, you will make them happy
twenty years hence by the memory of it."*
—Kate Douglas Wiggan

B y dictionary definition "special" is of a kind different from others; distinctive, peculiar, or unique. A "project" is an organized undertaking. An organized undertaking? Sure. A birthday party for twenty-three third-graders is an organized undertaking. What kind of medication are these people on?

There are days when I wish there was a medicine that would make organizing special projects or any other aspect of family life painless.

But, alas and alack, there isn't. So, like millions of my sisters in this country, I've had to make do with pulling off projects and making memories as best I can. Actually, despite the opportunities for humor and catastrophe (often the same thing in my book, not to mention my life), I have grown over the years to like special projects, especially since I discovered the importance of the "d" word. No, I'm not Cleopatra, Queen of Denial. The "d" word in question is delegation.

For years I felt frustrated, and I couldn't put my finger exactly on either the problem or solution. When we went on family vacations, I hardly ever felt rested, renewed, or like I was having much fun. On Christmas Eve I was way too tired to savor the fancy buffet, not to mention staying awake for the magic of the candlelight midnight service at church. After my kids' birthday parties, I wished I could ban all future ones—not so they'd stay little forever. So I'd never have to face paper hats, gooey cake, and screaming children again.

> "Imagination is more
> important than creativity."
> —Albert Einstein

Then one day, I was having coffee with a friend who manages her own house and her job as a busy book editor. She used management-type terms—like planning, research and development, delegation, deadlines—to describe her latest book project. Then, as we moved into talking about our personal lives, she used words like overworked, tired, and stressed out. She was in the midst of planning for her daughter's high-school graduation—where to put out-of-town relatives, what to serve for various meals, how to coordinate all the activities and still enjoy this special time in her only daughter's life. While listening to her frustrations and trying to figure out how to help her, it occurred to me—another lightning bolt—that the same words she used for overseeing a work project could be used for overseeing a home project.

The Family Manager is usually the one who organizes and coordinates the special events or projects in her family's life each year. These projects may be small or large, once-in-a-lifetime or annual events.

What they all have in common is that they fall outside the normal routine of daily activities. Birthdays, vacations, Christmas and other holidays, parties, weddings, anniversaries, family reunions, and garage sales are all special projects. Building or remodeling a house, and heading up a school or community fund-raiser would also fall into the category of special projects. Each project calls for a certain amount of planning, research, compiling data, delegation, meeting intermittent deadlines. Each requires careful follow-through until it comes to a definite close—just like a work project. That's right, each project, even if it's a fairly spontaneous one. As a matter of fact, sometimes the ones that work the best are quite spontaneous and can become family traditions.

"An opportunity grasped and used produces at least one other opportunity."—Chester A. Swor

THINK ABOUT IT

That same friend who was planning her daughter's high-school graduation discovered a revered family tradition by accident when her daughter was old enough to stay up until midnight on New Year's Eve. Trying to think of a way to make the evening festive, she found a lot of old candle stubs in her cabinet. (She says this wouldn't have happened if she were a better housekeeper.) She covered the coffee table with two layers of butcher paper to protect it from melting wax, then covered the surface with candles in candle holders, glasses, aluminum foil, and such. About 11:00 they lit all the candles and talked about their dreams and goals for the coming year. At the stroke of twelve they blew them out. What began as a spur-of-the-moment activity became a tradition. Now, as my friend plans her family's New Year's celebration, she includes their candle ritual.

> **"You've got to think about 'big things' while you're doing small things, so that all the small things go in the right direction."**
> —Alvin Toffler

Finding the Handle

Once I had the insight that a project is a project is a project, whether it's conceived and implemented in the office with colleagues or at home with husband and kids, I didn't have any less projects to deal with or any less work to oversee. It's just that I finally felt like I had a handle on how to pull off projects without pulling my hair out.

One special project that changed tremendously for the better was Christmas. I used to wonder who came up with the idea of happy holidays. To me, the Christmas season meant driving from store to store in bumper-to-bumper traffic trying to locate gifts for every name on my list; putting up decorations in between school pageants, office parties, and neighborhood get-togethers. Trying to fit in a few hours of sleep between addressing Christmas cards, gift-wrapping, and baking. And all the while trying to keep the spirit of the season in my heart. Trust me—it wasn't happening.

But when I saw that Christmas was a special project that needed planning, research and development, delegation, follow-through, and deadlines, just like any other project, I was able to accomplish everything I needed to do with less stress, and enjoy the season more.

> "It is a very hard undertaking to seek to please everbody."
> —Publilius Syrus

Looking at a special project as a work project probably changed my attitude more than it changed anything else. Even though I was well into being able to delegate and manage other areas, I was feeling responsible for special projects in a way that seemed more like the old me. If everybody wasn't having fun all the time on vacation, it was my fault. If our Christmas decorations weren't the brightest on the block, it was my fault. If my children's teachers asked me to undertake a school project, three of them at the same time, well, I just had to do it. How could I let them down?

But when I began to look at special projects as work projects, the first thing I realized is that I don't expect every work project I undertake to turn out perfectly. Things change on the way from inception to completion, and nobody gets too bent out of shape.

Another thing I realized about special projects, in home or office, is that usually it's essential to share the load with other people. I decided that if I needed an accountant, I would hire an accountant. If I wanted to add a room to our house, I would call a builder. So, if I needed some help with cooking, decorating, errands, invitations, organizing, anything that had to happen to pull off a special project, I could share the load.

Almost overnight, or so it seemed, although I know I'd been laying the groundwork in one way or another for years, I began to look forward to special projects. Since I was no longer responsible for making everybody happy or doing the whole thing by myself like the Little Red Hen of fairy-tale fame, I could be more flexible. Special projects didn't have to be scheduled six months in advance and happen in a certain way and at a certain time every year (although some of them do). I became more spontaneous, open to new ideas, new ways of doing things, and I had a better time. In business terms I became a better manager. I began to appreciate a special project for what it is, and actually do more of them, with more enthusiasm.

Beginning in the Middle

To get you started thinking about managing Special Projects in your own family, I want to begin at the end, or at least in the middle, with the "m" word. M for memories.

Memories. We talk about them as though we have a choice of whether or not to make them. We act as if the circumstances of life are like disappearing ink—only there for a moment. We forget our children's minds are like computer

> "It isn't the big pleasures that count the most; it's making a great deal out of the little ones."
> —Jean Webster

disks—constantly recording information. Who's to know which memories will be erased and which will be indelibly etched in their minds?

Psychologists say it's the unusual or out-of-the-ordinary happenings—good and bad—that form the strongest memories. This means our kids won't remember how many shirts we ironed, how many deals we closed, or if the kitchen floor was mopped daily. But they'll remember the April Fool's Day you put an apple in their lunch with a gummy worm coming out of it. They'll remember the time you cleaned out the attic and basement, had a family garage sale, and split the money. They'll remember the family reunion when you broke your neck to get to the "luxurious" campground and had to sleep in a cabin (vintage Davey Crockett), but had the time of your lives. Times like these are crucial to a family's culture and cohesion.

There's just something about being able to say, "This is the way our family always does it" or "Remember when . . . that was hilarious!" Traditions and common experiences cement a family. Every child's mind is a curator of memories. Fun family times and special traditions go a long way in building a rich museum of positive remembrances for our children. I try to get at least one special project a month on the calendar. Given the various holidays, five birthdays, and other assorted occasions, that's not hard to do. Depending on who you are and what you consider a special project, you may have anywhere from six to sixty of them a year. (At the risk of repeating myself, they needn't all

> "People need joy quite as much as clothing. Some of them need it far more."
> —Margaret Collier Graham

be scheduled in advance. Some of them can be quite spontaneous. They still require planning and execution, which might happen in twenty-four hours instead of over a period of weeks or months.)

What can tip us over the edge, more than the planning or even the events themselves, are expectations—our own and others' (as we perceive them). I had to decide that I'd welcome fun in whatever way it came—through my carefully prepared plans or through laughing at the failure thereof. I couldn't be married to my agenda for the sake of my expectations—I had to set a relaxed, "roll with it" model, which everyone could then follow.

Sanity belongs not to those who have the best circumstances, but to those who make the best of their circumstances.

Even though we may believe that special projects are the greatest memory-makers for our family, it's easy to let days, weeks, even months slip by without making any memories—any positive ones at least. Just the thought of planning one more thing may make you want to reach for a sedative. And maybe you feel like your budget is already stretched to the limit. If you're thinking, This woman is nuts. She wants me to spend more time and more effort and more money, and I'm already overdrawn in the sleep, money, and energy departments, I ask you to do this instead. Fix yourself a cup of tea or your favorite coffee, sit down in a quiet place, and just remember. Remember the happiest times you've had as a family. Remember the disasters that seem funny now, even if they didn't then. Remember the time you were proudest of yourself for pulling off a special project of any kind. You may want to jot these down. You may also want to make a short list of things you'd do differently for special projects that didn't work out the way you wanted them to. But the important thing is just to remember. Because it's those memories— your own and your children's—that you're after.

It's the special projects—traditions, family occasions and activities, and holidays—that bind a family together. These are the times when we can laugh, love, and enjoy life together—three things we all need large doses of.

So what's an already-overwhelmed Family Manager supposed to do? Here are seven suggestions:

1. As you think about how you spend your time, put special projects—carrying on family traditions and making memories—high on your priority list. It's okay to jealously guard your calendar and "just say no" to people and organizations asking for your time because you want to plan meaningful times for your family. You're always saying "no" to something—try not to let it be your family.

2. Keep in mind that special projects provide great opportunities for family bonding. Like your family, our family is busy. Very busy—and not so much with things we do together. We each have a lot of individual interests and activities. It concerns me that each of us could very easily end up living in our own separate world, everyone doing his or her own thing. I don't want our family to become fragmented, with no ties, no common threads to hold it together. Therefore, I am always on the lookout for special projects we can do together as a family.

"A wise man will make more opportunities than he finds."—*Francis Bacon*

3. Don't forget that it's a good investment to spend money on making memories. If you have the choice of whether to take a family excursion or buy a new piece of furniture, go for the trip. The furniture will get dirty, scratched, torn, and could end up some day in a garage sale. The family memory will last forever. Instead of amassing a big savings account or buying expensive furniture (our house is furnished in garage-sale finds that we've refinished and worked on together), we have

spent a lot of money over the years on taking vacations, hosting parties, celebrating ordinary and extraordinary occasions, traveling hundreds of miles to spend holidays with loved ones—and we don't regret it a bit.

"That man is the richest whose pleasures are the cheapest"—Henry David Thoreau.

 THINK ABOUT IT

4. As you work on special projects, remind yourself that the process is part of it. It's not just the party, the trip, or the holiday itself, it's teaching your kids the value of planning for something, working on details together, feeling the satisfaction of making progress, and watching all your hard work come together in a wonderful occasion. These are all part of the memory-making experience.

5. Cut yourself some slack. Remember, the object is to have fun and make positive memories. Managing special projects is not a good time to expect perfection of yourself. For years I made myself and everyone else in a five-mile radius miserable while I tried to create my notion of meaningful traditions and perfect holidays. Finally, I decided I was trying to do too much, I was doing things my family didn't necessarily like, and I was making myself crazy. Now, I've cut back on my "project have-tos" and our family works together to make special projects more enjoyable for everyone.

6. Don't wait until you "have enough money." Even though you can't do it exactly the way you want it the first time, it's better just to do it. Don't let lack of funds influence your decision to celebrate Grandma and Grandpa's fortieth anniversary; if you wait for their fiftieth because then "we'll have more money," you may never celebrate at all. If you wait until you can afford

to plan a family vacation, you may be stuck at home for the rest of your life.

7. Learn to laugh. Some of the fun and positive memories will be made because you are able to laugh with your family about your own flops.

> "He who waits to do a great deal at once will never do anything."
> —Charles Simmons

Accept the fact that calamity and confusion are often uninvited guests at family celebrations and events. Do yourself and your family a favor by finding humor in those inevitable mishaps that plague us all.

Making Molehills Out of Mountains

There's no doubt that most special events are big events—in one way or another. Maybe planning a nine-year-old daughter's birthday party doesn't seem as big as hosting a backyard barbeque for fifty neighbors. But in the mind of that young girl, her birthday party is a real big deal. And it's just as important to take care of her party's details as it is for the barbeque. So, I decided I needed to create some guidelines that I could follow each time I had to manage a project—no matter what the size of the undertaking. The guidelines turned into my seven-point special project strategy that I use for everything from holidays to vacations to parties.

Special Project Strategy

1. Do some long-range planning.

First, get out your calendar and, month by month, list the special projects you know will occur—birthdays, holidays, vacations, etc. Then list the special projects you want to occur—add in a tenth anniversary trip for you and your husband, a Super Bowl party, an end-of-the-year dinner for the teachers at your child's school. Then leave blanks for spur-of-the-moment projects like throwing a party for your best friend who's moving out of state, overseeing fund-raising for your neighborhood to put up special signs or streetlights, and hosting a victory celebration for your son's football team.

Now you'll be able to look ahead and know what projects are on the horizon, and you can work on them a little at a time. When you know way ahead of time that you're hosting a Fourth of July barbecue for out-of-town relatives, you can be on the lookout for menu ideas. When you see something on sale you'll need, you can buy it—saving time and money later.

Once or more a year it might be a good idea to devote a family meeting to think about special projects. Brainstorm fun things you'd like to do as a family, places you'd like to travel, occasions you'd like to celebrate. Think of a work of charity you'd like to do as a family.

Exercise some "executive neglect."

In business, this is a term that means wisely and carefully choosing to spend time, energy, and resources only on those things which are important to you. It's the same with family management. First of all it's important that you involve yourself in only those projects that are important to your family's priorities. This means you need to evaluate. Perhaps you've organized the used-clothing sale at your daughter's school for the past three years and helped raise a lot of money for the school. And this year, maybe your family wants you that day for a special trip or occasion. In such a case, it's time to say no when the PTA President calls and asks you to do it again.

Executive neglect is about choosing the special projects that are right for your family, not being pressured to do something just because you've always done it, or your mother's always done it, or somebody asked you to do it, and it's for a good cause.

Executive neglect is also about not going broke doing the quarter jobs while the dollar jobs go begging, which is just another way of saying: Pick the most important things. When you're busy with a special project, can you delegate daily chores to someone else? Or maybe that's the time to reevaluate whether the kitchen floor really needs to be scrubbed once a week. You might let some daily chores slide for a week or two. You might even discover there are things you've been doing more frequently than you actually need to for your family's happiness and peace of mind.

Executive neglect can also be about lowering your standards and expectations a little and neglecting some details that are driving you nuts. Do you really need to make the potato salad yourself when the deli offers a perfectly good substitute? If you're hosting a holiday dinner for your extended family, can you ask others to bring some of the food? Or someone to come early and help set up? Or stay late and help clean up? Sometimes it's better to carry on the tradition in a scaled-down way than to go to either of the other extremes—doing it so big that it drives you crazy or dropping it completely.

STRetCH YOUR MIND:

"We have left undone those things which we ought to have done; and we have done those things which we ought not to have done." —*The Book of Common Prayer*

3. Conduct research and development.

Commonly referred to in companies as R&D. Here you figure out what needs to be done and how you're going to do it. This is where you begin using your project planning-sheet in earnest. Get on the phone and collect data, write letters requesting information about dates and rates for resorts for a vacation or a hall to rent for an anniversary party. Ask your friends who've done a similar event for ideas. Be sure to ask: What's the main thing you wish you'd known beforehand? The hardest things to remember are the things you don't know about. Make lists, compare notes and figures, create the to-do list for the project of everything that needs to be done, bought, cooked, prepared, set up. Add approximate dates things should be completed by, and decide who's going to do each task and who their backup person is going to be.

4. Delegate.

Here it is, the "d" word. This is the part where you remind your family, "We're all in this together." The idea is not only to save yourself a trip to the therapist by not doing everything yourself, but to promote family bonding, team spirit, and memories as well.

I know I've said this before, but this is important. When we work on projects together we do bond, build team spirit, make memories, and have fun. We also give our children the lasting legacy of additional skills, a sense of responsibility, and the ability to work together with others to reach a common goal. That's an accomplishment any CEO would be proud of.

When you begin to delegate for a special project, go back and review the basic concepts in Chapter 2, Building Your Team. Remember to let team members, even the smallest of children, volunteer for some jobs. Remember to work with people's strengths and to pitch in together to do the unpleasant parts that no one likes to do.

Once you've roughed out a to-do list for a special project it might be a good time to call a family meeting to go over the plan, inviting people to add things they'd like that you haven't thought of, or to talk about how they might like to do something different this year.

5. Finally, execute and enjoy.

When I first used the term execution, which is, of course, a perfectly normal business way to talk about a project, one of my kids said "Who's going to get killed?" So, lest you get the wrong idea, please know I am not talking about capital punishment (although some Family Managers might think special projects are something they would rather die than do.)

> "I value this delicious home feeling as one of the choicest gifts a parent can bestow."
> —Washington Irving

What we are talking about here is the end toward which you've been working—the birthday party, Christmas Day, the family reunion, the family vacation. All the work we did—collecting brochures, making phone calls and reservations, studying the map, getting the car serviced, packing the clothes, getting the house vacation-ready, driving eighteen hours—is now worth it because we're enjoying mountain climbing, fishing, and exploring Colorado. Everyone will still have responsibilities to fulfill, even on vacation, or during the party, or on Thanksgiving Day, but you're all reaping the fruit of your efforts and enjoying the special project together.

6. Allow time to appreciate.

This happens after the project is completed. This step has two very important components. Never, no matter what went wrong, forget to do these two steps. First, give credit where credit is due. Make sure to compliment and thank your team members for their effort—even if it's for something they did wrong but it ended up as a funny story for the family joke bank. Secondly: Rest on your laurels. Give yourself credit as well. You've just finished managing a very important memory in your family's legacy.

7. Then recap.

After the project is over, what have you learned? What would you do differently? What information do you need to store in a safe place for next time? Make sure to jot all these particulars down on your project planner. On our third cross-country trip to Colorado, it occurred to me when we were trying to figure out where to stop for dinner along the road, that it would make a lot of sense to write down everything I learned from year to year—locations of restaurants and roadside parks, motels and campgrounds, distance and miles between towns.

Also, think about the intangibles. What memories do you want to save? Perhaps after you develop the vacation pictures, you'll have a mini special-occasion dinner to look at them, tell stories, and put them in a photo album. If one or more of your children or you likes to write, perhaps you'll write stories or anecdotes to collect in a memory book or to put in the photo album.

Recap by yourself, or, for more fun, have a family meeting in which everyone talks about what worked, what didn't, what went right, what went wrong. (And believe me, you can't stop people from talking about what went wrong. At my house they're still talking

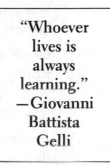

"Whoever lives is always learning."
—Giovanni Battista Gelli

about the time I planned a family vacation at what we thought was a Dude Ranch. In our book it turned out to be a Dud Ranch.)

52 Special Project Ideas

Remember, every special project doesn't have to be a huge undertaking, mini special-projects can produce wonderful moments and memories for your family as well. Here are 52 ways, one for each week of the year, to make any occasion or non-occasion special.

- Create a fun picnic memory for kids by serving cupcakes decorated with plastic ants.

- Make inexpensive taper candles look like fancy, expensive candles by painting designs on them with non-toxic, non-flammable T-shirt paints.

- Create birthday cone cakes. Fill the flat-bottomed ice-cream cones one-third full with cake batter. Bake according to instructions for cupcakes. When cool, top with a scoop of ice cream and a birthday candle.

Have a western party. Make a centerpiece by arranging tall, dried flowers in a cowboy boot. Carry out the theme with a tablecloth made from ordinary burlap. Use raffia to tie up cutlery in bandanna napkins and have metal pie pans for plates. Serve nachos, bean dip, or other western-style food in cast-iron frying pans. Tie a bandanna around the pan handles to brighten them up.

 Create a glamorous atmosphere on a party table by tying up a small piece of dry ice in cheesecloth and putting it into a bowl of punch. (There will be a lot of smoke, but the punch won't be affected.)

 Fix a fun fall lunch. Carve out miniature pumpkins and fill them with chicken, tuna, or pasta salad.

For a last-minute celebration, hang curly ribbon from the chandelier over your dining table. Tie small balloons onto the ribbons at different levels.

 For a child's slumber party, make a giant sugar cookie on a round pizza pan. Let children decorate it with icing, candies, and colored sprinkles.

 Let your kids be servers, door-openers, or coat-checkers at a party. Use paint pens to decorate T-shirts to look like tuxedos for them to wear. Buy inexpensive plastic top hats at a costume or toy store.

Encourage your teenagers to invite their friends over after a ball game or party for a midnight breakfast. Serve breakfast burritos. Fill bowls with cooked sausage, shredded cheese, chopped green chilies, tomatoes, green peppers, and salsa. Provide warm tortillas and let them make their own burritos.

When you have small children at an event, create a table just for them. Cover the table with craft paper. Use markers to draw pretend place mats at each seat. Put a cup of markers on the table for children to decorate their place mats.

Keep a large hurricane lamp on hand to make a decoration for any occasion. Fill it with seasonal items such as small pumpkins, oranges, and walnuts, apples, glass Christmas balls, or dyed eggs. Tie a raffia or plaid bow around the top and surround the hurricane with greenery.

Plan a "This is Your Life" celebration on a loved one's birthday. Look at old photos and tell stories from the past. Tell the honoree how much his life means to you.

Keep an airtight container of chocolate curls in your freezer to make a dessert look exquisite. Melt chocolate in a double boiler and spread a thin layer on the back of a cookie sheet. Refrigerate until firm, then use a metal spatula to scrape the chocolate from the cookie sheet, forming curls.

For a last-minute dessert, melt eight ounces of chocolate in a double boiler, stirring occasionally until smooth. Add one-half teaspoon of peppermint extract. Pour into a heat-proof serving bowl and surround with round, butter-flavor crackers for dipping.

Take photos at a special celebration. Write the date and event on the back of each picture and send copies to each guest who attended.

Add excitement to a plain chocolate cake mix by adding two teaspoons of peppermint flavoring to the ingredients called for on the box. Frost with chocolate frosting and sprinkle crushed peppermint candies on the top.

Host a "New Kid on the Block" party for a new neighbor. Make it potluck, and have old neighbors exchange names and phone numbers with the newcomers.

When a family member or friend can't be with you to celebrate an occasion, have everyone present hold up a big sign that says, "We miss you!" Take a picture and mail it to the missing person.

 Keep tiny American flags on hand to decorate foods on patriotic holidays.

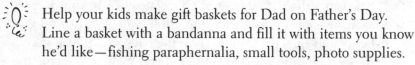 Make a princess cake for a young girl. Bake a bundt cake according to directions. Unmold it, then place a ten- to twelve-inch doll in the center hole. Frost the cake to look like the doll's formal gown.

 Help your kids make gift baskets for Dad on Father's Day. Line a basket with a bandanna and fill it with items you know he'd like—fishing paraphernalia, small tools, photo supplies.

 Dip the rim of iced-tea glasses first in lemon juice, then in sugar for a special effect.

Have a family awards night. Give personalized awards for silly categories such as fastest dish washer, best lawn mower, and quickest to answer phone.

 Give events added meaning by keeping a special-occasion scrapbook. Include pictures of recitals and parties, signatures of teachers and friends who attended, and souvenirs such as ticket stubs and programs.

 Let your child decorate her bedroom door for various holidays.

 Get out the nice serving pieces you usually save for company and use them for your family.

Mail a college student inexpensive door or room decorations for different holidays and seasons.

Keep a party journal. Record the date, time, location, guest list, menu, decorations, and costs. After the party, make notes of what you did right and mistakes you want to avoid next time. This will be valuable information when planning your next party.

Decorate the room of a hospitalized family member or friend with balloons, crepe paper, and inspirational posters. Create a giant get-well card from poster board. Take it to the patient's office or school for friends to sign.

Make your ceiling shimmer for a party. Cut out dozens of silver stars in various sizes and hang them from your ceiling with fishing line and straight pins.

Dress up and be your own singing telegram to a family member or friend.

Use toothpicks to roast miniature marshmallows over candlelight with a child.

When your family gathers for the holidays, videotape the oldest living relative reading the Christmas story. Continue this tradition through the years and build a treasury of memories of grandparents, aunts, and uncles.

Use sparklers to decorate birthday cakes.

Have a "Grandmother Shower" for a friend who's going to be a grandmother.

Collect pretty fall leaves. Press them in a book for a few days, then use them to form a runner down the center of your dining table. Place an arrangement of fall vegetables and candles in the middle.

Call your local high school to inquire about band students who play in string quartets or combos. This is usually an inexpensive way to have live music for an occasion.

For a teenager's party make a three- to five-foot submarine sandwich. Line up foot-long sandwich buns on a long piece of foil-covered cardboard. Layer favorite sub-sandwich toppings and cut the sandwich into serving pieces so it looks like one long sandwich.

 Host an around-the-clock wedding shower. Assign each guest to a different hour of the day and ask them to bring a gift that the newlyweds can use during that time of day.

 Organize a neighborhood yard-decorating contest at Christmas. Appoint a committee of judges. The winner receives a plate of goodies from the losers.

To celebrate a special day in someone's life, send a letter and a self-addressed stamped envelope to friends of the honoree, asking them to write a warm greeting and send it back to you secretly. Collect the messages and present them to the honoree.

Give someone a gift of personal coupons. Instead of buying a present, write down different "gifts" she can redeem.

Help your children celebrate the end of each grading period with their favorite dessert.

On New Year's Day decide on a family motto for the year, like "Life's too short not to celebrate," or "Every day's a gift."

Decorate your child's bedroom on a special day with streamers, balloons, and small hidden presents.

 Give your son or daughter an old-fashioned hope chest for his or her thirteenth birthday. Begin to stock it with items they will need when they leave home—cookware, tools, linens—items pertaining to their special interests.

 Give a potted geranium to a friend who is moving away. The geranium symbolizes remembrance.

Organize a neighborhood Fourth-of-July parade on your street. Decorate bicycles, wagons, and other riding toys with streamers and balloons. End up at your house for watermelon.

 Plan a surprise weekend for your family, and enjoy the pool, health club, and maid service at a local hotel. Many have inexpensive weekend packages that include breakfast.

 Take an impromptu family bike-hike to an interesting picnic spot.

 If school's out because of snow, have a neighborhood snowman contest. See who can create the biggest, fanciest, and most unique snowman. Take photos, award small prizes, and serve hot cocoa to all.

(From *How to Make Any Occasion Special* by Judie Byrd, Word Publishing, 1993.)

Because a special project is something extra added to your already-too-long To-Do list, it's easy to get tired, stressed out, and wonder why you're doing it in the first place. At this point, it's important to remember that there's something bigger going on than icing the forty-ninth cupcake or trying to cram a baby stroller, high chair, walker, wind-up swing, portacrib, fourteen changes of clothes, and two giant economy-size packages of disposable diapers into your car so you can spend a leisurely week camping out. You're making memories. You're helping create opportunities for your family to get to know each other better and enjoy life together. You're carrying on traditions. That's big.

> "The trouble . . . is that we constantly put second things first."
> —Lyndon Baines Johnson

"We find
in life
exactly
what we
put in
it."
—Ralph
Waldo
Emerson

chapter 9

Family and Friends

"Life in common among people who love each other
is the ideal happiness."
—George Sand

I f I could share only one part of our family and its management thereof, it wouldn't be the way we organize our closets, how we manage our schedule, or how we saved money by putting a new roof on our house by ourselves.

It would be to tell you about the rapport, the responsibilities, and the rewards we experience day in and day out as a family made up of five human beings who love and respect each other. We are committed to each other's best interests, and we enjoy relationships with many other people—relatives, friends, and acquaintances in a meaningful way.

The way I've gotten a handle on this is to look at the business analogy and think Human Resource Department. Human Resource departments offer employees opportunities to continue their education and build their skills. They inspire and entice employees to perform at their best by offering tangible rewards, such as promotions and bonuses, and intangible rewards, such as the feeling of taking personal responsibility, of enjoying the satisfaction of a job well done.

Like other managers, I am responsible for "my people." I'm responsible to help them learn to fulfill their roles, to help them build their skills—in short, to orchestrate opportunities so each one can develop into the best person he or she can be.

Managers of Human Resource departments send their people to classes and seminars; they work with them to evaluate performance and set new goals. In some companies, they're also the people who organize activities and events like the company picnic or the softball team or corporate volunteer opportunities. These things don't necessarily add to the "bottom line" for companies, but they benefit them in the long run because they provide opportunities for people to learn how to work together, to communicate better, and to clarify their priorities.

> "It's no good saying you can't afford to look after your staff. You can't afford not to. Treating your staff better will make your business perform better. It's that simple."
> —Tom Peters

There's a lot in this book about things I think are important—how to save time, money, and energy, how to carry on traditions, how to create a warm, welcoming home. But there's something more significant going on beyond the ideas in ink on these pages. One of the main reasons we save time is so we'll have more time to spend in meaningful ways with the people we care about. We save money so we'll have more money to spend on family trips, enhancing our lives, or giving to others. We save energy so we'll be awake to enjoy the finer moments of life—a night out with our husband, reading a book to a child before bed, having friends over for dinner. We carry on traditions that bond this generation of our family with preceding and succeeding generations. We create a warm and welcoming home so that human beings—family members and friends—can enjoy a place of acceptance and love.

It is beyond important to me—it is vital—to help my family (and myself) be all we were created to be. I want to bring out the best in those I love and have them bring out the best in me. In fact, the "bring out the best" principle is what I want our family to keep in mind when we deal with others as well. Accounting firms or computer manufacturers have a vested interest in bringing out the best in people because it helps them do a better job at whatever their mission is. Managing human resources in the family may be the most important category. A Family Manager's mission is to develop people. Period.

Assignment Accepted

I don't want to take this business analogy too far. Some people might chafe at talking about "managing" relationships. This chapter is not about cold and calculated manipulation to get other people to do things one way or another to serve some personal end. It's not about fixing other people, making them who we think they should be. This chapter is also not so much about what we do or how we do it (although I talk about those things) as it is about living with a conscious awareness that our most important job as wives, mothers, daughters, friends, and Family Managers is to build loving, lasting relationships. (And, of course, that's the most important job for children and husbands as well.)

Again, our most important job is to build loving relationships. Said that way, everything seems to fall into place. I take time to talk with my husband about his frustrations and dreams for the future because it's important to our loving relationship. I take Joel off to look at colleges because that's part of who he's becoming, and I want him to know that it's important to me.

That's also why I stood in line with James for two hours this morning to sign him up for baseball. And why I spent an hour reading aloud with him last night. And why I call my mom long distance just to chat. It's also why I take my kids (and myself) to the doctor and dentist for regular checkups. And why I make sure that Bill and I have time alone together, sometimes to work out difficulties we might be having and sometimes to enjoy each other's company. That's why I send my niece a birthday gift. And why I call to encourage a friend who's going through a hard time. And why I get my neighbor's mail and paper while she's out of town. Taking care of minds, bodies, and souls. That's what managing family and friends is all about to me.

People are more important than projects. THINK ABOUT IT

Projects Don't Fail; People Do

This is also the department that can produce more stress and guilt than the others; first of all because we're dealing with human beings who have feelings; second, because a lot of what we do in this department is constantly under scrutiny and, at the same time, is not measurable. Think about it. When your house needs painting, it doesn't cry, get angry, and tell you you're a horrible homeowner. The paint just peels off. When you set a goal to save one hundred dollars a month and at the end of the year you only have nine hundred dollars, the automated teller won't tell you you're a loser. But let's say you decide to spend more quality time with your child, and after doing so, your child still whines. And when you call your mother-in-law every day to check on her, she still complains that she feels neglected. It's hard not to feel frustrated.

People are people. And Family Managers are people. Could anything be simpler? Could anything be more profound? When we talk about managing projects of any kind, from getting dinner on the table to pulling off a family celebration for a huge crowd, we're dealing with the project and we're dealing with the people involved in that project. All of us have feelings and needs and want to feel appreciated and loved. We want to know that there are others in the world who care where we are, what we do, who we become.

"The happiest people are those who do the most for others."—Booker T. Washington

THINK ABOUT IT

Doing things for others does make me happy. There's the possibility for great fulfillment in doing for others. When we sincerely do something for someone else, give them the gift of our time, energy, and love, we are blessed. Genuine giving always gives back to the giver.

But what do you do if it seems there are too many others and too much to do? How much fulfillment can one person stand?

I am a people pleaser, and that's good news and bad news. It's good news if you hire me to do a job for you, to speak at a banquet, to write an article for your newsletter, because you can count on a 110 percent job. My motto is to always do my most excellent work and to deliver at least as much as I promise, hopefully more. I want you to be pleased. But that's the bad news too—at least it is for my emotional and physical well-being. I want to operate at that 110 percent level in every relationship. Of course, that's unrealistic, not to mention, humanly impossible. The outcome of trying to live like this is taking on too much responsibility in too many relationships, spreading myself, my energy level, my love too thin. As a result, no one really gets more than a small percent of me.

It's a daily tension, the tug between the desire to give of myself to others and knowing that if I give myself to too many others or promise more than I have to give, I'll end up giving and getting very little. So once again, I find myself needing a way to manage this area of my life, to prioritize, to decide which people are the most important to me and how much I can give to those people.

> "One is taught by experience to put a premium on those few people who can appreciate you for what you are . . ."
> —Gail Godwin

About the time my life went out of control and I landed in the hospital (the story I told in the Time Management chapter), I realized two things about priorities and giving. One was that when I set priorities about time, I was indeed setting priorities about people. Yes, I love the feeling of being wanted, and yes, there were too many people who wanted too many things from me. The second was that I was going to have to make some decisions. Some of those decisions would be based on who wanted me, some would be based on what they wanted. Clearly my family comes first. But no one person, I propose, no matter how giving and organized and efficient she is, can even come close to meeting all the needs and fulfilling all the desires of her family members.

James asked me recently if we could start talking about his upcoming birthday and the party he envisioned. He rattled off about six or seven possible party ideas, all of which involved renting a facility or paying for services. In other words, high-ticket parties. I told him an amount we would be willing to spend on a party, and he asked me to call and find out if any of his ideas would work within our budget. Remembering the old adage about teaching the cat to catch his own mice, I explained to James that he could do the research—that he could make a list of the places and look up the phone numbers. He called and inquired about prices and wrote them down on his list. He figured out by himself that the parties would be too expensive. This led to a brainstorming session about less expensive, but fun parties.

> "Don't take in a stray cat unless you can teach it to catch mice."
> —Anonymous

STRETCH YOUR MIND:
Managerial memo:
A part of managing people, especially children,
is helping them learn to help themselves.

The Three Rs of Relationship:
Rapport, Responsibilities, Rewards

By dictionary definition, to have a relationship with someone means we have a continuing attachment or association. This chapter is, of course, about building and maintaining relationships—relationships between the people in our families, as well as our own individual and family relationships to other people in our circles: extended family, friends, acquaintances.

A relationship, of course, isn't a thing. It's not a project. It's ongoing. It has to do with process, development, and communication. As I think about what goes into relationships, I picture a pinwheel, one of those multi-colored plastic wheels that twirls around on the end of a stick. When you blow on them, they spin round and round. The colors blur. They're fun to watch. You can't tell where one part starts and the other stops. That's sort of how I think of the three components—rapport, responsibilities, rewards—that go into making any relationship.

RAPPORT

We establish rapport at the beginning of a relationship, whether that's on a first date with the man who became our husband, when we first meet a new baby in the delivery room, when we first meet a friend at a neighborhood cookout. We could even say we established rapport with our own parents when they met us when we were born. Every relationship begins someplace. But I think it's important to remember that rapport changes over time. What I mean is this: We make connection with infants by holding them, maybe babbling at them in baby talk, trying to communicate on their level. As our infants grow, we need to establish a different kind of rapport. We don't talk to a three-year-old the same way we talk to an infant. But we do try to talk to him in a way he will understand, using words we think he knows, concepts he can latch on to. A lot of people I know understand this concept when it comes to smaller children, but it breaks down when it comes to teenagers. I admit it can be difficult to establish rapport with a teenager. They change, sometimes minute by minute. Sometimes it can feel like we're talking to a ten-year-old going on thirty. The important thing with this relationship, as well as others, is to keep trying to find common ground, which is what rapport is all about.

> **"Yield to a man's tastes, and he will yield to your interests."**
> —Edward Bulwar-Lytton

I'm talking about rapport first because I think of it as the beginning of any relationship. But really, it's the beginning, the middle, and the end, depending on what's going on in the relationship at any given time. My rapport with my mother has changed over the years. We no longer talk from the point of view of Kathy, the college kid who needed gas in her car, clothes in her closet, and money to pay college tuition. Our rapport with people changes because people change, but rapport is constant in any lasting relationship.

"Times change and we change with them too."
—*From Owen's Epigrammata*

THINK ABOUT IT

RESPONSIBILITY

The depth of a relationship determines the level of responsibility. Like rapport, responsibility changes over time. "Level of intimacy" is what we're talking about. When we hear the word intimacy, we usually think of two things: physical closeness and emotional transparency. But it's more than that. It involves intellectual and spiritual closeness as well. I have some degree of intimacy with each person with whom I have a relationship. For example, my neighbor: she lives across the street, our children play together, we let each other know when we're going out of town. Although I really like my neighbor and enjoy our relationship, our level of intimacy, and therefore our responsibility to each other, is not as great as the level I share with my husband or children or mother.

246

This is where those of us who have a hard time saying "no" can really get into trouble. A friend calls and asks you to host a tea for a political candidate. A neighbor calls and asks you to walk your block for a particular charity. Your mother-in-law calls and asks you to take her for an eye checkup. A coworker calls and asks you to cover for her at an after-hours meeting. You say "yes" to all of the requests, rationalizing that they're all worthwhile endeavors. In fact, it is good to do good to others. The problem occurs when we take on too much responsibility with those with whom we have a lower level of intimacy, to the neglect of those with whom we have a higher degree of intimacy—like our husband and children.

Good words from Will Rogers. But my ongoing struggle is to know what (or who) to turn down when I'm trying to balance being a wife, lover, mother, daughter, friend, neighbor, sister, coworker—while at the same time running a home, a company, and my legs off.

When relationship responsibilities seem overwhelming, when I feel like everyone needs a piece of me and there's not enough of me to go around, I try to remind myself of the wisdom in Ecclesiastes 3:1: "There is a time for everything, and a season for every activity under heaven . . ."

> "Don't just grab the first thing that comes by . . . know what to turn down."
>
> —Will Rogers

When I read this verse in the Bible I think about the seasons of the year, how they change, how we do summer things in summer and winter things in winter. And sometimes I think of seasons of death and life, a time to grieve and a time to dance, a time for war and a time for peace. There is a time for everything under heaven—and everything includes the relational responsibilities in my life. All I need to do is figure out which relationships and which responsibilities are most important. And if I take this verse at face value, I must recognize that if I am called to do a job, a person to care for, a responsibility to fulfill in a relationship, there will be time for it. On the other hand, if I take on too many responsibilities, from guilt, insecurity, or just unwise choices, I've mismanaged time. In the economy of life and God's time and seasons, not everything will fit.

We can't be responsible for the whole world. We can't do everything that needs to be done, regardless of its value. Realizing this means we won't meet everyone's expectations. If a friend calls and asks you to take her to pick up her car at 5:00 and your child has to be at soccer practice at 5:00, you take the child without feeling guilty that you couldn't help your friend. This means if you plan a much-needed weekend getaway with your husband and your mother calls and asks you to help clean out her attic, even though she thinks it has to be done immediately and if you were a good daughter you'd drop everything and come help her, you don't break your date with your husband. We simply can't be committed to every person with the same intensity. Therefore, every sane person has to live by priorities in relationships. And since every day is a new day with new opportunities, challenges, and people moving in and out of our lives, managing this department is not an easy formula. It is a constant process.

> "All things are to be examined and called into question. There are no limits set to thought."
> — Edith Hamilton

REWARDS

Sometimes, not always, the result of managing rapport and responsibility well is getting a reward, whether it be a feeling of well-being, a sticky kiss, a listening ear, or a returned favor.

In my mind there's nothing much better than a young child snuggling up and saying "Mommy, I love you." Or a teenager mumbling "Thanks Mom" as he hands you a bouquet of wilting flowers. Or a husband reminding you of his unconditional commitment to you. Or a mother saying how proud she is of you. Or a friend who knows you're in a busy season of life right now but is there waiting for you when you can find the time to go to lunch. These are only a few of the priceless rewards of relationships.

It's important to understand, though, that, more often than not, rewarding relationships come on the backstroke. You don't chase after a fulfilling relationship—with your husband, child, friend, neighbor—for your own good, your own happiness, your own fulfillment. Most of the time we are rewarded in a relationship because we have given of ourselves, loved sacrificially, sought the good of the other person.

Rewards: The Three Cs

There are numerous rewards in relationships. My experience has been the more I look for them, the more I'll see them. Having a relationship implies commitment—usually on the part of both participants. I know I can count on Laurie to be there if I have surgery. That's a reward. I know I can count on Bill to love me even when I'm tired and cranky. (Not to mention I can count on him to tell me when I'm taking my cranky mood out on others.) Those are both rewards I get from commitment. There are lots of times when I feel like I haven't "earned" someone's commitment to me. Yet I still get it. It's a great reward.

Another reward in relationships is communication. It's a grand thing to share ideas, problems, encouragement, and dreams with another human being. When John calls me (almost daily) from college to talk about his future, whom he's dating, or the problem he's having at his job, that's not a bother. Likewise it's a huge reward to have a child who wants to communicate with me. It's a reward when my father shares his business expertise with me, what he's learned over the years about working with people and products.

A third reward is camaraderie—enjoying shared interests and activities with someone—backpacking with your husband, working out at the gym with your teenager, comparing insights with a friend who has similar taste in books and authors.

We all enter into relationships for a number of reasons, but my experience is that if we enter into them thinking of the rewards that will come our way, they don't work. In other words, relationships are not exactly transactional, at least on a business model where an agreement is carried out in a way that satisfies the negotiating parties. What they are is, well, relational, which means they are covenantal rather than contractual. We may well choose to change or end a relationship because the reward part is no longer working for us, and this could be anything from practicing tough love with a kid who has chosen to run away from home to ending a friendship because a friend never calls us, never returns our calls, only wants to talk about herself. You can't judge or enter into a relationship based on its rewards, but the presence or lack of rewards is a good clue as to whether things need to be fixed or changed in the relationship.

> "It's the friends you can call up at 4 A.M. that matter."
> —Marlene Dietrich

Clearly, the equation that often works—RAPPORT + RESPONSIBILITY = REWARDS—doesn't always work smoothly. We all inherit certain relationships. We can't avoid having relationships with some people—our parents, our children, or perhaps a difficult neighbor or coworker or in-law. The rapport-responsibility-reward cycle might work in a different order. If a relationship isn't working out right, if your expectations and your understanding of the level of intimacy involved, or the responsibilities (the amount of time and energy you're willing to commit) are totally different from what the other person expects, sometimes going to rapport is a good way to approach a solution. What common ground can you find with that person? Are you speaking the same language? Are you reading from the same page of life? Perhaps you need to sit down and explain where you're coming from. And really make an effort to listen to that other person.

> "One who looks for a friend without faults will have none."
> —Hasidic Saying

The concepts of rapport, responsibility, and reward don't work as a reliable mathematical equation because the reality is, people are people. None of us is perfect, and sometimes we take our imperfections, our hurts, our disappointments out on those we love. From time to time, we'll all be hurt in relationships. There are no guarantees . . . except one: If we don't work at making our relationships work, we won't get the rewards we want or need—ever.

When I began to seriously look at relationships in terms of the concepts of family management, my first task was determining what relationships I had to manage. My second task was determining what my responsibilities were in terms of the Family Manager credo, in those relationships. Each category—husband, children—relatives, friends—calls for different responses from me as a Family Manager.

None of the following ideas are revolutionary. They have to do with what I've seen work in my family and in others. It's uniquely difficult in this department of Family Management to pass along a set of procedures; much depends on the age and stage of your marriage and family. As you look at these, adapt and apply what makes sense to you.

"People change and forget to tell each other."
—*Lillian Hellman*

Husband

People change. Families change. Relationships change. The best thing we can do—it sounds simple and it's often hard to remember to do—is to tell others when we change. And to listen for signs that they change.

There's probably not a couple in the world who entered marriage thinking, No way will this marriage work. Our goal is to make each other miserable. But somewhere along the way we realize that if it is going to work, if we're going to enjoy rather than endure each other, it's going to take some work.

> **"There is no more lovely, friendly, and charming relationship, communion or company than a good marriage."**
> —**Martin Luther**

Although Bill and I haven't "arrived" in our marriage by anyone's standards, there are a few things we've learned over the past twenty-five years about healthy relationships. First, we must accept each other as unique individuals— as is. Many women, including myself, said "I do" with a civilize-the-barbarian mentality. All this man needs is a woman's touch. I'll whip him into shape in no time, we secretly strategize.

Men have designs of their own too. As they envision their fantasies becoming reality, they think, Now she's mine, to meet my every need and fulfill my every desire . . . I've been waiting years for this.

Of course, when we take this approach the most likely result is that rather than changing our mates into what we think they should be, we actually drive them even farther away from where we are trying to take them.

A marriage is built of two individuals, who inevitably will have differences. But criticizing each other is no way to resolve them. I'll never forget the day Bill told me he would strive to accept me like I am and never criticize me again. You'd think I would have been elated. Instead, I felt frustrated and even a little mad. If he stops criticizing me, I pondered silently, that means that I'll have to stop criticizing him . . . and how will he ever become the man he needs to be without my help?

After stewing for a few days I realized that I need to accept Bill "as is." We made that decision almost fifteen years ago, although I'm sorry to say we've both reneged more times than we care to make public. Embarrassingly, the cutting words come all too easily when we forget our decision to stop the criticism and celebrate our differences. We often have to remind ourselves that neither one of us is perfect and that our own weaknesses and strengths can complement the other's—giving breadth to our "oneness."

Second, we must learn to say I love you in a way that communicates to the other person. Bill and I are very different. When it comes to our relationship, he wants me to sincerely praise him in private. I, on the other hand, feel so proud when Bill compliments me in front of others and demonstrates his love openly for the world to see. So what do we find ourselves doing more times than we care to confess? He demonstrates his love to me privately, and I broadcast my adoration for him to anyone who will listen. It is hard for me to understand why this means nothing to him, when I can think of nothing I'd like better.

Since the way we would like to be loved does not come naturally for either of us, we have to discipline ourselves to be sensitive

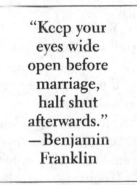

"Keep your eyes wide open before marriage, half shut afterwards."
—Benjamin Franklin

about this. Bill tries to remember that I love an audience and I want the whole world to know he loves me. And I have to write notes to myself about showing Bill my love one-on-one. Otherwise I forget.

Third, we both must proactively look for things we enjoy in common. Because Bill and I are so different, we constantly try to find things we like to do together. We don't want to end up living in two separate worlds. Years ago we discovered that we both enjoy art and decided to start collecting paintings to fill the walls of our home. We began to purchase favorite works of art at places we visited on vacations. Now our home is filled with memories of these trips.

We've also learned we enjoy doing projects together that will en-hance our home, such as upholstering, refinishing antiques, stripping and staining hardwood floors, laying tile, and remodeling the kitchen, to name a few. Working on a project bonds us together. When we fin-ish a job, we feel a shared pride and sense of accomplishment.

We've learned to give each other space for different interests as well. When we individually pursue various hobbies, friendships, and aspects of our careers, we become more interesting to each other as we share what we've experienced.

And fourth, we must give ourselves sacrificially to each other. Before we were married, no request was too big, no chore was a bother, no favor was too much trouble. We couldn't do enough for each other. But when the newness of marital bliss began to run thin, so did our patience.

The bottom line is that marriage takes time and commitment, two commodities we always seem to be short on. Quite frankly, I got mar-ried with the unrealistic expectation that we'd have two children, a yard with a picket fence, and a dog. As a good mom (or so I learned from Harriet Nelson), I'd wave good-bye to my family each morning before beginning my household chores. Each night our family would eat dinner together in the dining room. Any problems we encountered could be worked out in thirty minutes.

It didn't take long for reality to set in. With our calendars filled with work, kid's activities, community projects, and meetings, some days we feel we're scheduled up to eternity. Stressed-out and living on a fast track, it's hard to spend any quality time together as husband and wife.

We often get dangerously close to the crash-and-burn stage in our marriage before we realize we're desperate. When we let our relation-ship deteriorate to a place where we endure instead of enjoy each other, commitment to not bail out is sometimes the only thing we have to hang on to. It is then that we step back, take stock of the situ-ation, and remind ourselves that a good marriage doesn't just happen. It takes not only time, but a lot of work, patience, and prayer.

It takes two to make a really great marriage, but I'm only responsible for me. And what I do on my end can make a big difference. Here's a list of ideas and personal goals I have for my marriage. Some of them won't apply in your situation. Many of them, I'm sure you can improve upon.

- I try to remember that love is a verb and act on it every day. On my pre-printed list of daily to-do's I wrote, "Do or say something encouraging to Bill that shows my love."

- Plan at least two getaways a year without the kids—even if it's only for a couple of days. We need this.

- Set aside some time once a month to meet over coffee and discuss our schedules and family goals.

- Try to be intellectually stimulating to Bill. Introduce him to a new book or author regularly.

- Never go to bed angry. (On the nights I disregard this goal, I always regret it the next day.)

- Listen to tapes together when we go on short trips in the car. Talk about what we learn.

- Pray together regularly. This is very important to Bill and me.

- Concentrate on what I like about Bill. Cut him some slack when he falls short of my expectations. Remember that I do the same.

- Exercise together regularly and encourage each other to live a healthy lifestyle. Take walks together.

- Help Bill develop hobbies and recreational interests. Encourage him to take time off and go on a hunting or fishing trip with like-minded friends.

Ask Bill to make a list of ways he likes for me to tell him I love him. Review the list regularly.

 Coordinate our schedule with the kids' so we can go out on dates often.

 Be actively interested in Bill's world.

"One's best asset is a sympathetic spouse."—Euripides

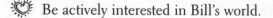

Children

Motherhood is one of the greatest privileges of life. It's also a huge responsibility and a highly important position—for which no one is qualified. Since I'm not a sociologist or a child psychologist by any stretch of the imagination, I can't quote exact statistics about which circumstances impact a child's life the most profoundly. And I don't know specifically which negative influences affect personality development to the greatest extent. But I do know a mother's attitudes and actions and the atmosphere in the home have a profound influence on her children.

A wise older mother gave me some advice when my first child was born. She told me that a mother needs to be fair, firm, and fun. I thought about her advice and set a goal to be a mother characterized by those three words. Now, twenty-two years into the process, if I had to start over again, I would do so with the same goals.

> **"My mother was the making of me. She was so true and sure of me I felt I had something to live for—someone I must not disappoint. The memory of my mother will always be a blessing to me."**
>
> **—Thomas Edison**

> "The hand that rocks the cradle is the hand that rules the world."
> —William Ross Wallace

Be fair.

My authority is not unbridled. When I become unreasonable in my demands or if I discipline my children in anger, I am the one who needs the discipline. I need to be both fair and appropriate.

In order to be fair, it's extremely important to discover why the child is misbehaving—before I select the appropriate disciplinary response. I've discovered and recorded at least five reasons why children disobey and violate my expectations. I strive to remember that each reason demands an appropriate, fair response.

Why Children Disobey

#1. They don't understand. Sometimes a child simply does not know he or she did something wrong. This can stem from either our failure to communicate or the child's ability to comprehend. If this is the case, the child needs clarification of the issue—not punishment. Especially with a young child, a fair response is to ask, "Did you understand you were not supposed to . . . ?"

#2. They didn't remember. Sometimes children forget because they don't take us seriously, but honest memory lapses should be handled as such. This is a constant problem with younger children. Sometimes it helps to give a child a reminder and a warning concerning the consequences of regular forgetfulness. If she forgets to take her lunch to school, she'll have to deal with it. If he leaves his baseball glove outside and it rains, he'll have to use a wet glove at practice.

#3. They are not capable. Sometimes children are either physically, mentally, or emotionally incapable of following the rules. A chronic problem for many parents is having unrealistic expectations of younger children. Milk will be spilled, not because a five-year-old is being careless, but because his hands are small and uncoordinated. Before I react harshly to apparent mis-behavior, I need to stop and ask myself if my expectations are appropriate to the child's capability to respond. It's not fair to ask children to behave beyond their years.

#4. They may not trust us. There can be a vast difference in a child's perspective and a parent's perspective of a problem. For example, it was a long time ago, but I'll never forget the day I was getting madder by the minute because I thought John was just being stubborn about a little splinter in his finger. When I said, "Sit still. This won't hurt," his crying escalated to screaming and his wiggling to writhing. I calmed down when I realized getting a splinter out with a needle was as traumatic to a young child as minor surgery was to me. He didn't know that he would feel better once the splinter was out. He had no basis to trust me because instead of listening to his fears, I told him he was making a mountain out of a molehill. Sometimes molehills are mountains from a child's perspective.

#5. They simply may want their own way. Much misbehavior simply comes down to a battle of the wills. When a child thinks I'm going to do what I want to do when I want to do it, fair and appropriate discipline is the only answer.

Be firm.

I try hard to remember that the goal is to change the way my child thinks so he can—in turn—change his own behavior. I've found these five forms of discipline invaluable.

Instruction or Preventive Discipline: Our kids need to know that there is such a thing as right and wrong. Children need to know what is good, and they need to know what is bad. And they need to have clear limits.

Modeling or Illustrated Discipline: Like it or not, more is caught than taught. If I want my children to behave a certain way, I must model that behavior in my own life.

Guidance or Corrective Discipline: Our kids need to be warned when they start to get off course. A rebuke should serve not to humiliate the child, but to encourage and protect the child from the consequences of continuing on his present course. It is not to demonstrate our authority, but to call on the child's internal character to change. A word of warning does three things: makes the child aware of the error, clarifies the consequences for the error, and outlines the desired alternatives. For example, "James, we don't call each other stupid. You know that, and I will have to punish you if you do it again. If you have a problem with your brother, ask him politely to stop bothering you. If he doesn't cooperate, come see me; but you may not call him stupid."

Reward or Persuasive Discipline: Behavior that achieves desirable results will be repeated. Of course our children need to learn to do the right thing because it's the right thing to do. But rewards can make learning fun and can give the child pleasure—which reinforces good behavior and attitudes. Unfortunately the law of reinforcement can work against us as well, by reinforcing poor behavior. If I reward a temper tantrum with attention a child is otherwise not getting, I can be sure I'll see more of the same.

But we should never use rewards as a bribe. The goal of discipline is to produce a disciplined person. You want to reward discipline. If you bribe for good behavior, you are reinforcing irresponsibility.

Punishment or Punitive Discipline: It's bound to happen. Instructions have been clearly given and warnings have been made. Bad behavior continues. Negative reinforcement must be brought to bear. Retribution has nothing to do with it. Anger has no place in it.

The goal of punishment is to teach the child that self-centered behavior leads to pain and emptiness. Controlled punishment and denial of certain privileges that teach this principle without harming the child physically or emotionally are important tools of discipline.

Be fun.

Strange as it seems, having fun with your children has a great deal to do with how they respond to your firmness. The moments you spend laughing, playing, and enjoying life together make large deposits in your child's emotional bank account. They understand your love and commitment to them in tangible ways.

Watch the Wiring

Something else that's always on my mind as I mother and "manage" my children, is that that every child has a unique design, and there's no such thing as standardized mothering. Nor are there boxes or categories we can neatly fit our children into and expect to understand them. We must approach each child as the unique individual he or she is. I try to be a student of my own children—seeking to understand how they're wired so I can help them develop to their full potential. This means I'm always on the lookout for ways I can enhance each of my children's education, physical fitness, emotional well-being, spiritual growth, and social development in ways that are in harmony with who he is.

What we leave in our children is more important than what we leave to them.

THINK ABOUT IT

I've been a mother for almost twenty-two years now. I've found my three kids are all different. Some things that captured the imagination and heart of one didn't appeal to the others at all. Some things worked well with all three. There are tons of books written about parenting, and they probably include tips enough to last until the twenty-second century. So I'm not going to give you Kathy's one hundred and one ideas about what do to with kids. Instead, since this is a chapter about relationships, I'm going to share with you some ideas I've found useful about setting kids off on the right path to relationships. It's like teaching them a lifelong sport.

In order to be able to relate successfully with others, kids need good self-esteem. One important way to build their self-esteem is to keep their emotional tank full by regularly doing something together. Sitting in front of the TV at the same time doesn't count. It can, though, be doing something as simple as working on a model or taking a walk in

> **"The best way to have a friend is to be one."**
> **—Ralph Waldo Emerson**

the park. Or you might try something out of the ordinary—learn to rollerblade, conquer a computer program, or invent a new cookie recipe together.

Another way to build self-esteem is to remind a child of his or her positive attributes. I like to find a new way each day to say to each child, "You're a special person!" I try to use phrases like "You're such a blessing to our family when you make us laugh," "Your kindness mean the world to me," and "I appreciate how hard you try."

It's also important to be interested in your children's world, of which school is a big part. When they arrive home from school or you arrive home from work, ask specific questions about their day. For example . . .

- What was your favorite class or subject today?

- Tell me something interesting that happened to you today.

- Who did you sit with at lunch?

- What are some of the upcoming events at school?

- What can I help you with?

Show your interest by providing a good study environment for your children. Have plenty of school or "office" supplies on hand (remember, their school is their career right now, and we should treat it as such), and turn off the TV. Try to do something fun together each night after homework is finished, even if it's only for a few minutes. Play a board game, put a few pieces in an ongoing jigsaw puzzle, read a book together. Many nights, James and I take turns reading to each other from *The Book of Virtues* and *The Chronicles of Narnia*.

Another part of self-esteem is discovering things your child is good at and enjoying the process of working at them, learning more, getting better. You might begin a notebook and keep a record of the things your child loves to do. Expose your child to a variety of interests: Check on classes and events offered through your local library, museum, YMCA, Boys or Girls clubs, community colleges, or parks and recreations departments. Then you can provide opportunities for dabbling in those things.

Teaching children values is another way we help them learn to get along in society. When our children were small, we wrote down the values we embrace and want to pass on to our children. In the end, our list boiled down to the principles of the Ten Commandments. We set a goal to look for ways to teach the principles of the Commandments to our children in ways they could understand.

You may need to evaluate your home and your family's activities to discover what and who, besides you, is influencing your children's values as they grow up.

Probably the most important thing to remember about teaching children to relate successfully with others is that they need to see you living out what you are teaching—modeling the behaviors you want them to embrace. If you want your children to live by strong values, respect other people, exhibit good manners, be a giver not a taker, you must model it yourself—when dealing with friends (yours and theirs), relatives, and business associates. I've found that I need to honestly examine my own life regularly. Maybe you feel the need to do the same.

Are there areas where you know you're not setting a good example for your children?

Practice Makes Perfect

One of our jobs as Family Managers is to provide opportunities for our kids to practice what we're teaching them and build relationships with others. You can initiate activities with other families, friends, and relatives, and encourage involvement in group activities—sports teams, music groups, Scouts. And if possible, send your children to summer camp. There are many excellent camps across America. I've found that going away to camp teaches children flexibility, independence, and responsibility. It helps with their social skills and enables them to observe positive role models and broadens their understanding of other people from different walks of life.

> "I get many letters from you parents about your children. You want to know why we people up here in Princeton can't make more out of them and do more for them. Let me tell you the reason we can't. It may shock you just a little, but I am not trying to be rude. The reason is that they are your sons, reared in your homes, blood of your blood, bone of your bone. They have absorbed the ideals of your homes. You have formed and fashioned them. They are your sons. In those malleable, moldable years of their lives, you have forever left your imprint upon them."
>
> —Woodrow Wilson, when he was president of Princeton University

Relatives

Everybody has them. Sometimes they're the butt of stupid jokes. Sometimes they're the source of frustration. Sometimes they're a wonderful secondary support system. Many times they help us and our children understand our past. They add a depth and diversity, a sense of belonging, that the nuclear family on its own can't provide. Often they're all of the above.

> "Our ancestors are very good kind of folks; but they are the last people I should choose to have a visiting acquaintance with."
> —Richard Brinsley Sheridan

Many of us don't live in close proximity to our extended families and have learned to forge relationships over distance, while relying on nonbiological related groups of friends for many of the traditional roles of the extended family—i.e., helping out in times of crises. Some of the ties that bound our families together in times gone past simply don't apply anymore. For instance, we don't all have to work together on the farm to harvest the crops before the first frost. We can't just drop in on our brothers, sisters, aunts, uncles, cousins, parents, and in-laws if they live two thousand miles away. But, we do ourselves and our children a disservice if we don't find ways to connect with our extended families.

There's an old saying that we don't get to choose our relatives. That's basically true. But what we do get to choose is how to be in relationships with them.

"The interests of childhood and youth ar

As I've gotten older, family connections have taken on new significance. Our family has been to a number of reunions since our children were small. They've learned a lot about their family this way. They've met aunts, uncles, and cousins who lived at a distance. They've heard family stories about "the good old days" I never would have thought to tell them. They've figured out where I get my sense of humor. They haven't figured out where I get my sense of cooking, since everybody, and I mean everybody, from the smallest child to my oldest living aunt, cooks better than I do.

> "Heirlooms we don't have in our family. But stories we've got."
>
> —Rose Chernin

At family reunions our children sometimes learn facts about our own childhoods, some of which we hoped would remain secret. But, more importantly, they learn a lot about their heritage. They learn family and country history by hearing stories about Granddaddy's stint in the navy during World War II. They figure out that peas and corn don't come from plastic freezer bags when they hear great aunts and uncles reminisce about hoeing weeds and picking corn. They find out about the "old country," wherever in the world our families came from, and often hear about the traditions or sample foods from those places for the first time at family reunions.

Getting to know their relatives can also stir up a strong sense of family pride in kids. They meet cousins who have performed on stage, won academic prizes, or have the same funny cleft in their chins as they do. They hear about or see grandmother's latest handiwork. They meet uncles who run companies or aunts who write books.

Simply put, when extended families get together, traditions are passed from generation to generation. Grandparents and parents enjoy telling stories and reliving the past. Kids may roll their eyes in disbelief or groan in embarrassment when Dad tells about walking to

the interests of mankind." — E. S. Janes

school three miles through the snow, uphill both ways. But spending time together, even if only a day or two every few years, hearing stories, and having fun together strengthens family ties and helps to instill a love of family in children, even though they are usually too busy enjoying their long-lost or seldom-seen cousins to realize that something significant is taking place.

If your extended family provides back and forth support and love and friendship, there's probably not much you need to do as a Family Manager except keep it going. Make sure your kids have opportunities to interact with their grandparents, aunts, uncles, and cousins. Model behavior like phoning Grandma, sending birthday cards to cousins, making every effort to attend reunions, in short, keeping in touch.

Divvy Up the Work

How you conduct your relationships with family and who assumes responsibility for what and why might be the occasion for a family meeting and/or ongoing discussion. One thing's for sure. Mom the Family Manager can't do it all by herself. Talk about the relatives with whom you have a relationship and the responsibilities involved— taking Grandpa to get his blood pressure checked each month, sending birthday cards to all the aunts and uncles, organizing an annual Labor Day campout so the cousins can get together. However long or short your list, let all of your family take part in taking care of the rest of the family.

Touchy Issues

Sometimes I venture to say, at least once in a while in every family, some relationships will go awry. There may be family members you don't particularly want your children interacting with. I think two truisms apply here: If you can't say something nice, don't say anything at all AND tell the truth. There's no need to tell children, particularly young children, details of the people's lives and difficulties. And there's certainly no need to put other people down by telling them any version of "Uncle So-and-So is a no good bum." However, if Uncle So-and-So has, say, a drinking problem, and you have decided not to spend time with him when he's drinking, this might be an opportunity to be up-front with your older children about what you've decided and why.

"What families have in common the world around is that they are the place where people learn who they are and how to be that way."
—*Jean Illsley Clarke*

Friends

I learned the value of friendships from my parents. Starting at an early age I watched them keep their own friendships in constant repair. Many of the friends they had when I was in kindergarten are still their good friends forty years later. They've been through hard times and good times, rebellious children, failed businesses, death, and divorce. It's a joy for me to see my parents enjoying the later years of their life with their friends today, many of whom are the same people I've seen all my life.

> **"If we advance through life and do not make friends, we shall soon find ourselves alone. We must keep our friendships in constant repair."**
> **—Samuel Johnson**

Although my parents never formally taught me any principles of friendship, I watched their lives and learned. I've also learned a lot from Bill. He suggests that there are three stages of building friendships:

1. **Take the Initiative:**
    Be friendly; be the first to say hello
    Say the other person's name often
    Show genuine interest in the other person's life

2. **Establish Rapport:**
    Think to yourself, "I accept you as you are."
    Listen attentively—for feelings as well as thoughts
    Express approval and affirm when appropriate
    Give sincere compliments when due
    Look for ways to give, not take
    Watch for occasions to spend time together

3. **Build the Relationship:**
    Let them know what you are thinking
    Seek their advice
    Make time for them
    Remember important dates
    Share personal resources
    Honestly share your joys and pain
    Avoid being possessive or controlling

*"You cannot do a kindness too soon because you never
know how soon it will be too late."—Ralph Waldo Emerson*

True Wealth

Although I certainly don't pretend to understand or relate to Helen Keller's deprivation, I understand, in my own limited way, the value she placed on friends. My banker may deny this, but I am a very rich woman. I enjoy the friendships of many people on many levels.

> "Life is nothing without friendship." —Cicero

I dedicated this book to three longtime friends—Judie Byrd, Kathryn Waldrep, and Peggy Zadina. Kathryn, Peggy, and I have been friends since college days. Judie and I have been friends since our boys became friends at age three. Today, our boys are still friends and roommates at college. I have other good friends, ones I've known for years with whom I keep in contact, and new friends I'm enjoying getting to know better and better. Whatever the level of the relationship, it all comes back to the three Rs—rapport, responsibilities, and rewards.

> "It is that my friends have made the story of my life. In a thousand ways they have turned my limitations into beautiful privileges, and enabled me to walk serene and happy in the shadow cast by my deprivation."
> —Helen Keller

Probably most of us are constantly making new friends—in the neighborhood, at the office, at school or community meetings, and at church. We have a great deal to do with how far each relationship goes. The reality of friendships—the rapport, responsibilities, and rewards—is that they ebb and flow in our lives. And perhaps one way to know if a friend is really a friend is if they understand this.

A Very Valuable Position

If you suddenly won the lottery or inherited a large sum of money and were able to hire a full-time cook, housekeeper, chauffeur, gardener, handyman, social director, accountant, and secretary, there's one department you'd still have to personally oversee: Family Members and Friends. No one else can be a wife to your husband, a mother to your children, a daughter to your parents, a daughter-in-law to your in-laws, a sister to your siblings, or a friend to your friends. This is the department where you manage the people in your life—raising your children, keeping your extended family together, taking soup to a sick neighbor, working on your marriage, keeping up with old friends and making new ones. What could possibly be more important?

chapter 10

Personal Management

"By and large, mothers and housewives are the only workers who do not have regular time off. They are the great vacationless class."
—Anne Morrow Lindbergh

"Friendship with oneself is all-important, because without it one cannot be a friend with anyone else in the world."
—Eleanor Roosevelt

We live in a day of activity overload. Despite technological advances—appliances and machines designed to increase productivity and save energy, money, and time that were unthinkable twenty years ago—we are more exhausted than ever before.

- -

Dr. Juliet B. Schorr describes our plight in *The Overworked Woman*. She says:

". . . Millions of ordinary Americans fall victim to the shortage of time. The most visible group has been women who are coping with a double load—the traditional duties associated with home and children and their growing responsibility for earning a paycheck. With nearly two-thirds of adult women now employed, and a comparable fraction of mothers on the job, it's no surprise that many American women find themselves operating in overdrive. Many working mothers live a life of perpetual motion, effectively holding down two full-time jobs. They rise in the wee hours of the morning to begin the day with a few hours of laundry, cleaning, and other housework. Then they dress and feed the children and send them off to school. They themselves travel to their jobs. The three-quarters of employed women with full-time positions then spend the next eight and a half hours in the workplace.

At the end of the official workday, it's back to the 'second shift'—the duties of housewife and mother. Grocery shopping, picking up the children, and cooking dinner take up the next few hours. after dinner there's cleanup, possibly some additional housework, and, of course, more childcare. Women describe themselves as "ragged," "bone-weary," "sinking in quicksand . . ." and "busy every waking hour." . . . Ann Landers pronounced herself 'awestruck at the number of women who work at their jobs and go home to another full-time job. . . . How do you do it?' she asked. Thousands of readers responded, with tales ranging from abandoned careers to near collapse. . . ."

An Epidemic of Burnout

Every week I get mail from women telling me how desperate they feel. They're tired, frustrated, burned out. And it's not just women with two jobs—one in the marketplace and one at home. More often than not, I've found that women who choose Family Management as their full-time career find themselves busier and more exhausted than ever. I think there are a couple of reasons this happens. First off, it's easy to rationalize that since you're not "working," i.e., receiving a paycheck, you aren't "worth" as much. And you have a lot of time you need to account for. So, you end up saying "yes" to far too many requests for your time and energy, and become terribly overcommitted. Simply put, full-time Family Managers often don't have the outside validation they need and/or want. It's always nice to have someone say you've done a great job, and one way to get those positive strokes is to do a lot of volunteer jobs. But while extreme busyness will fulfill that ache to be needed and noticed, it won't alleviate the real issue that cries to be recognized: What about me?

> "One half of knowing what you want is knowing what you must give up before you get it."
> —Sidney Howard

Many women recognize that they've let their own needs go unmet. Some of them feel too busy, extremely tired, and like they're spinning their wheels. They talk about working on school projects, helping their spouses, taking care of aging parents and in-laws, "doing for" coworkers, community agencies, and friends. Now they feel desperate. They want to know what they can do to feel better and usually, to be able to do more for others. They ask me for advice— books they can read, tapes they can listen to, seminars they can attend. They wish for a place to go get an overhaul—some necessary adjustments, a few replacements, a battery charge—in about eight hours and come home better than new.

I've always been a little leery of "experts" who want to change my life. They write books and teach seminars promising that if I commit to eating two tablespoons of wheat germ every day at 10:37 A.M., drink a gallon of water, and never again in my entire life eat processed sugar, I'll never have another argument with my children. If I throw out everything in my closet and buy seventeen black outfits with accessories color-coded by a NASA computer to coordinate with my skin, hair, and eyes, I will never again experience that sinking feeling of discarding the fifth outfit while my husband gives me one of those you-know-I-hate-to-be-late looks. The experts promise a quick fix, five easy steps, and painless strategies we know don't exist. And yet, they sound so convincing, there are times I think that if I follow their methods, my life will miraculously change.

"The great thing in this world is not so much where we are, but in what direction we are moving."
—*Oliver Wendell Holmes*

THINK ABOUT IT

The last thing I want to do in this book is say that if you don't organize your house a certain way, if you don't plan meals in advance, if you don't manage projects like I do, even if you don't manage your home by the seven departments, well, you might as well give up. As far as I know, you might manage your home according to three departments or nine, and that might make a lot more sense for you. I don't believe in easy answers or in one right way to do something. Human beings are too complex and too creative.

But there is one point I'll be dogmatic about, and I believe what I'm about to tell you with every cell of my being. A Family Manager has to take care of herself— manage herself—if she's going to be a good manager of the other departments.

Memorize the last sentence. It's important.

Remember these words when you're tempted to put your own needs on the back burner. Your children do not need a cranky, resentful, overworked, "unfun" mom. They need somebody who can be present for them. And you need somebody who can be present for you: Yourself.

It's really pretty simple. We can take some small comfort in the fact that we're part of a growing statistic. It's not just me. It's happening to everybody. There's an epidemic of burnout out there—and a lot of people want to help. Six dollars and ninety five cents will get us a new tube of lipstick or the latest mass market self-help book on how to solve our problems in thirty days—and if it doesn't work it's our fault. Or we can take charge of our

> **"Kids needs are best met by adults whose needs are met."**
> —**Jean Illsley Clarke**

> "Life develops from within."
> —Elizabeth Barrett Browning

lives, stop feeling like victims, and start making time for ourselves. And from experience I can say that when we do that, we begin to see what's really important and suddenly, almost miraculously, we have the time and energy for it.

Now memorize this sentence:

The person who is most qualified to figure out how to take care of you is you.

In hopes of encouraging you to take care of yourself, I'm going to tell you how I've learned to take care of myself over the years and share some stories from my friends and my work. The ideas here come from many sources and over many centuries.

Just one last thing before we start: The ideas here are not guaranteed to make your life perfect overnight. But they might just make you feel a little less frazzled, a little less tired, a little more content and productive as you face life's peaks and valleys.

"It is never too late to be what you could have been."—George Eliot

THINK ABOUT IT

Alter Your Vision and Your Life Will Follow

I can't pinpoint the precise day. It wasn't an abrupt change. It was more like a long, slow turn like a large ship would make. But there was a definite turning point in my life. Or maybe it's more accurate to call it a turning process. Since my first recognition of the need to change, around the time I found myself flat on my back in the hospital, there have been other crises and hard times, times when I was quite sure I didn't have enough time, money, or energy to take care of myself. Now, whenever I find myself thinking like that, I recognize it as a yellow warning flag. And I redouble my efforts to take care of myself. It always helps me through the rough patches.

I will hazard a guess that all of us, at one time or another, have had to deal with the presence of resistors in our lives. By resistor, I mean those inner voices or attitudes within us that retard, hinder, or oppose something we want or at least ought to do. I didn't have to think long to pinpoint the main resistor in my life. It's a disease. It lies dormant for a while, then becomes active when I decide to better myself. It's called the "If Only Syndrome," and its symptoms are debilitating.

> "If you want a place in the sun, you have to put up with a few resistors."
> —Abigail Van Buren

Maybe you're a carrier too. The disease settles at the back of your brain and perverts your perception of reality. It poisons your goals, dreams, and attitude about life with If Onlys . . .

- If only we had more money,

- If only my husband would change,

- If only my children weren't so much trouble,

- If only we could go on a trip,

- If only I had a better job,

- If only I didn't have a job,

- If only I were thinner, taller, younger, then . . .

- I would have more energy,

- I would get more done,

- I would take care of myself, and my life would be perfect."

- **If only this were true. It's not!**

"Things do not change; we change." —Thoreau

When I get a bad case of the If Onlys, I'm usually feeling overwhelmed about one or more areas of my life. The disease blows things even more out of proportion. For example, I might be thinking "If only I could lose twenty pounds and run a mile without stopping then I could buy new exercise shoes, which I really need to protect my ankles. But I can't buy them until I promise to wear them every day and go to the gym to work out for thirty minutes on the treadmill. But I don't have that kind of time, and I can't do that much exercise until I lose twenty pounds, so I guess I won't get the shoes, and I might as well give up."

The If Only disease causes us to focus on our liabilities—some of which are real—but greatly blown out of proportion, and some of which are imagined. What we must do instead is choose (and we do have a choice) to focus on our assets—what we do have and what we can do—even if it's only something small to begin with.

"Every little bit helps." My children hate it when I say that—especially when we're playing Monopoly. While they're holding out for the big properties—waiting to be able to put hotels on Boardwalk and Park Place, I'm stockpiling the cheaper ones. I save the small bits of rent money they owe when they land on my houses in the "low-rent district," as they put it.But guess who usually wins? I do, because all the little deals add up to a big win at the end.

I think the same principle holds true for taking care of ourselves—every little bit helps. Wise behavior daily adds to overall better condition.

> "The last of personal freedoms of which no one can deprive you is choice."
> —Dr. Victor Frankel

Although it took me a long time to learn this, it was a lesson worth waiting for. That is, I know today, beyond a shadow of a doubt, that I am a valuable person and I am worth taking care of. And I know that you are too. We have a lot to contribute—as Family Managers, wives, mothers, friends, community volunteers—as human beings in the world. But we can't contribute a whole lot of anything to anyone if we don't take care of ourselves first.

"First you make your decisions, then your decisions make you."—Howard Hendricks.

THINK ABOUT IT

I have this quote printed at the top of my daily to-do sheets. It reminds me that the little choices I make today—what I put into my body, what I watch on TV, what I spend my leisure time doing, how much rest and exercise I get, what I read—will determine who I am tomorrow.

What Things Look Like

When the truth settled into my being that I am valuable and worth great care, I had to figure out how to go about changing some of the self-neglecting habits that had become a part of me.

Since I am a visual person, I had to visualize what I would look like if I was really taking care of myself and operating at peak efficiency as a woman and a Family Manager. Just as I wrote what our ideal family would look like, when I was trying to get my life into a manageable state, I wrote what would be my ideal "end product"—what I would look like if I were operat-

---

EXAMINATION + EVALUATION + ACTION = ENHANCEMENT (OVER TIME)

- First, we *examine*—that is, list what is.

- Next, we *evaluate*—take the what is list and decide what we'd like to change.

- Then, we take *action*—even a small action, changing one thing, one day at a time.

- The result is *enhancement*—not instantaneously, not overnight, but we wake up one morning to find our life has been enhanced.

ing at peak performance. I described how I was growing intellectually—how many books I was reading, the subjects I was mastering; I described the condition of my body—how often I exercised, how many calories and fat grams I ate each day, the vitamins I took. I described my emotional state—how much patience, love, forgiveness, and kindness I exhibited. I described my spiritual condition—what I was learning and experiencing as a result of my relationship with God, how much I was praying, how I was living out what I said I believed.

"If you are ever in doubt about what to do,
it is a good rule to ask ourselves what we shall wish
on the morrow that we had done." — *Sir John Lubbock*

THINK ABOUT IT

Whether you're a visual person or not, this might be the perfect time to sit down and think about your life. Your life. Not your children's lives, your husband's life, or the life of the Perfect Family Manager. Next year at this time, what kind of woman would you like to see in the mirror? How have you changed for the better? That's one way to look at it. Another approach I've taken is to think about what I want people to say about me at my funeral. With that question in mind, I wrote my own epitaph, describing the person I wanted people to remember. You might consider doing the same. Or maybe you're a list person. You might want to make a list of things you'd like to know how to do, or characteristics you wish described you but don't now. I have a friend who cut out pictures from magazines that portrayed the characteristics she wanted to have in her own life. She cut out pictures of happy families, couples in love, pictures of women exercising, reading, taking a leisurely walk, having lunch with friends, sitting in church. However you do it, in one long session or in ten-minute

> "The greatest discovery of my generation is that human beings can alter their lives by altering their attitude of mind."
> —William James

increments over several weeks, take some time to begin to draw or list or write a description of who your best self is.

Four Areas to Explore

It probably won't come as a surprise to you that most things in life make more sense to me when broken down into categories or departments. After I look at the grand scheme of something—a job, a project, my life—and see the scores of tasks that need to be done, it becomes much less overwhelming and easier to handle when I break it down into manageable pieces or categories. There's nothing particularly ingenious about the categories I came up with, they just work well for me. They are: intellectual, physical, emotional, and spiritual. I studied these categories of my life and tried to honestly evaluate how I might not be taking care of myself. I tried to identify the "resistors"—those things that were holding me back from taking care of myself, keeping me from operating most effectively. And I studied my vision of myself to see what I could do, today, and each day, to move toward who I envisioned I could be in each of these four main areas.

> "The life which is unexamined is not worth living."
> —Plato

"We must never try to escape the obligation of living at our best."—*Janet Erskine Stuart*

Intellectual Best*

My vision of myself is someone who is open-minded and keeps on learning, someone who is interesting to herself, as well as to her hus-

---

* A word of caution here. Best means your best in any given year, month, day, hour, or moment. We're talking striving for your own top form, not comparing yourself to your mother, sister, friends, or women in your age and demographic group, or women from history. This is about you, not comparison or competition.

band, her children, and her friends. I am by nature curious, and even though I might not be able to spend all the time I want to reading and studying, I determined many years ago to spend at least part of my time learning new things. I don't want to grow up to be one of those grandmothers who has nothing to say to her grandchildren except, "When I was your age we didn't have such newfangled gadgets, notions, ideas." I want to keep up.

S T R E T C H YOUR MIND:
"When people are bored, it is primarily with
their own selves that they are bored."
—Eric Hoffer

When I set out to stay mentally astute, I found myself pursuing some things I thought I would like but didn't. I started some classes and didn't finish them—or finished them without a sense of satisfaction. But if I hadn't explored those things, I wouldn't have discovered others, including knowing a whole lot more about what I do and think.

Taking advantage of lectures or seminars offered in my community is a good way to explore new interests. It's quite inexpensive and requires a minimum time commitment at first. I also enrolled in classes (one per semester) at a local university and even took a correspondence course. You may want to consider finishing a degree you started years before or pursuing a post-graduate degree. There are also educational programs offered on public television. Taking courses or attending seminars and lectures helps us put new learning in context, introduces us to new people as well as new ideas, and keeps us stimulated.

> "Reading is to the mind what exercise is to the body."
> —Sir Richard Steele

If I wanted to learn new things, I knew I couldn't be a victim any more . . . hold on to the attitude "If only I had time to learn something new" or "If only I wasn't so busy meeting everyone else's needs." I knew these were excuses. If I really wanted to pursue a personal endeavor, I could choose to do it.

Besides, when I do learn new things and meet my own needs for intellectual stimulation, I come back to meeting my family's needs more refreshed and often with new ideas.

Over the years, as I developed my daily intellectual disciplines, I've searched for older people to emulate in this area. I've found a few people to be role models.

"You don't grow old. You get old by not growing."—E. Stanley Jones

THINK ABOUT IT

I loved Doris the moment I met her at a women's conference. Dressed in a colorful warmup suit and tennis shoes, she had just finished a brisk walk. When she smiled, her entire face lit up as each line enhanced her countenance. As we talked I learned that she reads two books a month and takes each of her grandchildren on an educational trip once a year. Last year when she learned to parasail, her only fear was losing her dentures over the ocean. At age seventy-five she lives each day to the fullest. Soon after meeting Doris, I wrote these guidelines for myself:

Keep-on-Growing Guidelines

1. Set a goal to study a new subject and learn something new each year.

2. Allow myself to be curious.

3. Give myself the freedom to fail.

4. Be jealous of my time and use it well.

5. Collect information even if I don't know how to use it.

6. Focus on the long-term benefits.

"The desirableness of a life is to be measured by the amount of interest and not the amount of ease in it, for the more ease, the more unrest." — George MacDonald

Growth Opportunities

Here's a sampling of ideas I've tried and suggestions I've picked up along my intellectual pilgrimage. Select the ones you like. Change any of them to suit your needs and goals. Do anything you like with them. Just do yourself the favor of doing something.

> **Five minutes a day spent growing intellectually may not seem like much, but that adds up to over thirty hours a year of personal "class time."**

 Always keep at least one good book going. Remember, we are influenced by what we choose. I read three or four at the same time. My mood decides which one I read that day.

Remember that education helps us live a more quality life by continually stretching our minds. Enroll in a class at a community college or take a correspondence course.

When you find an author who stimulates you, try to read everything he or she has written.

Buy a good dictionary, keep it close at hand, and use it. Try to learn one new vocabulary word each week. A New Word a Day calendar is an easy way to do this. Crossword puzzles and "It Pays to Increase Your Word Power" in *Reader's Digest* are also good vocabulary stimulants.

Write facts you want to remember or interesting quotes in a notebook or on index cards. Categorize and file them for future reference.

 Check out "how-to" videos from the library on a subject you've always wanted to know more about.

 Start a book club. Invite friends to read the same book, then get together once a month to discuss what you read.

 Find an older mentor to share his or her wisdom with you.

 Attend a lecture with a friend who stimulates you. Talk about what you learned.

 Create an environment conducive to learning. Surround yourself with good books, play stimulating music, keep your desk supplied with study supplies, and turn off the TV.

 Be accountable to a friend if you need an mental energy boost. I have a good friend who regularly asks me what I'm reading and learning.

 Organize a trip to take with friends who push you to be your best. You'll feel invigorated and refreshed when you return.

 Don't be afraid to go back to school. You'll be surprised at how much you remember. I was shocked when I did well on the graduate-school entrance exam at age thirty-seven.

Start a list of topics and ideas you're interested in. It's great to have such a list when you're feeling bored. And it's hard to think of new things when life seems uninteresting.

Physical Best

Weight control. It will always be a struggle for me, as it is for so many Family Managers. And when we don't take time to take care of our bodies—exercise, eat wisely, take vitamins, and drink plenty of water, we have double trouble. First, our bodies get out of shape, which causes us to not have as much physical energy and to be more susceptible to illness. Second, we don't feel good about who we are and how we look which drains us of emotional energy.

My friend Kathryn Waldrep, who is a doctor, told me that almost every one of her patients over the age of forty automatically gains five pounds each year because of metabolism slowdown. If this distressing trend is inevitable, I figure I have three possible responses: I can buy clothing with elastic waistbands—then sit back and let it happen. I can try extreme, expensive, unhealthy weight loss plans—which, by the way, almost guarantee that you will gain back the weight you lose within a year. Or I can commit to fighting the battle wisely through discipline, regular exercise, and sensible eating habits. In other words, take care of myself.

> "The excuse of not being able to find the time is a cop-out. We find time to sleep because it is mandatory. So is exercise."
> —Nathan Pritikin

But as we think of taking care of ourselves physically, it's also important to make sure our definition of a "good figure" is accurate. So many women—regardless of age—are dissatisfied with their bodies because they want to look like a media image. Let's face it—very few of us have "10" bodies. We take a giant step toward a healthy self-image when we give up this delusion and begin to love ourselves for who we are as unique individuals. My personal best may not match another woman's—nor does it need to. Comparisons have to go. When I feel good about myself I can be more others-centered instead of me-centered. When I take care of my body I feel more lovable, and I'm able to love my husband and my children more freely.

"If you rest, you rust."—Helen Hayes

And when I walk past a mirror and enjoy who's looking back at me, I am invigorated and more productive.

One Step at a Time

It seems to me that in our work and in our relationships with other people we understand that "Rome wasn't built in a day," but when it comes to us, and especially to our physical well-being, we can't apply it at all. If we miss exercising one day, we think we will NEVER IN THIS LIFETIME exercise again. We see that the little things we do to accomplish a work project all add up, even the mistakes we make, the parts that end up on the cutting floor.

> **Neither Rome nor a healthy lifestyle can be built in a day. . . . Developing a healthy lifestyle requires consistency, not perfection."**
> **—Gordon S. Tessler,**
> *Lazy Person's Guide to Better Nutrition*

But if we eat a hot-fudge sundae today, we "give in" to mistakes, deciding we'll never have what it takes to eat right on a daily basis.

What's really important is to realize that each day is a new day. And we can make the choices in that day that are going to make us more physically fit and healthy in the long run.

Take some time when you can be alone and honestly evaluate the condition of your body and your personal habits. Write down what would have to change for you to operate at your personal best. Then look through this list of ideas. Try a few that fit comfortably into your lifestyle. Make your overall goal be to make healthy, wise decisions every day about what you eat and drink, and how you take care of your body.

Growth Opportunities

Do one thing today. And the same thing tomorrow, or a different one, until you find the physical regime that best suits you. Then when you get bored—don't we all?—come back to this list for inspiration.

Commit yourself to a regular exercise program. Try to exercise aerobically at least three hours each week. Join an aerobic dance class, swim laps, ride a bicycle, jog, jump rope, or walk briskly on your lunch break. (I work out at the YMCA six times a week.)

 Squeeze your fanny muscles when you're riding an elevator, waiting in a long line, or caught in a traffic jam.

 Keep three-pound weights in an easily accessible location. Use them to firm up your arm muscles two to three minutes each day.

 Enroll in a nutrition course or physical-education class at a local college.

Float lemons in a pretty pitcher full of water. Drink six to eight glasses every day. If you work, take a favorite glass to keep on your desk. Refill it with fresh water regularly.

Try to let your digestive tract rest for twelve hours each day. If you eat breakfast at 7:00 A.M., don't eat after 7:00 P.M. the night before.

 Purchase a small inexpensive cotton rug or exercise mat. Do sit-ups each day.

 Buy a small stepstool with rubber-tipped legs so it won't slip. Step up and down 100 times. This is great for your gluteus muscles.

Limit your sugar intake. (I allow myself six sugary desserts each year. I save these for special occasions or dinner parties.)

Eat more complex carbohydrates. They fill you up without overloading your system with calories.

Do floor exercises while watching an old movie.

Eat slowly. Put your fork down between each bite. Studies show that most overweight people eat very fast. Never clean your plate.

 Exercise with your family in fun ways. Take a bike hike, throw a Frisbee, have a sit-ups contest, or a family softball game.

 Keep fresh vegetables cut up in your refrigerator.

 Don't eat standing up. Cows graze.

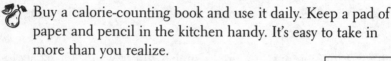 Play calm background music while you eat. Research shows that listening to fast music causes us to eat faster.

 Buy a calorie-counting book and use it daily. Keep a pad of paper and pencil in the kitchen handy. It's easy to take in more than you realize.

 Grab a piece of fruit when you're hungry.

 Enroll in a dance class that you've always dreamed of—ballet, tap dancing, clogging.

> "Never eat more than you can lift."
> —Miss Piggy

 Take the stairs whenever possible.

 Don't keep your favorite junk foods around the house.

Only allow yourself three small bites of a recipe you have to taste to get the seasoning right.

Install a full-length mirror in your bedroom or bath.

Wear tennis shoes and ankle weights when doing housework. Go about your work with an "attitude of exercise." Bend, stretch, and move briskly.

Don't always look for the closest parking place at the mall.

Take long strides and tighten your thigh and hip muscles when walking through an airport.

🍐 Find a friend and be mutually accountable to each other about what you eat and how much you exercise.

Emotional Best

"When one is estranged from oneself, then one is estranged from others too." —Anne Morrow Lindbergh

Along with burnout, the other big epidemic in this country seems to be depression. And the cure seems to be the latest pill. Now I in no way intend to belittle depression. I know it's real and it's debilitating, and if you feel like you suffer from this disease, I urge you to consult your physician. No pill is a miracle cure, but medication can bring relief for some types of chemical depression. In addition to medication, good counselors and many support groups are available, the former often on a sliding fee basis and the latter often free. If you are feeling like you need help getting out of an emotional slump, please look into those options.

Taking care of our emotional health, like taking care of our physical health, is an ongoing, day-by-day process. No life is all sunshine. Sometimes we feel down in the dumps for an obvious reason, sometimes for no reason we can determine. The point of taking care of our emotional health is not to feel happy all the time. It's to recognize our feelings, to live with them, and to live in a way that allows us to have less stress and more strength to deal with whatever the circumstances of our life are.

No matter what size family we manage, we are less efficient when we don't take care of ourselves and become emotionally stressed out. It takes us longer to do simple tasks, and we often make mistakes, creating more work, taking up even more time.

> "You can be pleased with nothing when you are not pleased with yourself."
> —Lady Mary Wortley Montagu

I have a friend who has been a great inspiration to me about taking care of myself emotionally. She told me the story of a time in her life when she was overwhelmed by undone work. Her phone messages had piled up, along with unfinished reports and correspondence. She was working long hours, trying to please everyone, and ended up pleasing no one. Nothing she did gave her satisfaction, and her self-esteem hit bottom.

Beginning then, a day at a time, she took time for herself. Sometimes just ten minutes, sometimes an afternoon. She took walks and naps and took herself out for lunch. She began to try to leave her work at work. She started being a friend to herself, which made her then a better friend to others.

I think we could all tell this same story, just changing a few of the details. Most of us let ourselves go too long without rest, refreshment, and allowing ourselves to do things that recharge our emotional batteries. All of a sudden we find ourselves close to crash-and-burn stage, unable to manage our life, much less our family.

Growth Opportunities

There's a little book on the shelf above my desk that has given me great comfort. It is *How To Be A Friend To Yourself* by Jan Johnson. The following list of ideas are from her book. Some of the ideas are things to do for yourself now and then, on special occasions, or at a time when you're feeling particularly sad, lonely, or vulnerable. Some of them are nurturing, some are thought provoking, some are celebratory. Some suggestions won't appeal to you at all. But hopefully a few of them will inspire you to think of things you can do to be a better friend to yourself, which will help you grow stronger emotionally.

 Think of ten things you wish a friend would do for you. Pick one and do it for yourself.

 Buy yourself some fancy soap or bath salts. Luxuriate in a warm tub. Let the water wash your cares away.

- Get your nails done, even if it's not a special occasion.

- Fix yourself something beautiful and healthy to eat. Put your favorite music on, and sit down to enjoy your own company.

- Put your nightgown on early, turn off the telephone, and climb into bed with a good book. Let yourself go to sleep early.

- Buy a book that teaches you to do something that pleases you—maybe making flower arrangements.

- Give yourself the gift of hiring someone to clean your house to help you catch up.

- Treat yourself to your favorite berries out of season.

- Treat yourself to lunch out, either alone or with a friend.

- Give yourself a facial.

- Make an appointment with a makeup consultant. Get a new look.

- Buy a bit of gourmet coffee in several flavors. Try them all out.

- Watch your tea cool. Let the rising steam carry off your worries.

- Buy yourself a big fluffy bath sheet. Use it to wrap yourself up in comfort after your shower or bath.

- Make your own list of how you can get to know yourself better, feel better about yourself, and become your own best friend.

- Pick a few good friends and approach them about being each other's support system when things are going badly for you. You may well do this on an informal basis right now. It's important not act like you are a mountain of strength, not to try to carry all your pressures alone.

Join a support group.

 Keep a journal you can tell your innermost feelings to.

 Take an occasional mental-health day, a break from work and routine, alone or with your husband or a good friend. Take a drive in the country. Go for a hike. Go to a matinee or a museum.

 Take yourself on a weekend retreat. Give yourself the luxury of time to pray, meditate, sleep, and play.

 When you make a mistake, write yourself a gentle, corrective note. Pretend you're writing to a child you love.

When you face a difficulty, remember past difficulties you've overcome.

Spiritual Best

Spiritual growth means many different things to different people. You may feel anxious at the mention of spirituality because of a past negative experience. Maybe you feel indifferent because you think spiritual matters are irrelevant to real life. Or maybe you resonate with joy because you have been spiritually enriched in deep and meaningful ways, and you have experienced great peace as a result.

The development of my own spiritual life over the years has allowed me to feel a connection with the larger purposes of life. I've found that spiritual understanding stretches us beyond our limited perceptions of reality and self-preoccupation and calls us to a gloriously larger world.

Recently I traveled to the West Coast to do some interviews about Family Management. Halfway through one interview, a reporter looked me in the eye in a way that made me know she was very serious. She said, "May I ask you a personal question?" She wanted to know how the spiritual part of my life affected my role as a Family Manager. The essence of that question—how spirituality affects our life, day in and day out—is not uncommon today. Women (and men) are searching for a larger reality than themselves.

I responded sincerely to the reporter by telling her that the principles of family management—being prepared, team-building, creating routines, establishing priorities, delegating, etc.—apply to every woman, no matter what her religious beliefs. But as far as my own role as a Family Manager goes, there is no way I could do all I have to do or be the woman I desire to be without significant spiritual roots.

I have come to understand that the God who created the universe also has a plan for every one of his creatures, and loves us more than we can possibly imagine. This confidence in God compels me to appreciate my uniqueness and individuality. C. S. Lewis said that joy is the business of heaven. As I discover more fully God's plan for me, it pulls me from being miserably preoccupied with myself, and I experience the joy of which Lewis wrote. As I grow in my understanding of how much God loves me personally, it is easier to believe that I am a very valuable person. I have found no greater source of security and significance than that.

> "Before you can do something you must first be something."
> —Goethe

I have also discovered another force working within me. A force that I dare not deny nor disguise, lest it destroy everything I am trying to create as a Family Manager. The sine qua non of family life is selflessness—generously giving of yourself for the welfare of those you love. (I'm not talking about self-destructive love that depreciates your own personal value by finding meaning in being the family martyr. But the giving of yourself—a whole and valuable person—with nothing to prove. In fact, only a person who has something to give can give themselves away.) Our own willingness to give ourselves away is the key to the warm loving relationships we all want to experience in our family. However, I find that all too often selfish attitudes well up within me. Every woman I know struggles with these ugly attitudes to one degree or another when life doesn't go our way or give us what we want. Before we know it, we are more interested in protecting ourselves than loving those God has put in our care. Angry words, unreturned affection, and bitterness can easily follow. Where does all of this come from? Where does the joy go? According to the Bible, joy is with God.

> In your (God's) presence is fullness of joy;
> At your right hand are pleasures forevermore.
> (Psalm 16:11) NKJV

To be connected with God brings joy. To be disconnected brings emptiness and pain, causing us to focus on ourselves and our needs. And when I am preoccupied with my own needs, the results are disastrous—both in time and eternity.

The problem is that I still, at times, try to live my life disconnected from God. It's not a pretty picture. However, I find great comfort in knowing that even when I am at my selfish worst, God has provided a way for me to reconnect with him, to be forgiven, and experience the joy only he can bring. The Bible tells me that the reconnection comes through Jesus Christ. Confronted with selfishness, Jesus did the unthinkable. He gave his life in selfless sacrifice to reclaim us from disaster. When we turn to Christ for forgiveness of our selfishness, our relationship is reconnected, and His Holy Spirit literally takes residence within us to work out God's purpose for us, empowering us to become the people—the Family Managers, wives, mothers, friends, professionals—He created us to be, filling us with joy.

> **A woman wrapped up in herself makes a small package.**

THINK ABOUT IT

"The treasure secretly gathered in your heart will become evident in your creative work."—Albrecht Dürer

Personally, as far as my own role as a Family Manager goes, or any other roles I play for that matter, if I did not receive spiritual nourishment regularly and continually grow in my relationship with God, I would have gone AWOL a long time ago. I depend on God's help, all day every day, in managing my family, in being a loving wife and mother, a good daughter, sister, friend, neighbor, and professional. In the Bible I find practical advice and relevant principles that directly apply to all aspects of family management—motherhood, child-rearing, marriage, friends, property, finances, time management. For many years I have been reading and keeping notes of what I'm learning in a journal. I also find solace and ideas in the great spiritual writers and thinkers from the ages—St. Augustine, John Wesley, Martin Luther, George MacDonald, Dorothy Sayers, Corrie Ten Boom, Francis Schaeffer.

> "The longest journey
> is the journey inward."
> —Dag Hammarskjold

Of course, we can't have a relationship with God, ourselves, or anyone else for that matter, without spending time on it. I've found that if I devote time to developing my spiritual life, other things start taking care of themselves. I understand more fully what I'm supposed to do, and, miraculously, I have time and energy to do it.

> "The kind of person a human being
> becomes is determined in large part by the
> kind of activities he elects to emphasize."
> —René Dubos

Wherever you are on your spiritual pilgrimage, take time to regularly be alone with God so you can be who you need to be for yourself and others. If this is a new idea to you, you might start by reading the book of John from a modern translation of the New Testament.

In our hurry, scurry world, solitude takes a bad rap. If we have ten or fifteen minutes we often feel like we should be doing something, something besides staring out the window at the sun on the snow, or meditating or praying, or simply daydreaming. But, we do need to be alone with ourselves and our Creator in order to be in touch with ourselves—the woman we were each created to be—which is essential to balanced personal management. And there's no time like the present to start.

chapter 11

Closing Thoughts

*"You've got to think about 'big things' while you're doing small things,
so that all the small things go in the right direction."*
—Alvin Toffler

Family Management is about things like saving money on groceries, serving nutritious meals, making sure your child's gym clothes get washed, spring cleaning, hosting dinner parties, planning vacations, and fixing drippy faucets.

But more importantly it's about nurturing human lives—including your own, creating a warm and welcoming home where family members feel good about where they live. It's about being a team; enjoying a vital relationship with your husband; enhancing your children's intellectual, physical, spiritual, and social development, providing opportunities for them to be creative and resourceful, helping them grow up with a healthy self-image. It's about believing that there's more to life's work than making money. It's about teaching your kids the importance of self-discipline, instilling in them a strong value system, and preparing them to make smart choices. It's about helping family members to love themselves and others, about helping them feel a sense of responsibility to be the best they can be and to share their skills, resources, and love with family, friends, and strangers. It's about loving your family members in ways they can understand and planning regular times to have fun together. It's about helping family members learn to laugh at themselves and with each other. It's about crying—together—over the hurts. And it's about giving yourself room and time to grow, getting the mental, physical, spiritual, and emotional nourishment you need.

Whew, that's a mouthful. Maybe it sounds too abstract for your taste. Maybe it sounds too lofty. But, for me, it's about balancing the little picture with the big picture. It's about remembering that small actions and attitudes, many of which may seem insignificant at the time, make a big difference in the grand scheme of life.

As I finish this book, I want to paint an impressionist word picture of what family management means to me. It's a collage of moments in time in my family.

Family management is . . .

treating each other with respect

Taking spur-of-the-moment picnics

Having lots of (at last count we had 116) pictures of your family lining hallways, on desks, tables, buffets, the kitchen window sill

Climbing a 12,700-foot mountain together

honoring what's important to each family member

Being available to help with homework

Laying a wood floor in the family room together

A *fire in the fireplace, popcorn, and quilts*

Not YELLING in the house

Having an annual Valentine's Day scavenger hunt for presents

USING CLOTH NAPKINS

Eating the same thing every year when we decorate the Christmas tree

Remembering that people are more important than projects

keeping a jigsaw puzzle going

Counting our blessings out loud at the end of a hard day instead of feeling discontent and wanting more

going roller blading together

Reminiscing about family vacations

Leaving an encouraging note on the bathroom mirror

Waking my children up gently in the morning

Letting my kids have a puppy even though it's a pain

Helping everyone in the family become computer literate

Reading a book aloud as a family

Having a marathon Spades tournament that lasts all summer

Bringing my husband a cup of coffee in the morning

building a treehouse in the backyard

My husband bringing me a cup of coffee in the morning

sending my children off to school on a positive note

TICKLE WARS

Watching hundreds of baseball, basketball, soccer, and football games, tennis matches, and golf tournaments

Going to church together

Saying something encouraging to every family member each day

being there when someone's hurting

Attitude Just Might Be Everything

Not too long ago, I was feeling pretty smug about the fact that I was doing a good job of balancing magazine-article deadlines, speaking engagements, media interviews, and book deadlines—while at the same time keeping up with Bill and the boys' needs, running the household semi-efficiently, and fulfilling my personal goals. I looked good on paper. Then our life fell apart, and I didn't have it nailed down nearly as securely as I thought I did. It didn't occur to me that the plumbing under my kitchen sink would spring a leak and the floor would have to be replaced; or that my ten-year-old would get the flu and get behind in school; or that a business deal would fall through causing serious financial repercussions; or that the transmission would go out in one car and the brakes in another; or that the dishwasher would go out; or that the septic system would back up—just to mention a few things that happened.

I wish I could tell you I had a rise-above-the-circumstances attitude.

I wish I could tell you I was a shining example of a woman who concentrates on what is right with life instead of what's wrong with it. I wasn't. And it didn't make matters any better. As a matter of fact, my attitude made things worse.

We laugh at the old saying "if Mama ain't happy, ain't nobody happy," thinking that those words apply to some fictional character from an Uncle Remus book. I'd like to suggest that we get honest and own up to the fact that as Family Managers, for the most part, we set the atmosphere in our home, and our attitude, disposition, and outlook on life make a huge difference in the "personality" of our family.

No one's life is perfect—or even close. Bad things happen to good Family Managers. But I'm convinced that it's not what happens to me that's so important—it's how I react to what happens to me. I don't have a choice about my past. I don't have a choice about a lot of things that happen to me every day. I don't have a choice about how some people will act toward me. I do, though, have the choice every hour of every day about what kind of attitude I'm going to have.

"Life is a grindstone. But whether it grinds us down or polishes us up depends on us."—L. Thomas Holdcroft

When my washer breaks down I can gripe, or I can choose to be thankful that it's not 1750 and I'm not washing all those petticoats by hand. When my roof leaks I can be thankful it has a house underneath it. When a child disappoints me, I can be thankful I have the privilege of being a mother. When we can't afford to take a vacation, I can be thankful for the state park nearby where we can camp out. When I fail at something, I can be thankful I'm good at something else.

S t r e t C H YOUR MIND:

We are given the privilege of influencing family members through thousands of small daily acts—doing laundry, changing diapers, running carpools. Our attitude when carrying out these acts make a difference in the personality of our home. How would you describe the personality of your home?

Ten Murphy's Laws for Family Managers

1. The new soccer shoes your child must have before the game Saturday will go on sale the following Monday.

2. Leak-proof thermoses—will.

3. The chances of a piece of bread falling with the grape jelly side down are directly proportional to the cost of the carpet.

4. The garbage truck will be two doors past your house when the argument over whose day it is to take out the trash ends.

5. The shirt your child must wear today will be at the bottom of the dirty-clothes pile.

6 Gym clothes left at school in lockers mildew at a faster rate than other clothing.

7 When you're running late, your car keys will be in the last place you look.

8 Sick children recover miraculously when the pediatrician enters the treatment room.

9 Things you use daily naturally gravitate toward the back of the refrigerator.

10 Your chances of being seen by someone you know increase exponentially when you drive your child to school in your robe and no makeup.

> "The future is something which everyone reaches at the rate of sixty minutes an hour, whatever he does, whoever he is."
> —C. S. Lewis

Remember that fulfilling your role as Family Manager is a lifelong pilgrimage. Don't expect miraculous changes overnight. Just start setting some goals and acting on a few ideas. Don't try to implement them all at once. Your family might run away.

A Worthy Goal

At a recent speaking engagement a young mother asked me what she could do be the best mother and Family Manager possible. Here are my suggestions to her—and to myself and anyone else who wants to get better at the job.

First, stay on a sharp learning curve. Read biographies of successful people, looking for information about the homes they came from. What can you learn about the atmosphere of that home? What were the mothers like who raised them? Devour good parenting books, read good articles about family management. Try to gain insights from the experts.

Be persistent in becoming a better Family Manager. This is a worthy pursuit.

Second, ask for help when you need it. Instead of feeling trapped by insecurity and incapability, find someone who is further along in their pilgrimage as a Family Manager. Pick the brains of older women you admire—asking them to share their wisdom about motherhood and family management.

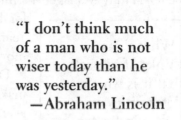

"I don't think much of a man who is not wiser today than he was yesterday."
—Abraham Lincoln

Third, have faith you will be the best Family Manager you can. This may sound simplistic, but it's true. Over and over, historians, psychologists, and theologians tell us we become how we see ourselves in our minds. What this means to you as a Family Manager is this: If you have the attitude, "I don't know a thing about preschoolers or cooking

"Nothing in the world can take the place of persistence. Talent will not: Nothing is more common than unsuccessful men with talent. Genius will not: Unrewarded genius is almost a proverb. Education will not: The world is full of educated derelicts. Persistence and determination alone are omnipotent."
—Calvin Coolidge

or college savings plans or how to teach my kids values"—whatever—"but I'm going to learn everything I can and be the best Family Manager I can be because this is an important job," then you'll be an effective Family Manager.

Think of yourself as a Family Manager on the road to becoming a better Family Manager. Picture yourself on the cover of a magazine

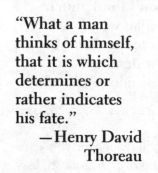

"What a man thinks of himself, that it is which determines or rather indicates his fate."
—Henry David Thoreau

for being chosen Family Manager of the Year. Envision why you were chosen and move toward that picture.

Don't get down on yourself when you make mistakes. No one has ever been or ever will be a perfect Family Manager. What's important is that we keep trying. Remind yourself of this daily.

You probably didn't receive a Family Management manual when you got married or when you brought your first baby home from the hospital. I haven't met a woman yet who felt prepared for her role as Family Manager. You will make mistakes. When this happens, cut yourself some slack, learn from what you did wrong, then get up and go on.

What we do every day as a Family Manager will determine what our homes will be like in the years to come. When our kids grow up, they will not remember if the carpet was vacuumed every day or if their towels were perfectly folded in sixteen-inch squares. They will remember, though, if home was a place they loved to be and if Mom, the Family Manager, was fun to be around.

Make This Book Your Book

I said at the beginning that I am a woman with a mission. It is my desire that every woman will understand the importance of her job as a Family Manager, take pride in her work, and recognize its value. I sincerely believe that you will benefit from this book if you will make it your book—adapt the principles to your own family, become comfortable with who you are and how you manage things best, add your own unique twists to the ideas. Make this book about your life and your family—and then, if you have time, write to me and tell me how you're doing. I'd love to hear!

Kathy Peel
The Family Manager
P.O. Box 50577
Nashville, TN 37205

Additional Information

If you'd like information about Family Manager seminars in your area, please call Ambassador Artist Agency (615) 370-4700.

If you'd like to know about other publications and products by Kathy Peel or would like to receive her newsletter, please write:

> **The Family Manager**
> **P.O. Box 50577**
> **Nashville, TN 37205**